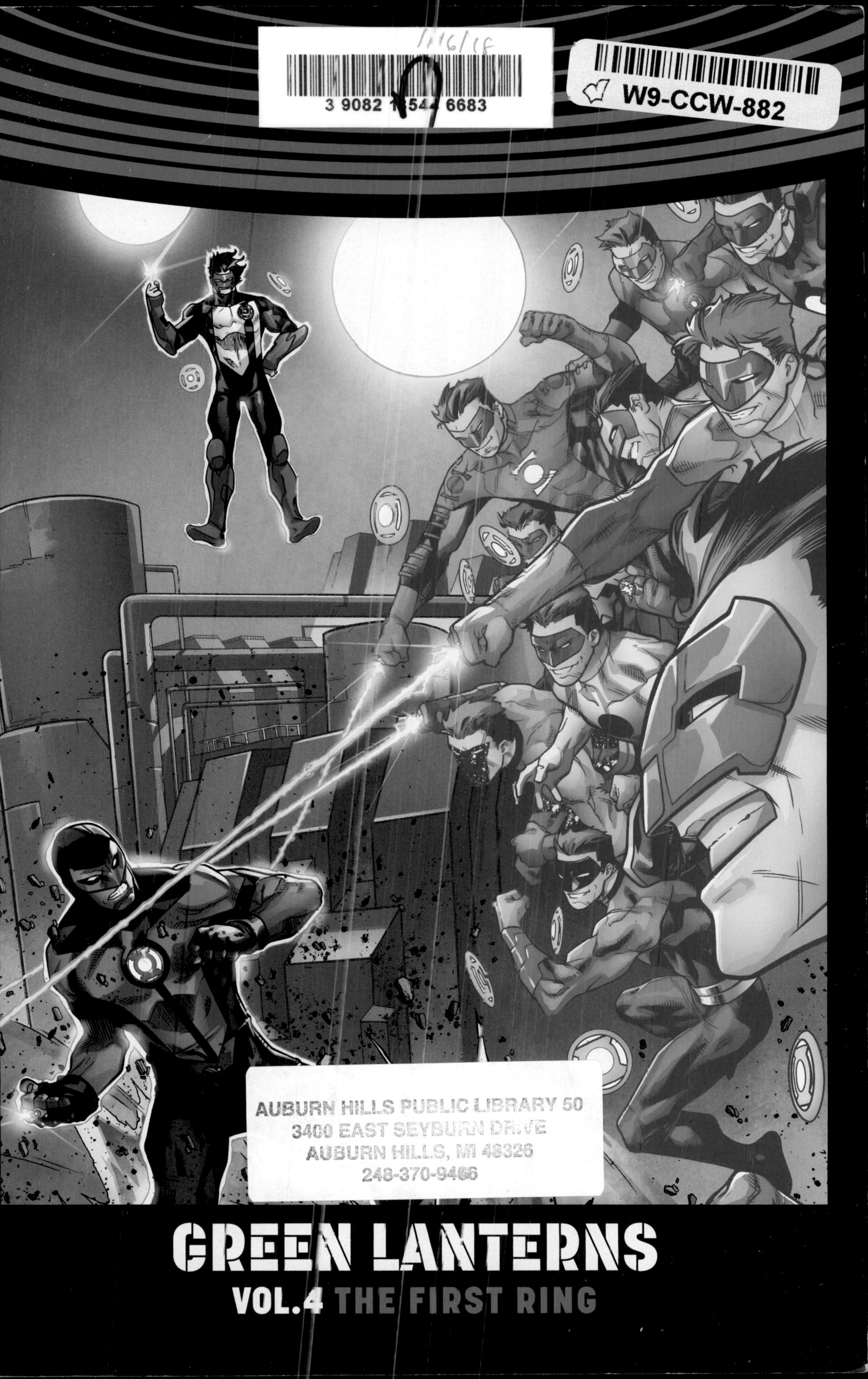

GREEN LANTERNS

VOL.4 THE FIRST RING

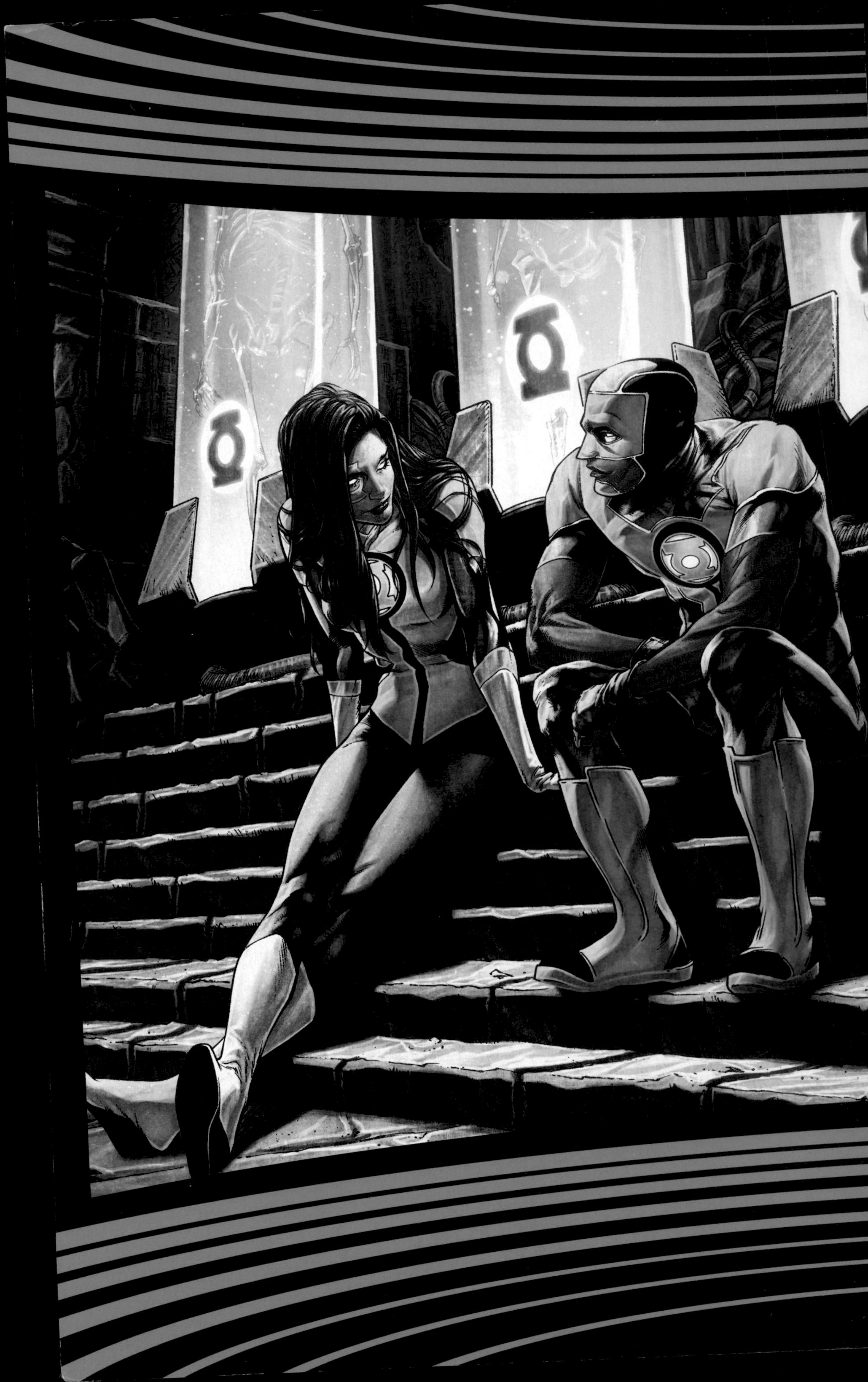

GREEN LANTERNS
VOL.4 THE FIRST RING

SAM HUMPHRIES
writer

RONAN CLIQUET * **CARLO BARBERI** * **JULIO FERREIRA**
DANIEL HENRIQUES * **EDUARDO PANSICA**
ROBSON ROCHA * **MATT SANTORELLI**
artists

ULISES ARREOLA * **BLOND**
HI-FI * **ALEX SOLLAZZO**
colorists

DAVE SHARPE
letterer

BRANDON PETERSON
collection cover artist

MIKE COTTON Editor - Original Series • **ANDREW MARINO** Assistant Editor - Original Series
JEB WOODARD Group Editor - Collected Editions • **BETSY GOLDEN** Editor - Collected Edition
STEVE COOK Design Director - Books • **MONIQUE NARBONETA** Publication Design

BOB HARRAS Senior VP - Editor-in-Chief, DC Comics
PAT McCALLUM Executive Editor, DC Comics

DIANE NELSON President • **DAN DiDIO** Publisher • **JIM LEE** Publisher • **GEOFF JOHNS** President & Chief Creative Officer
AMIT DESAI Executive VP - Business & Marketing Strategy, Direct to Consumer & Global Franchise Management
SAM ADES Senior VP & General Manager, Digital Services • **BOBBIE CHASE** VP & Executive Editor, Young Reader & Talent Development
MARK CHIARELLO Senior VP - Art, Design & Collected Editions • **JOHN CUNNINGHAM** Senior VP - Sales & Trade Marketing
ANNE DePIES Senior VP - Business Strategy, Finance & Administration • **DON FALLETTI** VP - Manufacturing Operations
LAWRENCE GANEM VP - Editorial Administration & Talent Relations • **ALISON GILL** Senior VP - Manufacturing & Operations
HANK KANALZ Senior VP - Editorial Strategy & Administration • **JAY KOGAN** VP - Legal Affairs • **JACK MAHAN** VP - Business Affairs
NICK J. NAPOLITANO VP - Manufacturing Administration • **EDDIE SCANNELL** VP - Consumer Marketing
COURTNEY SIMMONS Senior VP - Publicity & Communications • **JIM (SKI) SOKOLOWSKI** VP - Comic Book Specialty Sales & Trade Marketing
NANCY SPEARS VP - Mass, Book, Digital Sales & Trade Marketing • **MICHELE R. WELLS** VP - Content Strategy

GREEN LANTERNS VOLUME 4: THE FIRST RING

DC Comics, 2900 West Alameda Ave., Burbank, CA 91505
Printed by LSC Communications, Kendallville, IN, USA. 11/17/17. First Printing.
ISBN: 978-1-4012-7505-1

Library of Congress Cataloging-in-Publication Data is available.

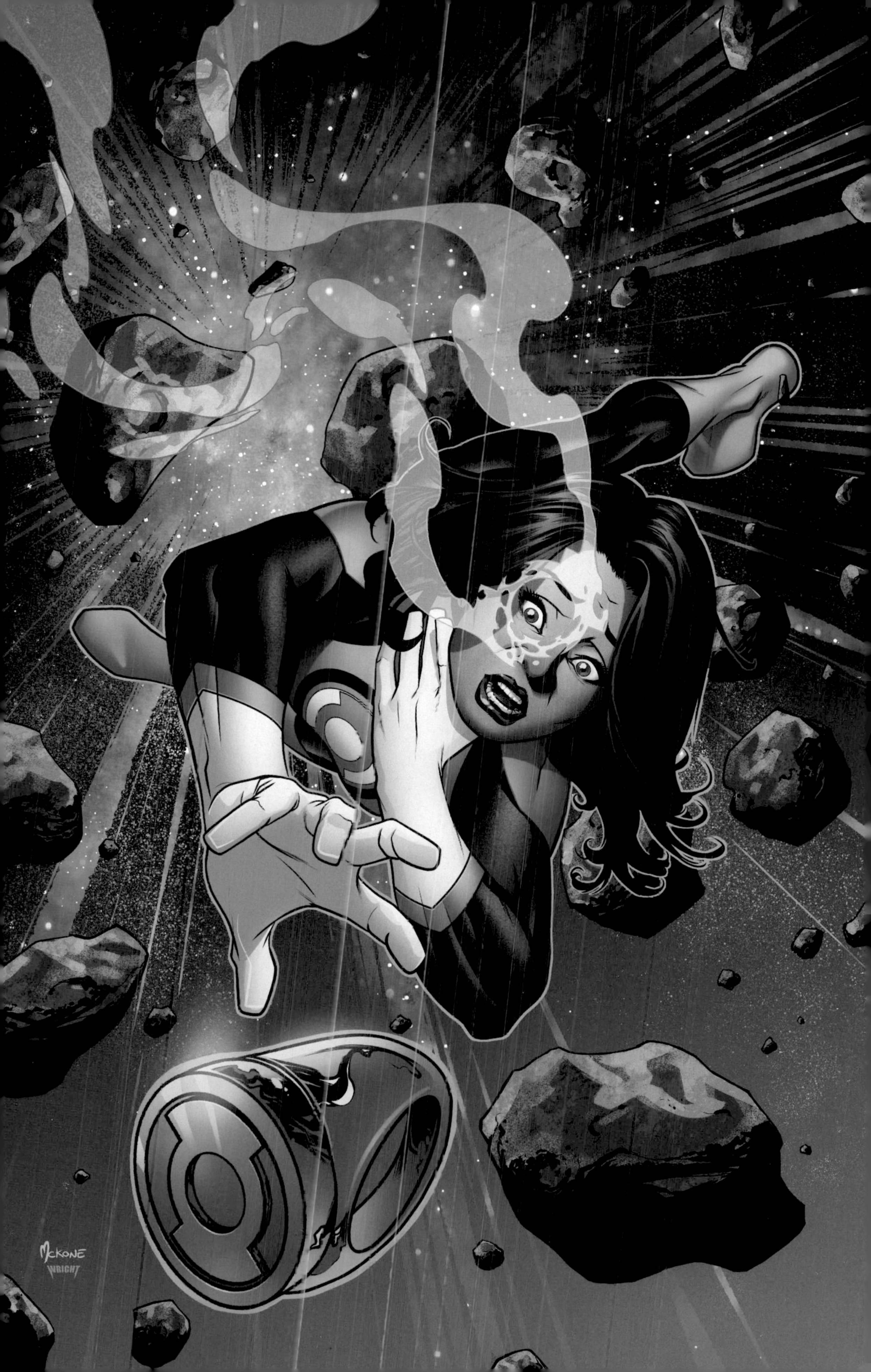
MCKONE
WRIGHT

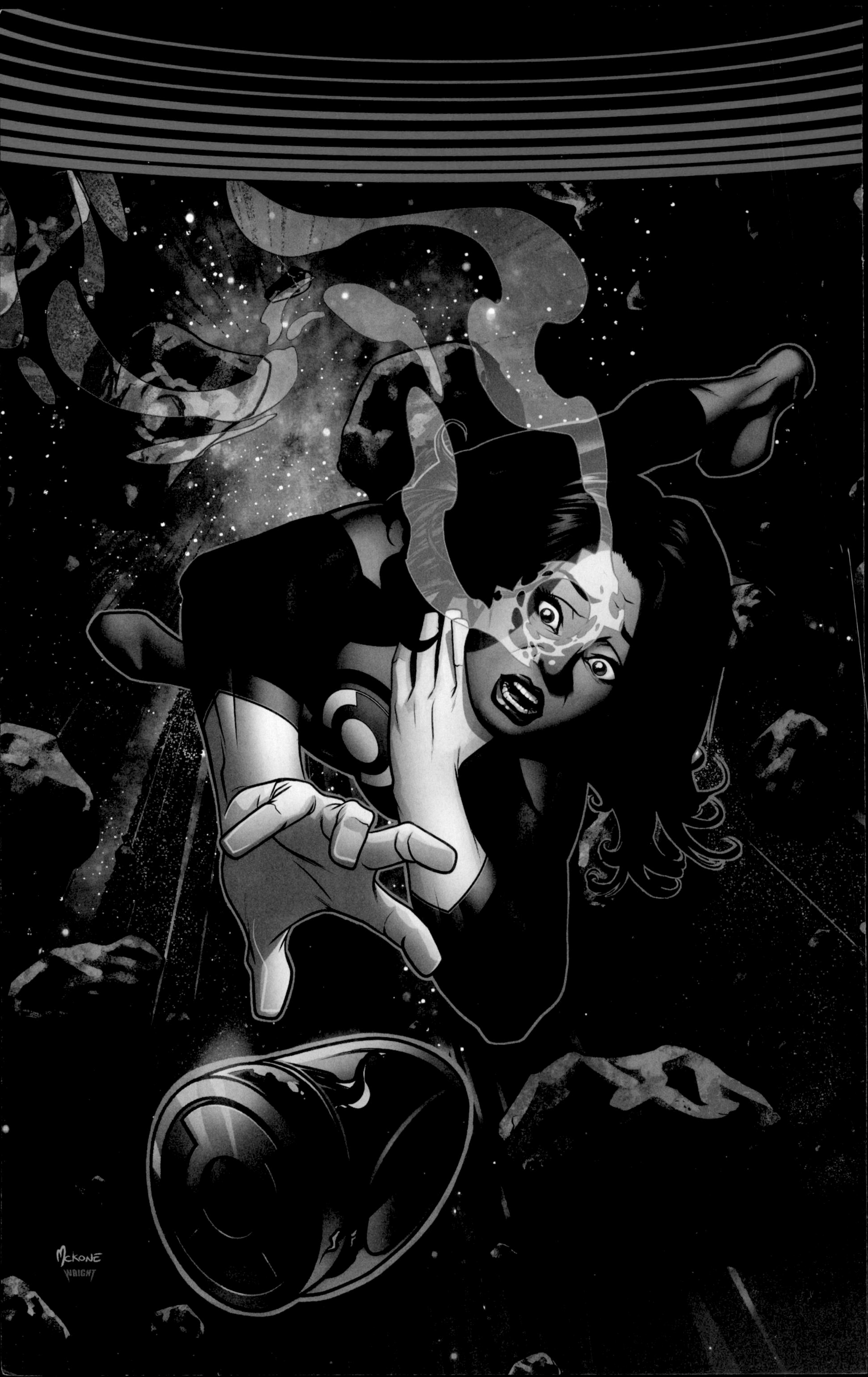
McKONE
WRIGHT

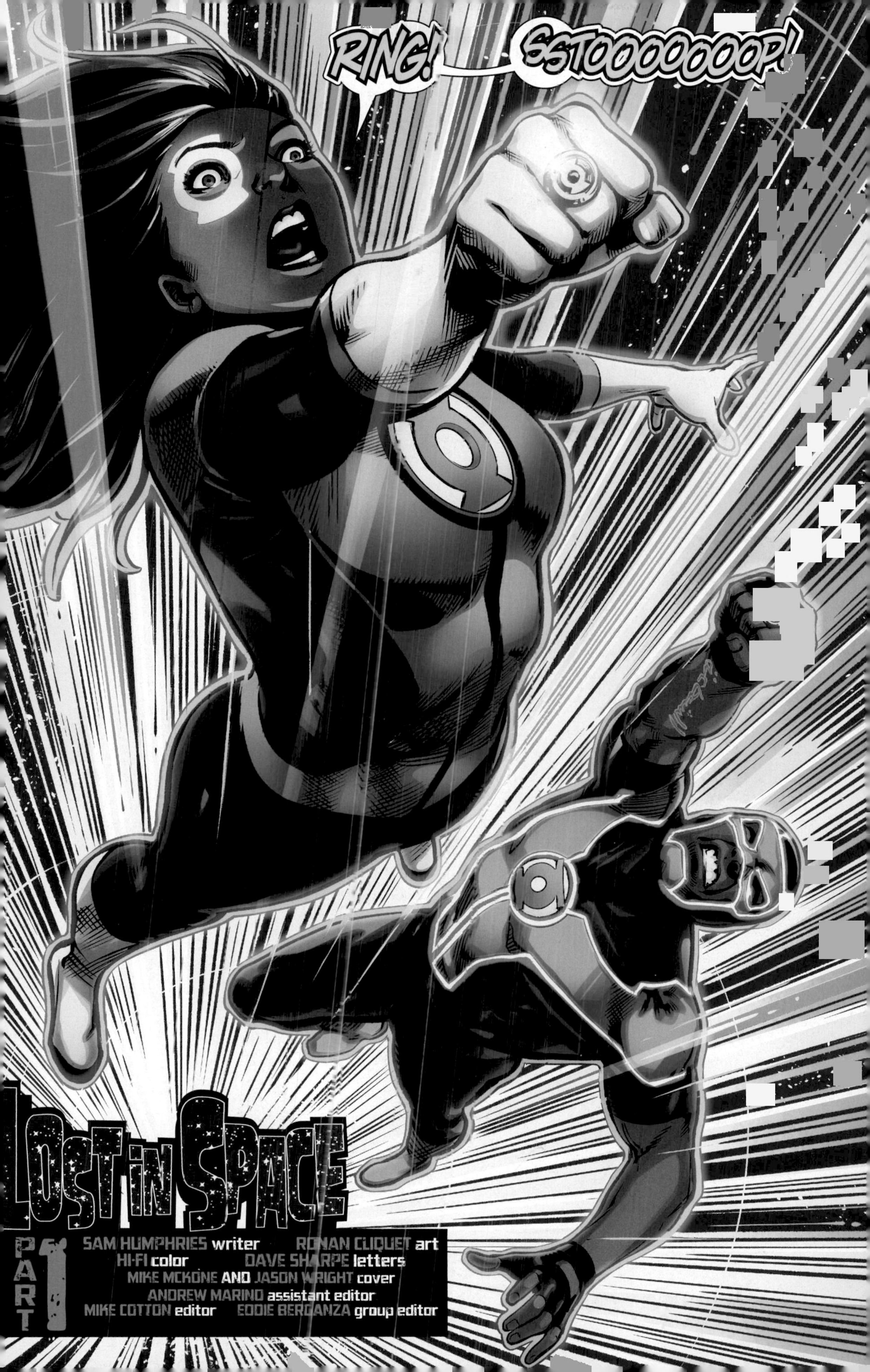

RING!
SSTOOOOOOOOP!
LOST IN SPACE
PART 1
SAM HUMPHRIES writer RONAN CLIQUET art
HI-FI color DAVE SHARPE letters
MIKE MCKONE AND JASON WRIGHT cover
ANDREW MARINO assistant editor
MIKE COTTON editor EDDIE BERGANZA group editor

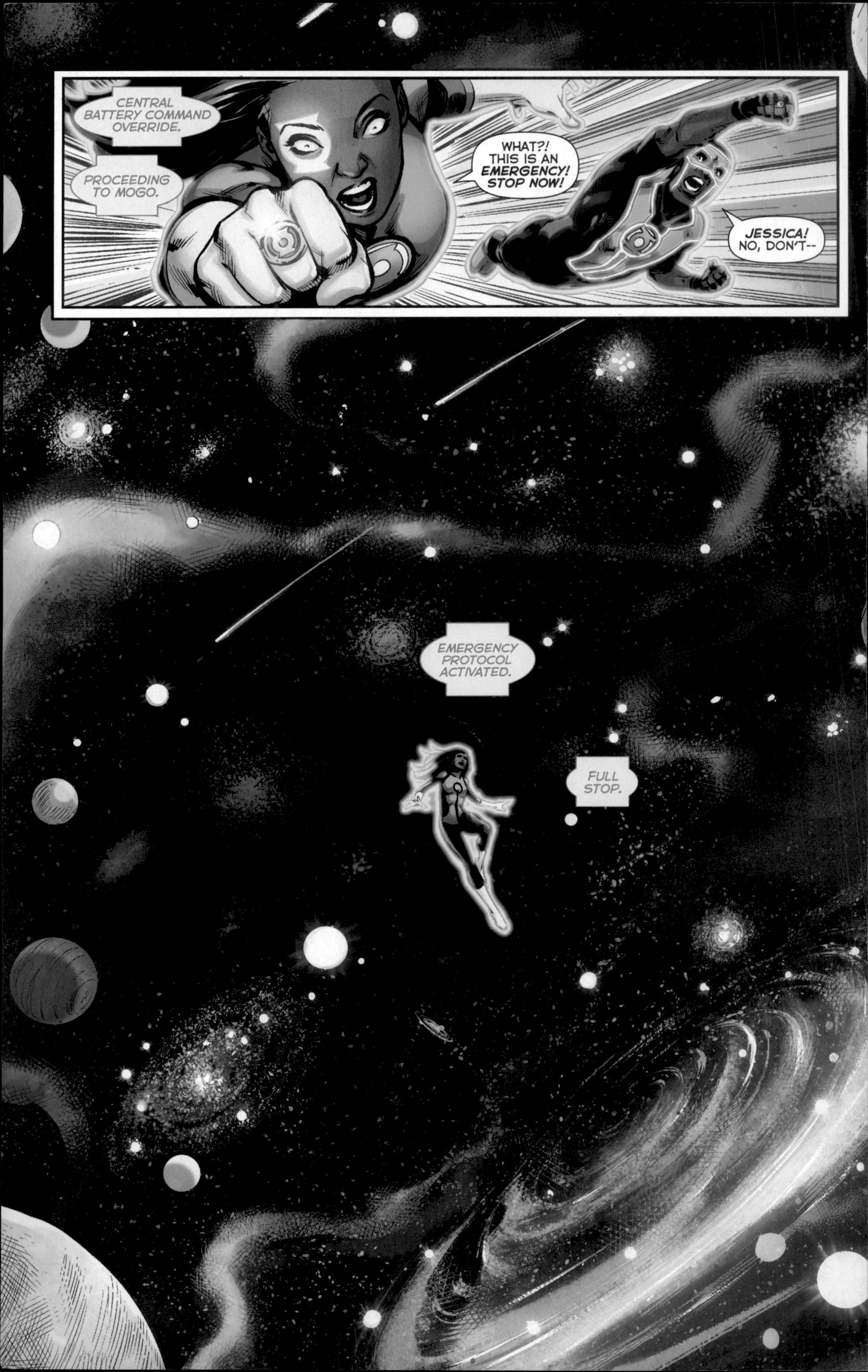
CENTRAL BATTERY COMMAND OVERRIDE.
PROCEEDING TO MOGO.
WHAT?! THIS IS AN EMERGENCY! STOP NOW!
JESSICA! NO, DON'T--
EMERGENCY PROTOCOL ACTIVATED.
FULL STOP.

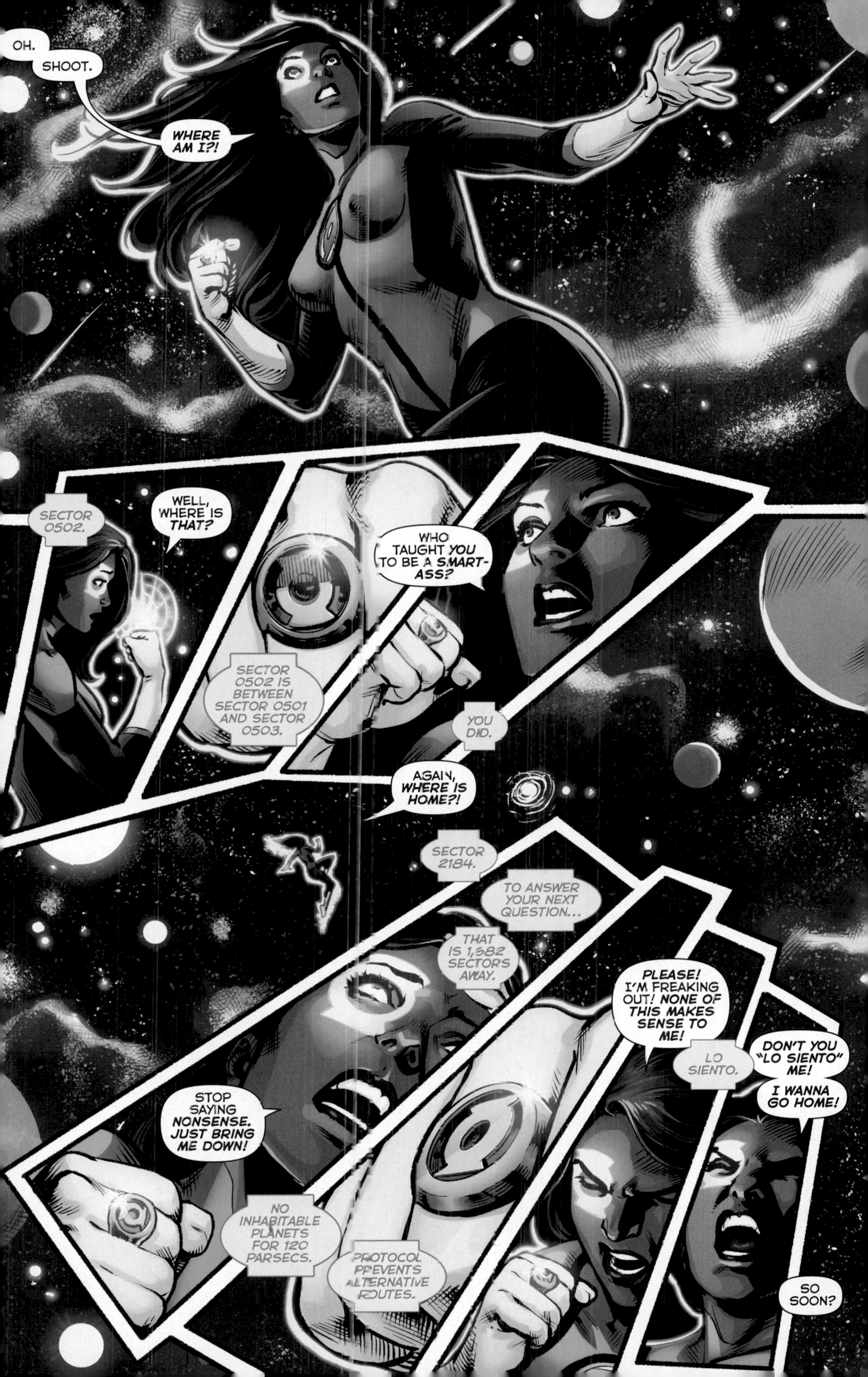
OH.
SHOOT.
WHERE AM I?!
SECTOR 0502.
WELL, WHERE IS THAT?
SECTOR 0502 IS BETWEEN SECTOR 0501 AND SECTOR 0503.
WHO TAUGHT YOU TO BE A SMART-ASS?
YOU DID.
AGAIN, WHERE IS HOME?!
SECTOR 2184.
TO ANSWER YOUR NEXT QUESTION...
THAT IS 1,682 SECTORS AWAY.
STOP SAYING NONSENSE. JUST BRING ME DOWN!
NO INHABITABLE PLANETS FOR 120 PARSECS.
PROTOCOL PREVENTS ALTERNATIVE ROUTES.
PLEASE! I'M FREAKING OUT! NONE OF THIS MAKES SENSE TO ME!
LO SIENTO.
DON'T YOU "LO SIENTO" ME!
I WANNA GO HOME!
SO SOON?

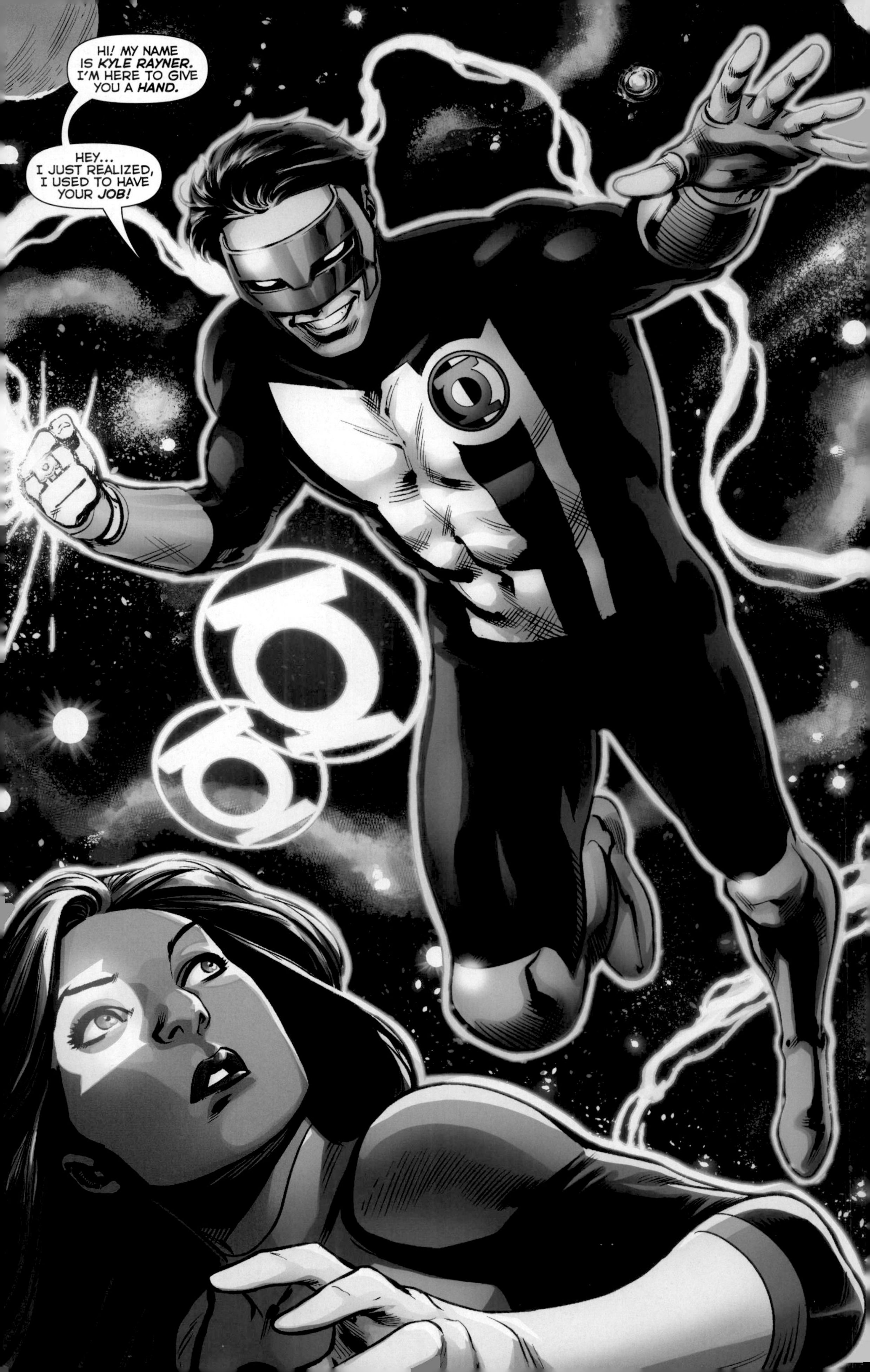
HI! MY NAME IS KYLE RAYNER. I'M HERE TO GIVE YOU A HAND.
HEY... I JUST REALIZED, I USED TO HAVE YOUR JOB!

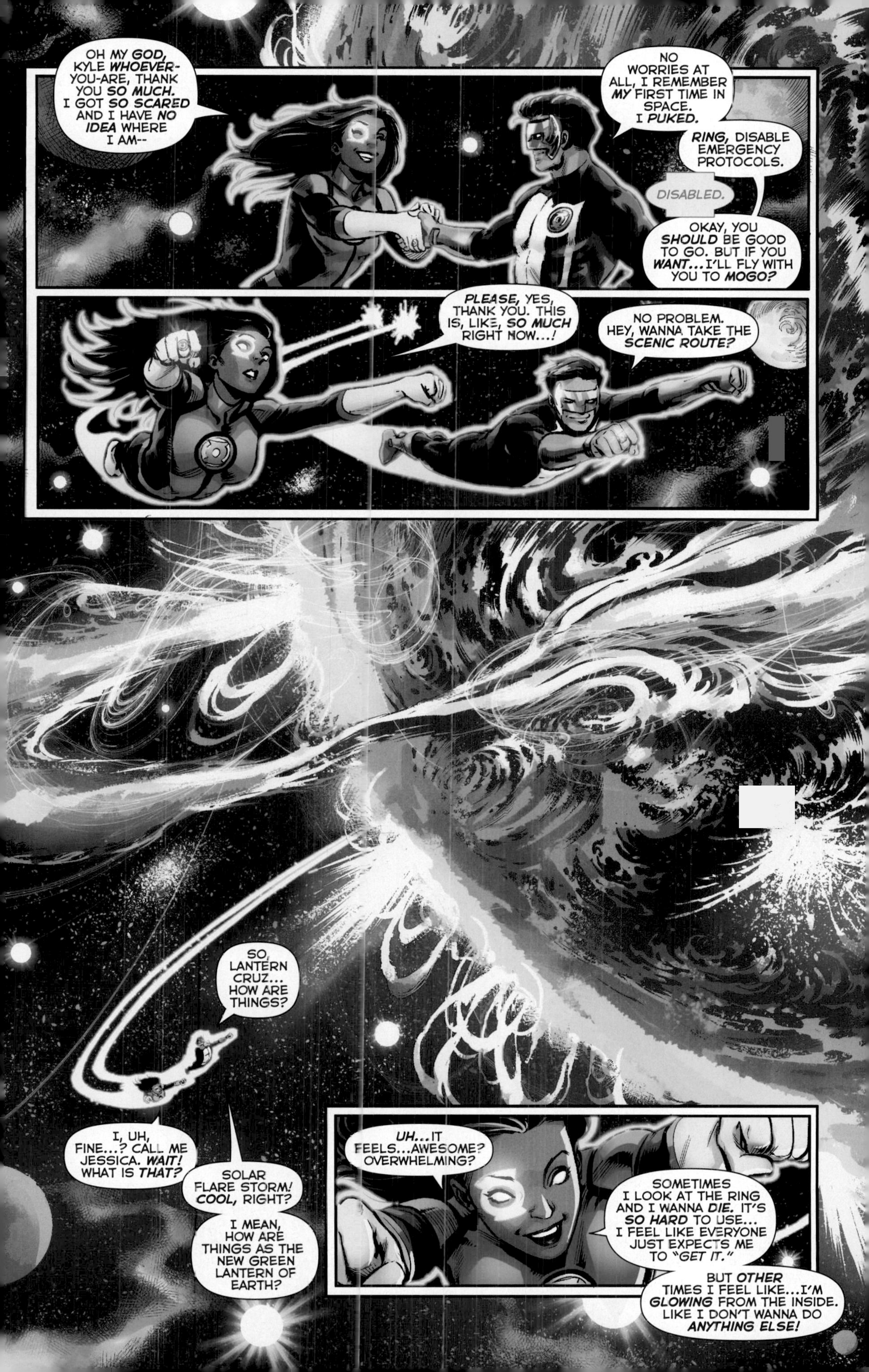
OH MY GOD, KYLE WHOEVER-YOU-ARE, THANK YOU SO MUCH. I GOT SO SCARED AND I HAVE NO IDEA WHERE I AM--
NO WORRIES AT ALL, I REMEMBER MY FIRST TIME IN SPACE. I PUKED.
RING, DISABLE EMERGENCY PROTOCOLS.
DISABLED.
OKAY, YOU SHOULD BE GOOD TO GO. BUT IF YOU WANT...I'LL FLY WITH YOU TO MOGO?
PLEASE, YES, THANK YOU. THIS IS, LIKE, SO MUCH RIGHT NOW...!
NO PROBLEM. HEY, WANNA TAKE THE SCENIC ROUTE?
SO, LANTERN CRUZ... HOW ARE THINGS?
I, UH, FINE...? CALL ME JESSICA. WAIT! WHAT IS THAT?
SOLAR FLARE STORM! COOL, RIGHT?
I MEAN, HOW ARE THINGS AS THE NEW GREEN LANTERN OF EARTH?
UH...IT FEELS...AWESOME? OVERWHELMING?
SOMETIMES I LOOK AT THE RING AND I WANNA DIE. IT'S SO HARD TO USE... I FEEL LIKE EVERYONE JUST EXPECTS ME TO "GET IT."
BUT OTHER TIMES I FEEL LIKE...I'M GLOWING FROM THE INSIDE. LIKE I DON'T WANNA DO ANYTHING ELSE!

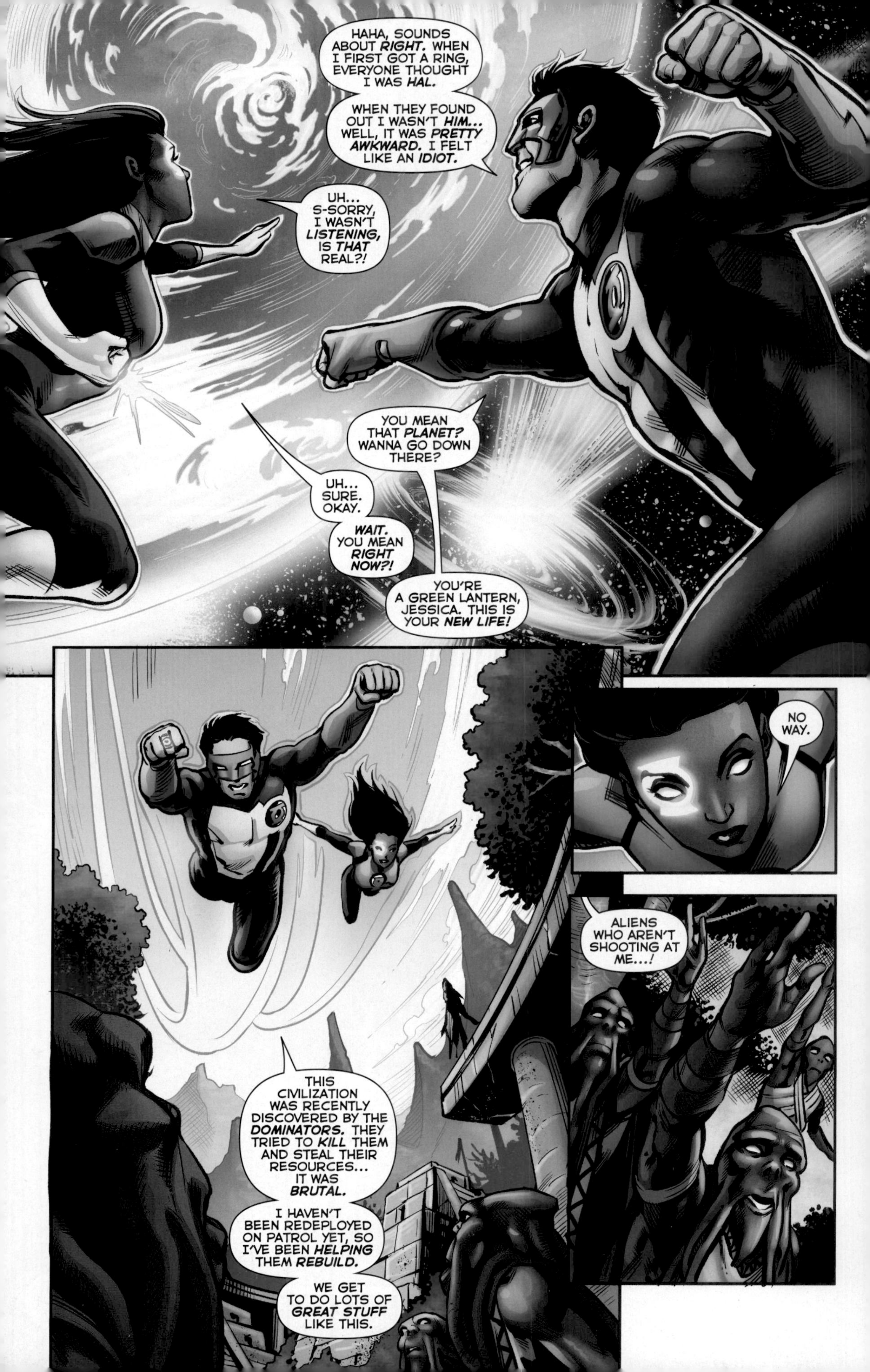
HAHA, SOUNDS ABOUT RIGHT. WHEN I FIRST GOT A RING, EVERYONE THOUGHT I WAS HAL.
WHEN THEY FOUND OUT I WASN'T HIM... WELL, IT WAS PRETTY AWKWARD. I FELT LIKE AN IDIOT.
UH... S-SORRY, I WASN'T LISTENING, IS THAT REAL?!
YOU MEAN THAT PLANET? WANNA GO DOWN THERE?
UH... SURE. OKAY.
WAIT. YOU MEAN RIGHT NOW?!
YOU'RE A GREEN LANTERN, JESSICA. THIS IS YOUR NEW LIFE!
NO WAY.
ALIENS WHO AREN'T SHOOTING AT ME...!
THIS CIVILIZATION WAS RECENTLY DISCOVERED BY THE DOMINATORS. THEY TRIED TO KILL THEM AND STEAL THEIR RESOURCES... IT WAS BRUTAL.
I HAVEN'T BEEN REDEPLOYED ON PATROL YET, SO I'VE BEEN HELPING THEM REBUILD.
WE GET TO DO LOTS OF GREAT STUFF LIKE THIS.

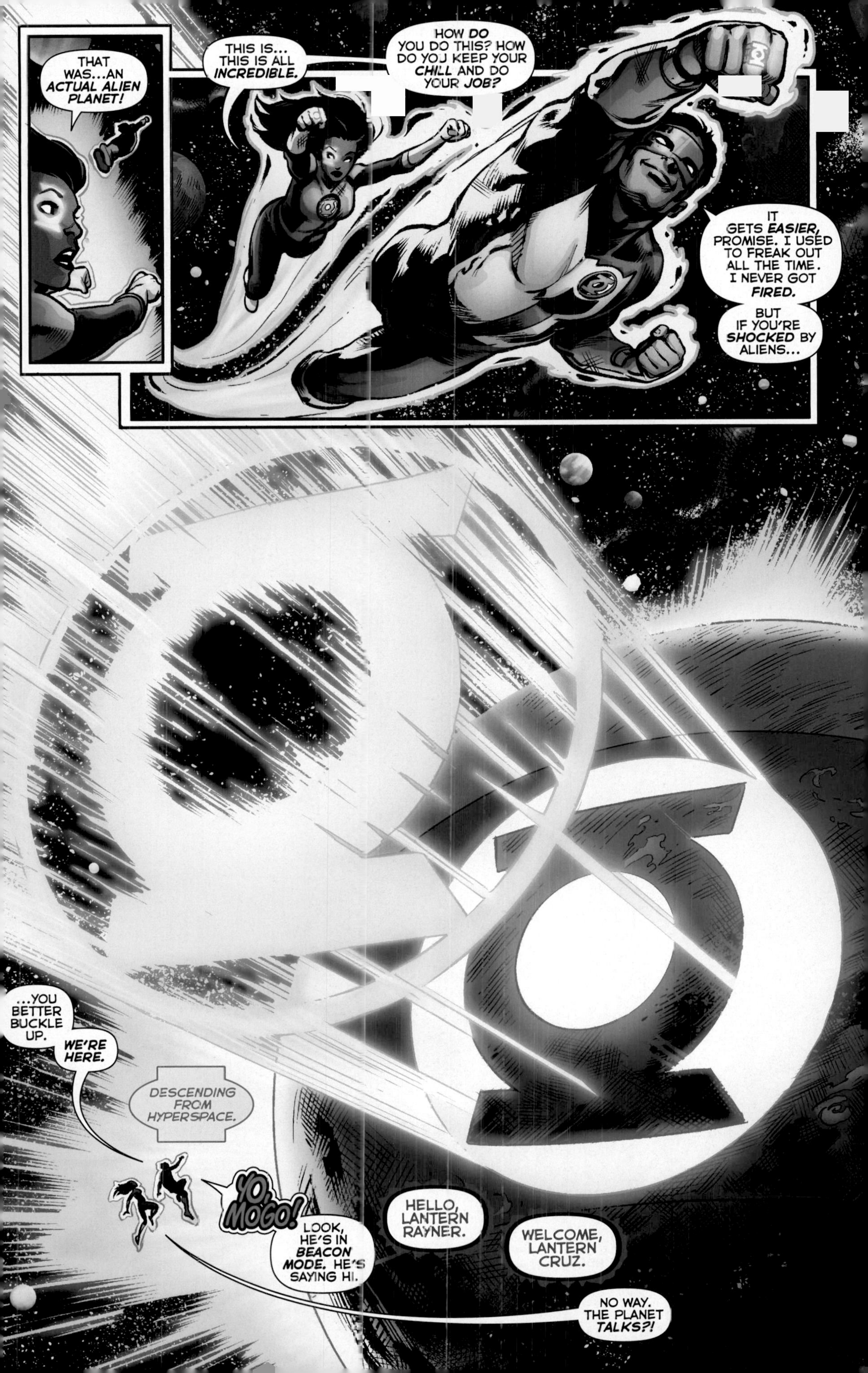

THAT WAS...AN ACTUAL ALIEN PLANET!
THIS IS... THIS IS ALL INCREDIBLE.
HOW DO YOU DO THIS? HOW DO YOU KEEP YOUR CHILL AND DO YOUR JOB?
IT GETS EASIER, PROMISE. I USED TO FREAK OUT ALL THE TIME. I NEVER GOT FIRED.
BUT IF YOU'RE SHOCKED BY ALIENS...
...YOU BETTER BUCKLE UP.
WE'RE HERE.
DESCENDING FROM HYPERSPACE.
YO, MOGO!
LOOK, HE'S IN BEACON MODE. HE'S SAYING HI.
HELLO, LANTERN RAYNER.
WELCOME, LANTERN CRUZ.
NO WAY. THE PLANET TALKS?!

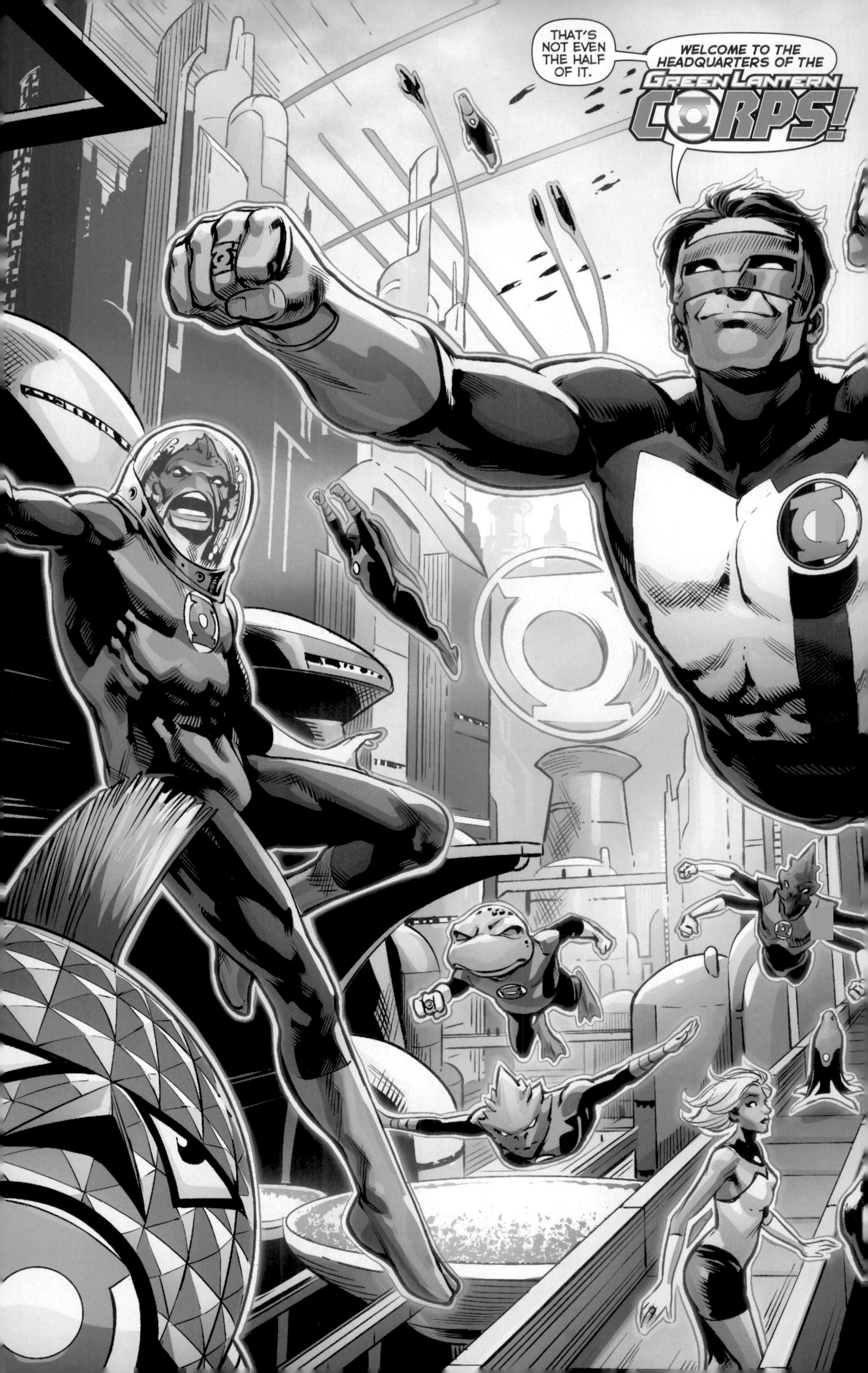
THAT'S NOT EVEN THE HALF OF IT.
WELCOME TO THE HEADQUARTERS OF THE GREEN LANTERN CORPS!

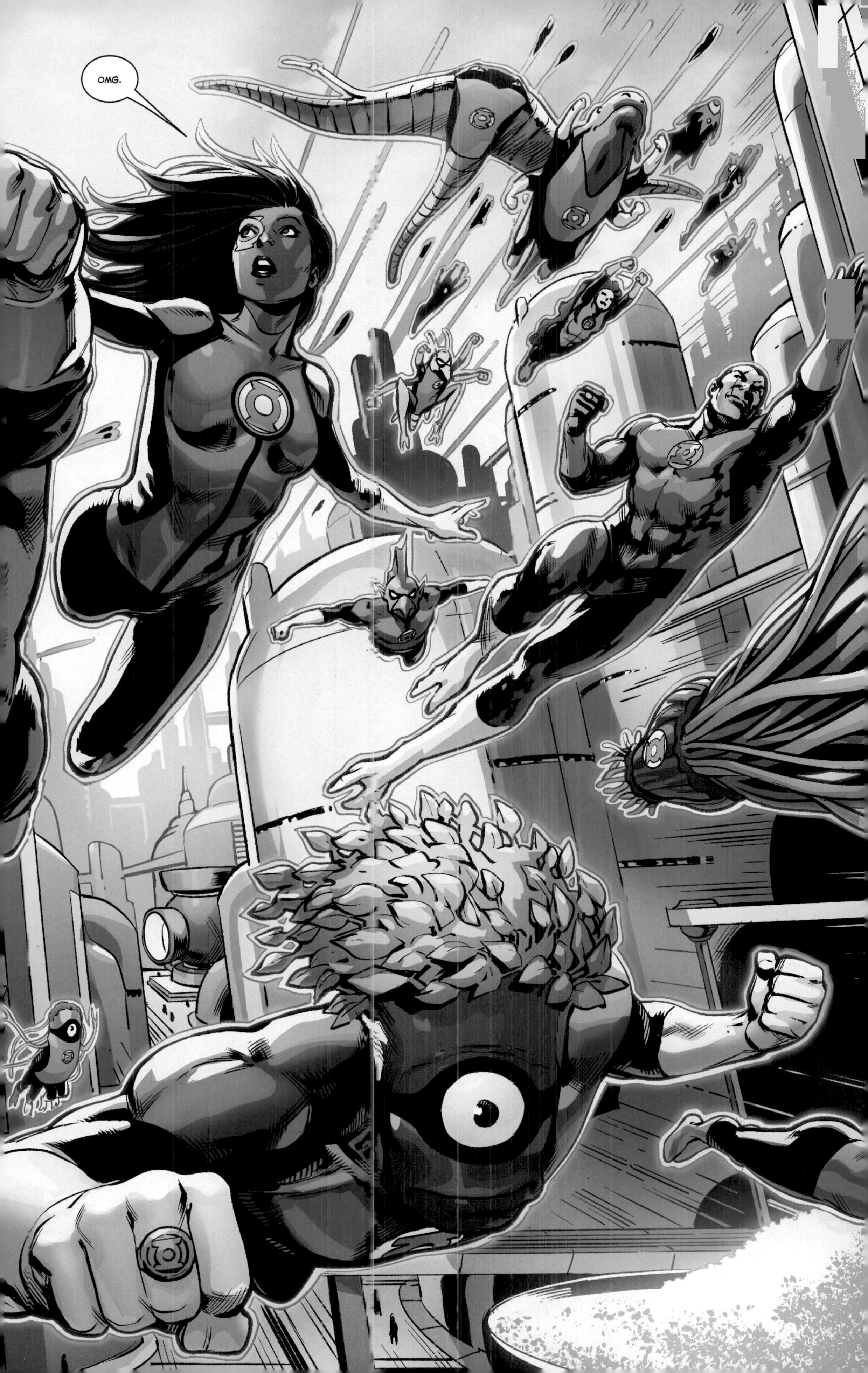
OMG.

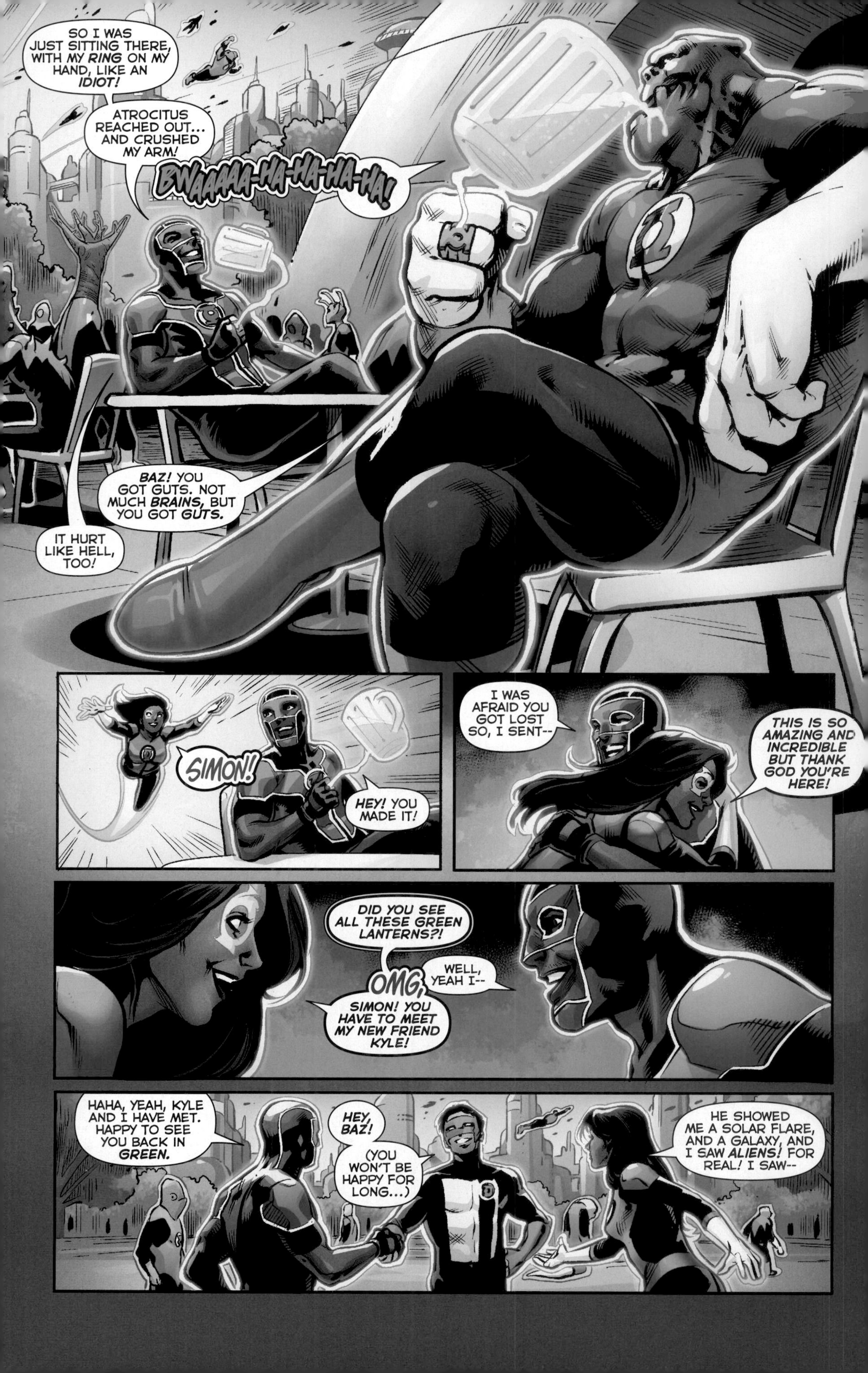
SO I WAS JUST SITTING THERE, WITH MY RING ON MY HAND, LIKE AN IDIOT!
ATROCITUS REACHED OUT... AND CRUSHED MY ARM!
BWAAAAA-HA-HA-HA-HA!
BAZ! YOU GOT GUTS. NOT MUCH BRAINS, BUT YOU GOT GUTS.
IT HURT LIKE HELL, TOO!
SIMON!
HEY! YOU MADE IT!
I WAS AFRAID YOU GOT LOST SO, I SENT--
THIS IS SO AMAZING AND INCREDIBLE BUT THANK GOD YOU'RE HERE!
DID YOU SEE ALL THESE GREEN LANTERNS?!
WELL, YEAH I--
OMG,
SIMON! YOU HAVE TO MEET MY NEW FRIEND KYLE!
HAHA, YEAH, KYLE AND I HAVE MET. HAPPY TO SEE YOU BACK IN GREEN.
HEY, BAZ!
(YOU WON'T BE HAPPY FOR LONG...)
HE SHOWED ME A SOLAR FLARE, AND A GALAXY, AND I SAW ALIENS! FOR REAL! I SAW--

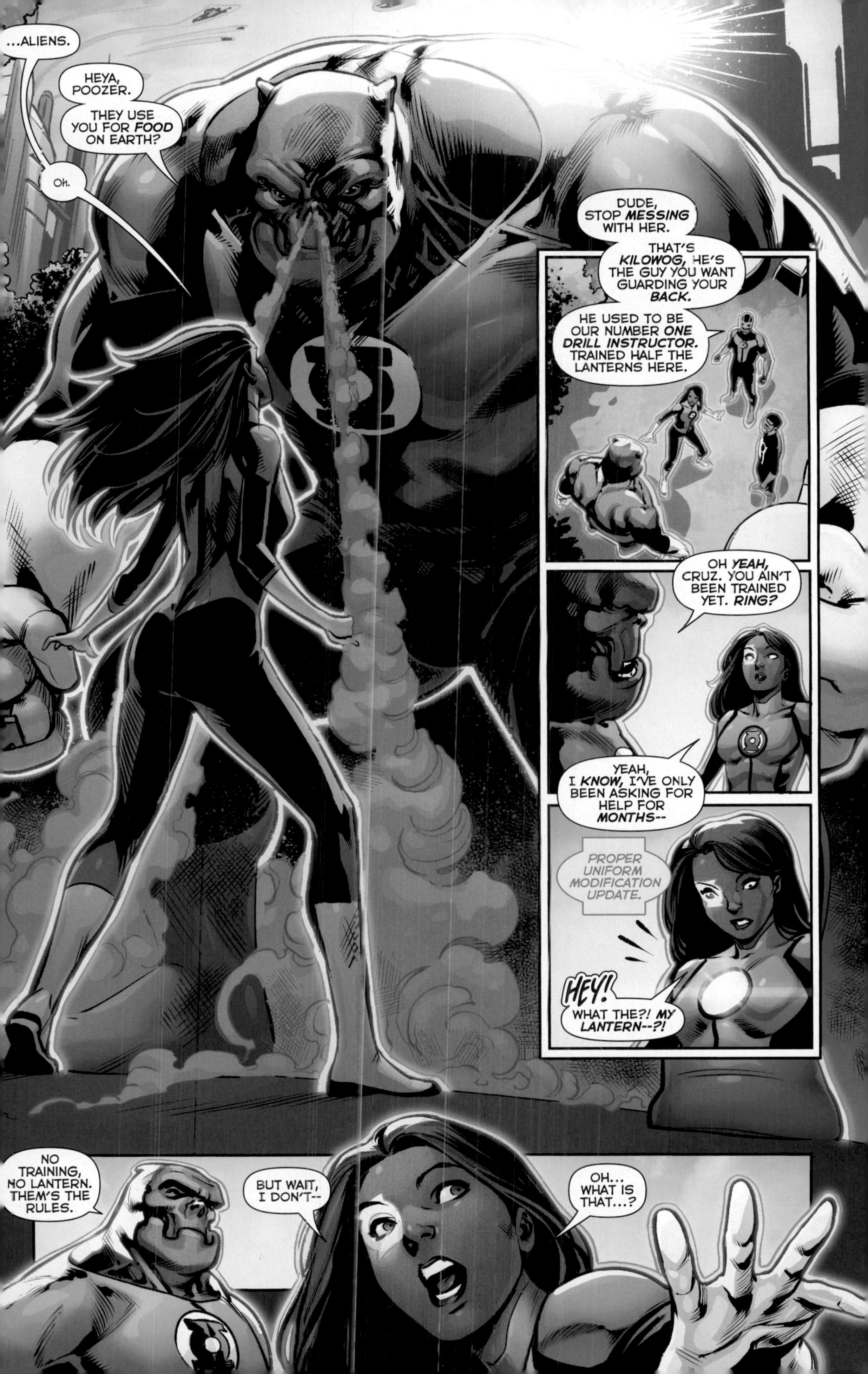
...ALIENS.
HEYA, POOZER.
THEY USE YOU FOR FOOD ON EARTH?
Oh.
DUDE, STOP MESSING WITH HER.
THAT'S KILOWOG, HE'S THE GUY YOU WANT GUARDING YOUR BACK.
HE USED TO BE OUR NUMBER ONE DRILL INSTRUCTOR. TRAINED HALF THE LANTERNS HERE.
OH YEAH, CRUZ. YOU AIN'T BEEN TRAINED YET. RING?
YEAH, I KNOW, I'VE ONLY BEEN ASKING FOR HELP FOR MONTHS--
PROPER UNIFORM MODIFICATION UPDATE.
HEY!
WHAT THE?! MY LANTERN--?!
NO TRAINING, NO LANTERN. THEM'S THE RULES.
BUT WAIT, I DON'T--
OH... WHAT IS THAT...?

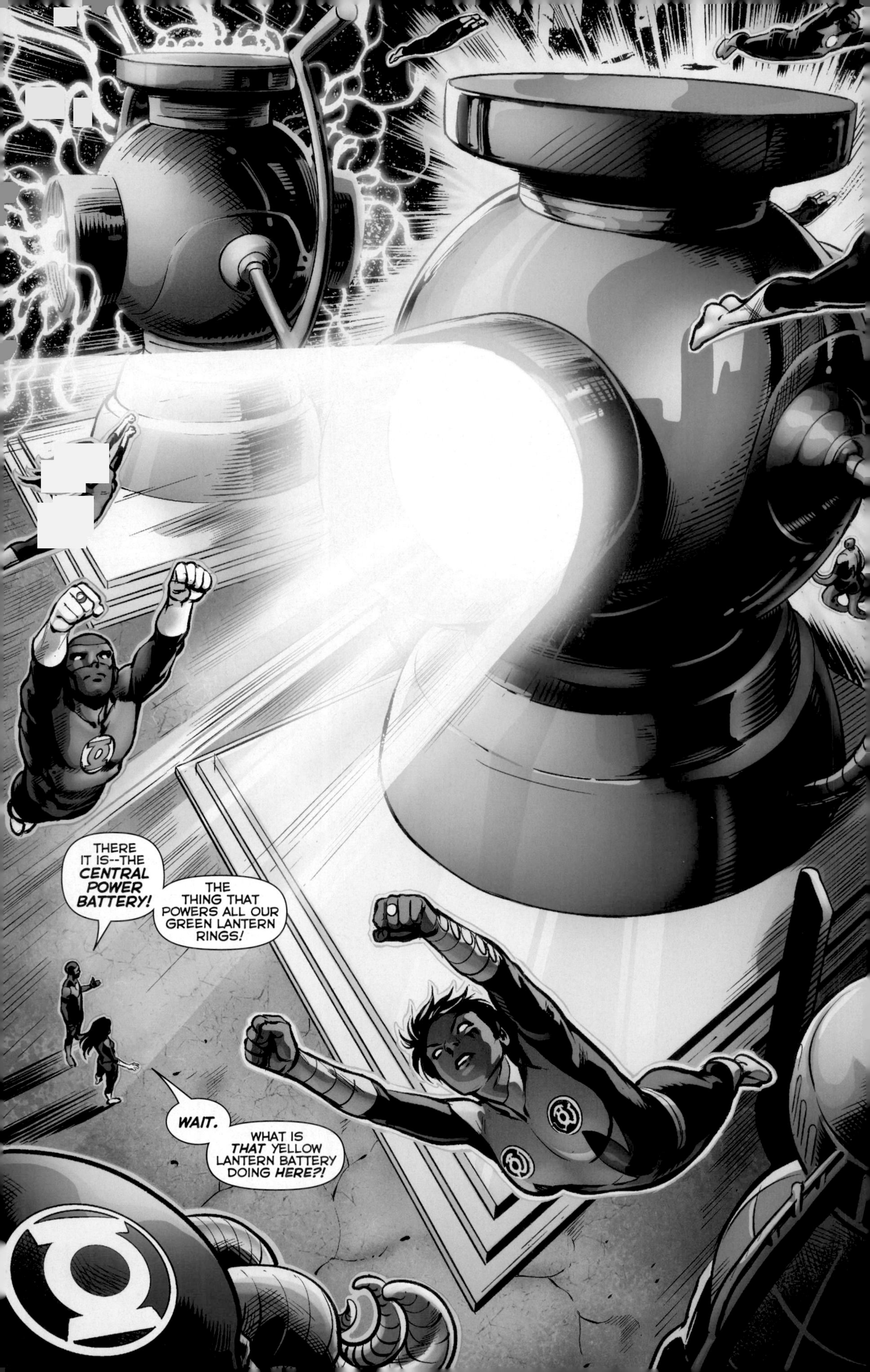
THERE IT IS--THE CENTRAL POWER BATTERY!
THE THING THAT POWERS ALL OUR GREEN LANTERN RINGS!
WAIT.
WHAT IS THAT YELLOW LANTERN BATTERY DOING HERE?!

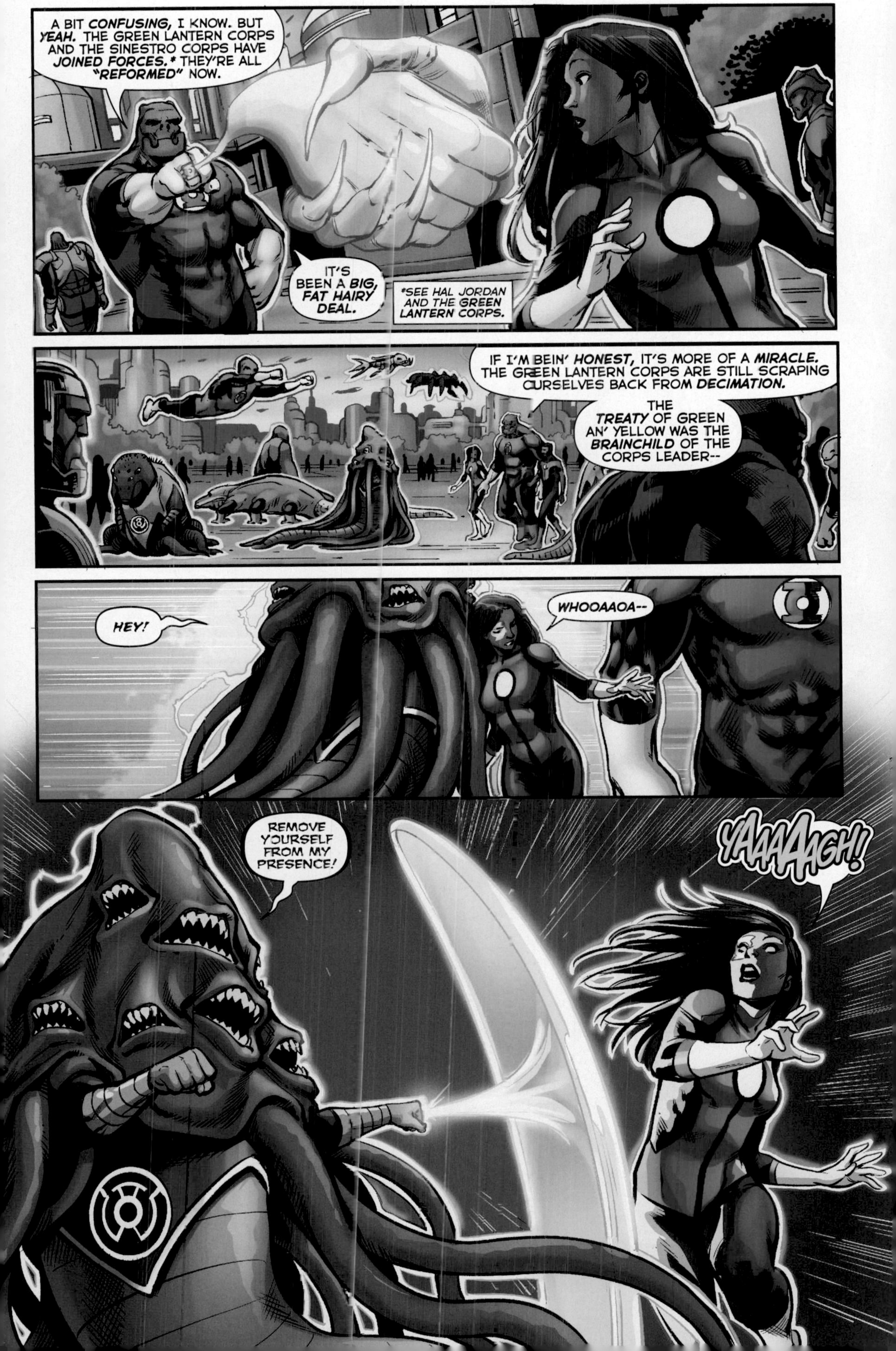
A BIT CONFUSING, I KNOW. BUT YEAH. THE GREEN LANTERN CORPS AND THE SINESTRO CORPS HAVE JOINED FORCES.* THEY'RE ALL "REFORMED" NOW.
IT'S BEEN A BIG, FAT HAIRY DEAL.
*SEE HAL JORDAN AND THE GREEN LANTERN CORPS.
IF I'M BEIN' HONEST, IT'S MORE OF A MIRACLE. THE GREEN LANTERN CORPS ARE STILL SCRAPING OURSELVES BACK FROM DECIMATION.
THE TREATY OF GREEN AN' YELLOW WAS THE BRAINCHILD OF THE CORPS LEADER--
HEY!
WHOOAAOA--
REMOVE YOURSELF FROM MY PRESENCE!
YAAAAAGH!

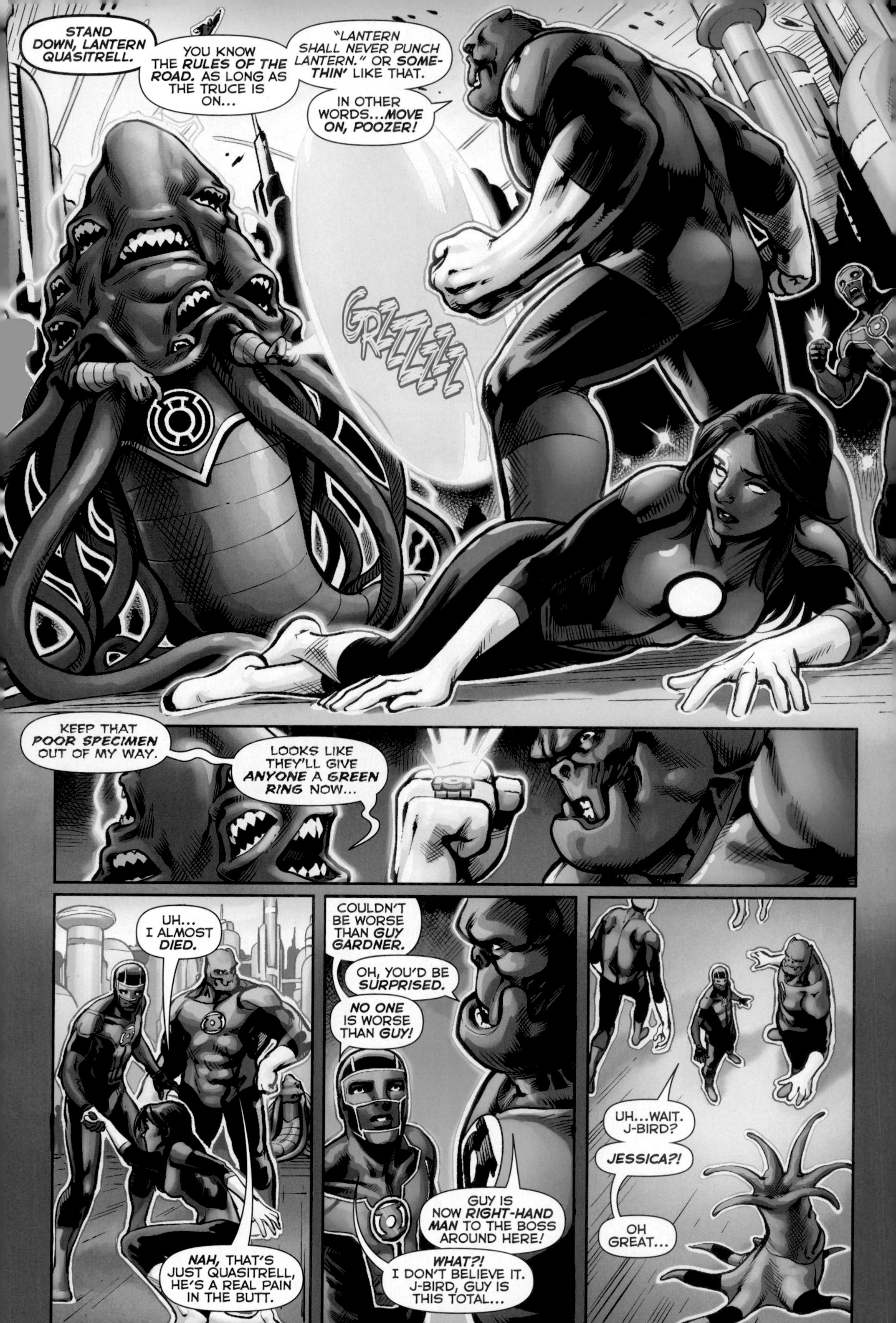
STAND DOWN, LANTERN QUASITRELL.
YOU KNOW THE RULES OF THE ROAD. AS LONG AS THE TRUCE IS ON...
"LANTERN SHALL NEVER PUNCH LANTERN." OR SOME-THIN' LIKE THAT.
IN OTHER WORDS...MOVE ON, POOZER!
GRZZZZZ
KEEP THAT POOR SPECIMEN OUT OF MY WAY.
LOOKS LIKE THEY'LL GIVE ANYONE A GREEN RING NOW...
UH... I ALMOST DIED.
NAH, THAT'S JUST QUASITRELL, HE'S A REAL PAIN IN THE BUTT.
COULDN'T BE WORSE THAN GUY GARDNER.
OH, YOU'D BE SURPRISED.
NO ONE IS WORSE THAN GUY!
GUY IS NOW RIGHT-HAND MAN TO THE BOSS AROUND HERE!
WHAT?! I DON'T BELIEVE IT. J-BIRD, GUY IS THIS TOTAL...
UH...WAIT. J-BIRD?
JESSICA?!
OH GREAT...

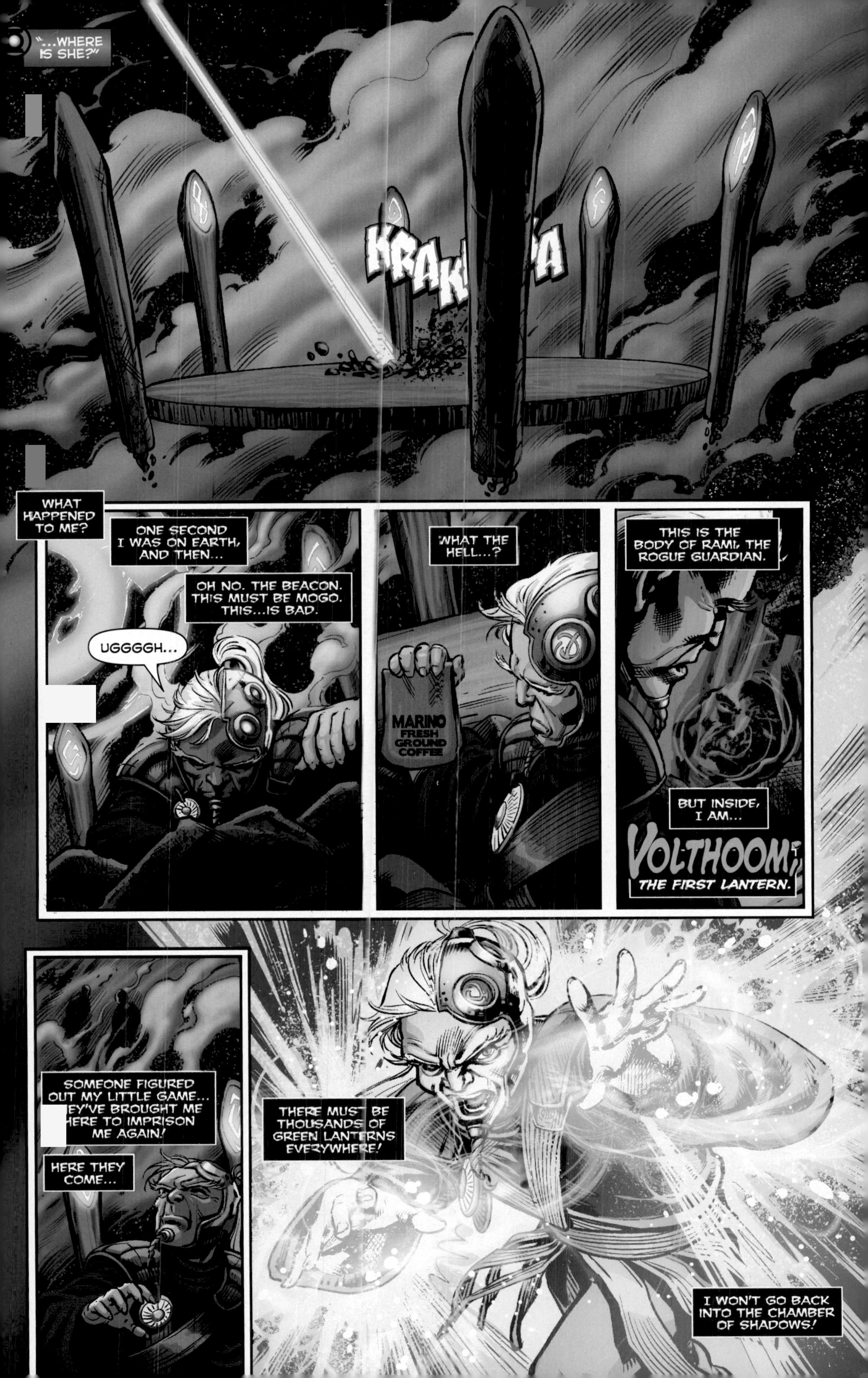

"...WHERE IS SHE?"
KRAK
A
WHAT HAPPENED TO ME?
ONE SECOND I WAS ON EARTH, AND THEN...
OH NO. THE BEACON. THIS MUST BE MOGO. THIS...IS BAD.
UGGGGH...
WHAT THE HELL...?
MARINO FRESH GROUND COFFEE
THIS IS THE BODY OF RAMI, THE ROGUE GUARDIAN.
BUT INSIDE, I AM...
VOLTHOOM,
THE FIRST LANTERN.
SOMEONE FIGURED OUT MY LITTLE GAME...
EY'VE BROUGHT ME
HERE TO IMPRISON
ME AGAIN!
HERE THEY COME...
THERE MUST BE THOUSANDS OF GREEN LANTERNS EVERYWHERE!
I WON'T GO BACK INTO THE CHAMBER OF SHADOWS!

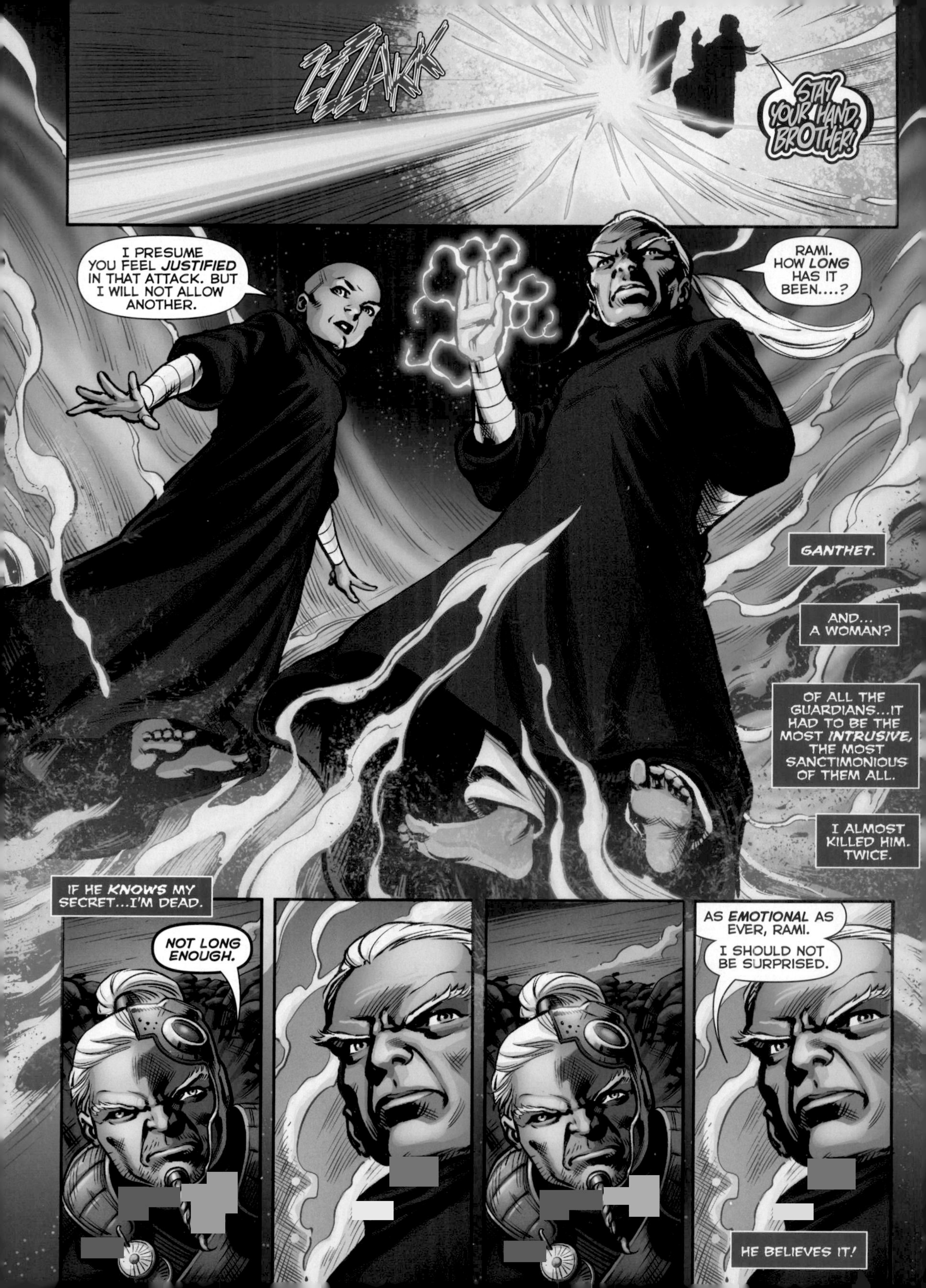

ZZZAKK
STAY YOUR HAND, BROTHER!
I PRESUME YOU FEEL *JUSTIFIED* IN THAT ATTACK. BUT I WILL NOT ALLOW ANOTHER.
RAMI. HOW *LONG* HAS IT BEEN....?
GANTHET.
AND... A WOMAN?
OF ALL THE GUARDIANS...IT HAD TO BE THE MOST *INTRUSIVE,* THE MOST SANCTIMONIOUS OF THEM ALL.
I ALMOST KILLED HIM. TWICE.
IF HE *KNOWS* MY SECRET...I'M DEAD.
NOT LONG ENOUGH.
AS *EMOTIONAL* AS EVER, RAMI.
I SHOULD NOT BE SURPRISED.
HE BELIEVES IT!

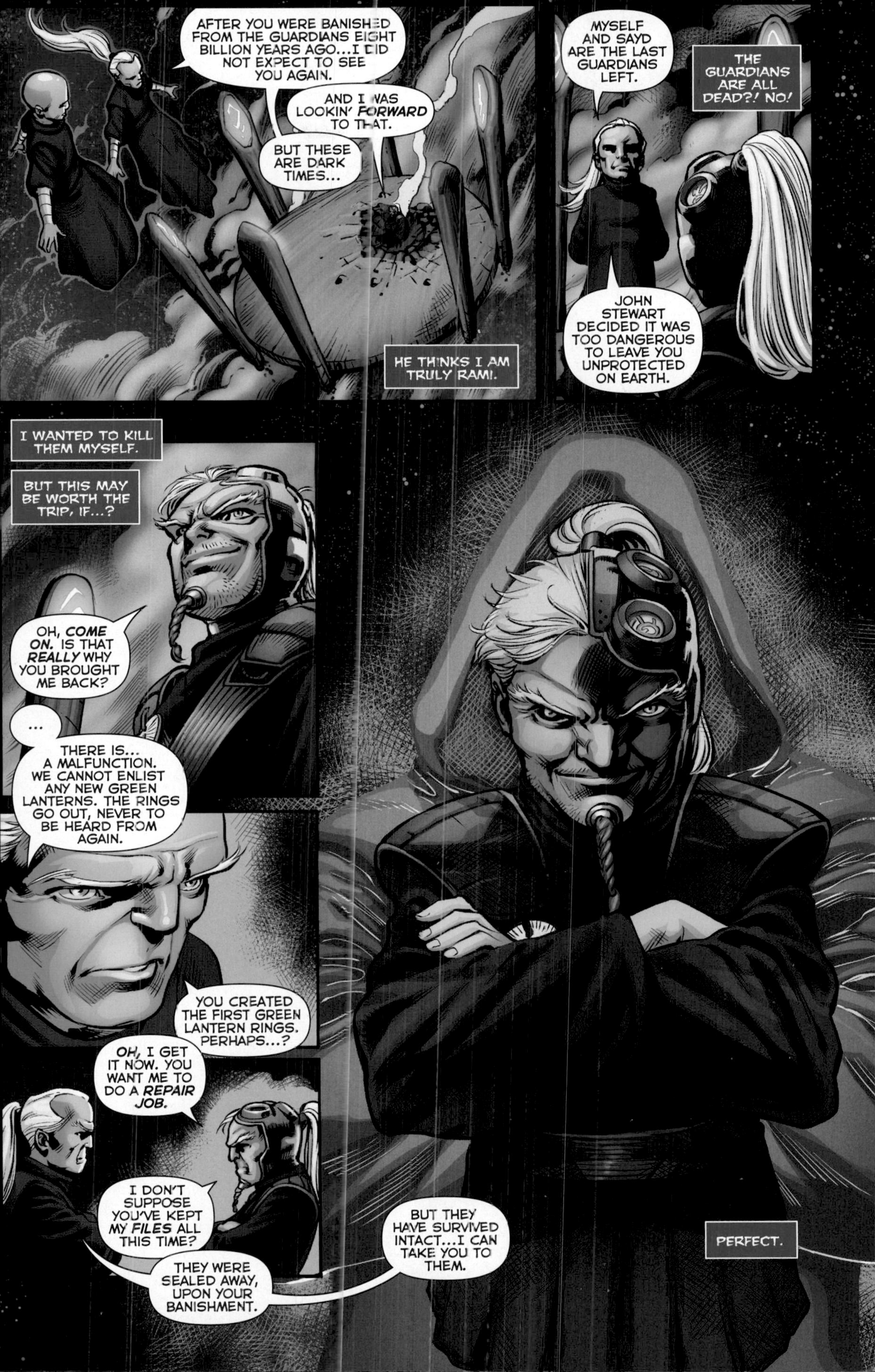
AFTER YOU WERE BANISHED FROM THE GUARDIANS EIGHT BILLION YEARS AGO...I DID NOT EXPECT TO SEE YOU AGAIN.
AND I WAS LOOKIN' FORWARD TO THAT.
BUT THESE ARE DARK TIMES...
HE THINKS I AM TRULY RAMI.
MYSELF AND SAYD ARE THE LAST GUARDIANS LEFT.
THE GUARDIANS ARE ALL DEAD?! NO!
JOHN STEWART DECIDED IT WAS TOO DANGEROUS TO LEAVE YOU UNPROTECTED ON EARTH.
I WANTED TO KILL THEM MYSELF.
BUT THIS MAY BE WORTH THE TRIP, IF...?
OH, COME ON. IS THAT REALLY WHY YOU BROUGHT ME BACK?
...
THERE IS... A MALFUNCTION. WE CANNOT ENLIST ANY NEW GREEN LANTERNS. THE RINGS GO OUT, NEVER TO BE HEARD FROM AGAIN.
YOU CREATED THE FIRST GREEN LANTERN RINGS. PERHAPS...?
OH, I GET IT NOW. YOU WANT ME TO DO A REPAIR JOB.
I DON'T SUPPOSE YOU'VE KEPT MY FILES ALL THIS TIME?
THEY WERE SEALED AWAY, UPON YOUR BANISHMENT.
BUT THEY HAVE SURVIVED INTACT...I CAN TAKE YOU TO THEM.
PERFECT.

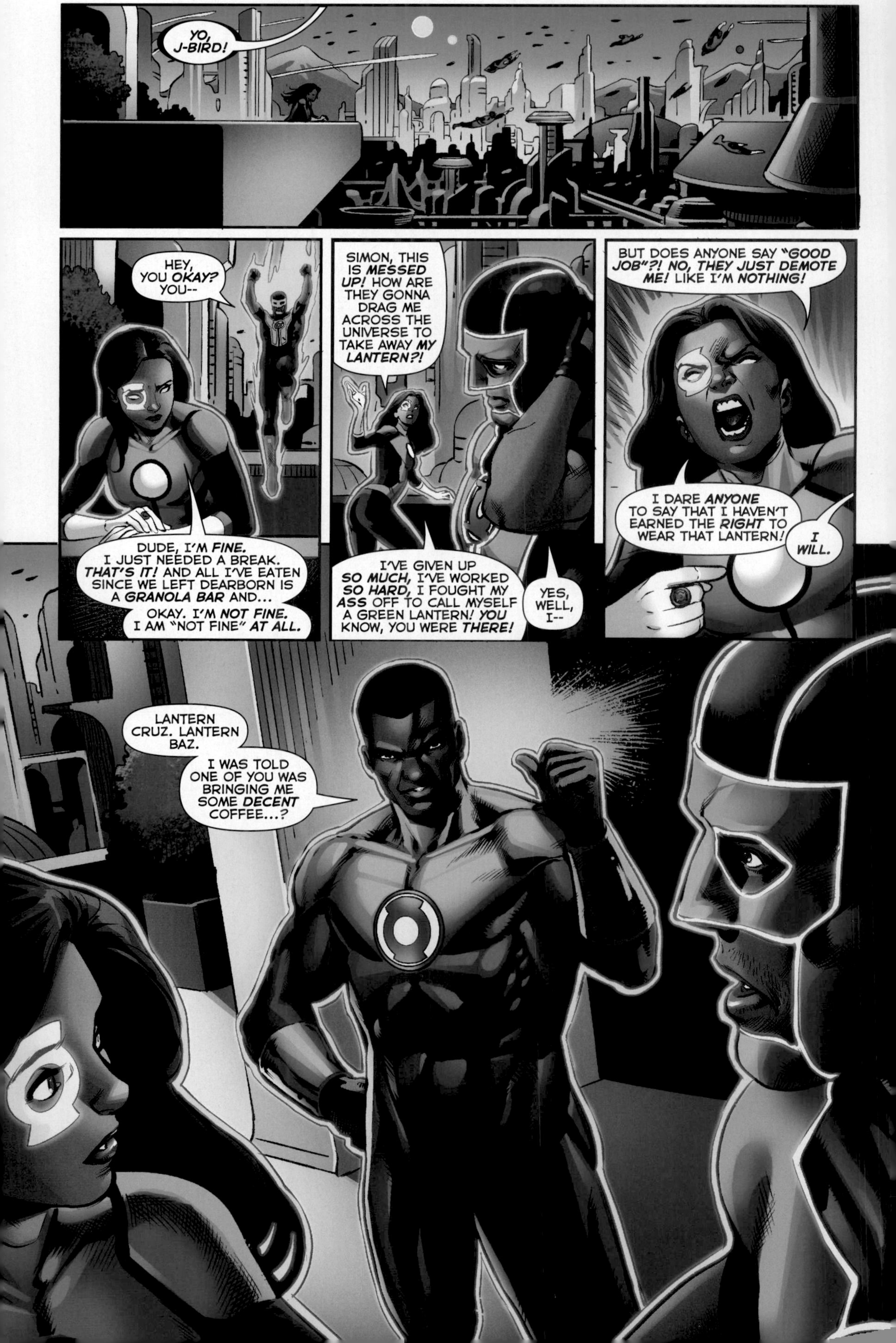
YO, J-BIRD!
HEY, YOU OKAY? YOU--
DUDE, I'M FINE. I JUST NEEDED A BREAK. THAT'S IT! AND ALL I'VE EATEN SINCE WE LEFT DEARBORN IS A GRANOLA BAR AND...
OKAY. I'M NOT FINE. I AM "NOT FINE" AT ALL.
SIMON, THIS IS MESSED UP! HOW ARE THEY GONNA DRAG ME ACROSS THE UNIVERSE TO TAKE AWAY MY LANTERN?!
I'VE GIVEN UP SO MUCH, I'VE WORKED SO HARD, I FOUGHT MY ASS OFF TO CALL MYSELF A GREEN LANTERN! YOU KNOW, YOU WERE THERE!
YES, WELL, I--
BUT DOES ANYONE SAY "GOOD JOB"?! NO, THEY JUST DEMOTE ME! LIKE I'M NOTHING!
I DARE ANYONE TO SAY THAT I HAVEN'T EARNED THE RIGHT TO WEAR THAT LANTERN!
I WILL.
LANTERN CRUZ. LANTERN BAZ.
I WAS TOLD ONE OF YOU WAS BRINGING ME SOME DECENT COFFEE...?

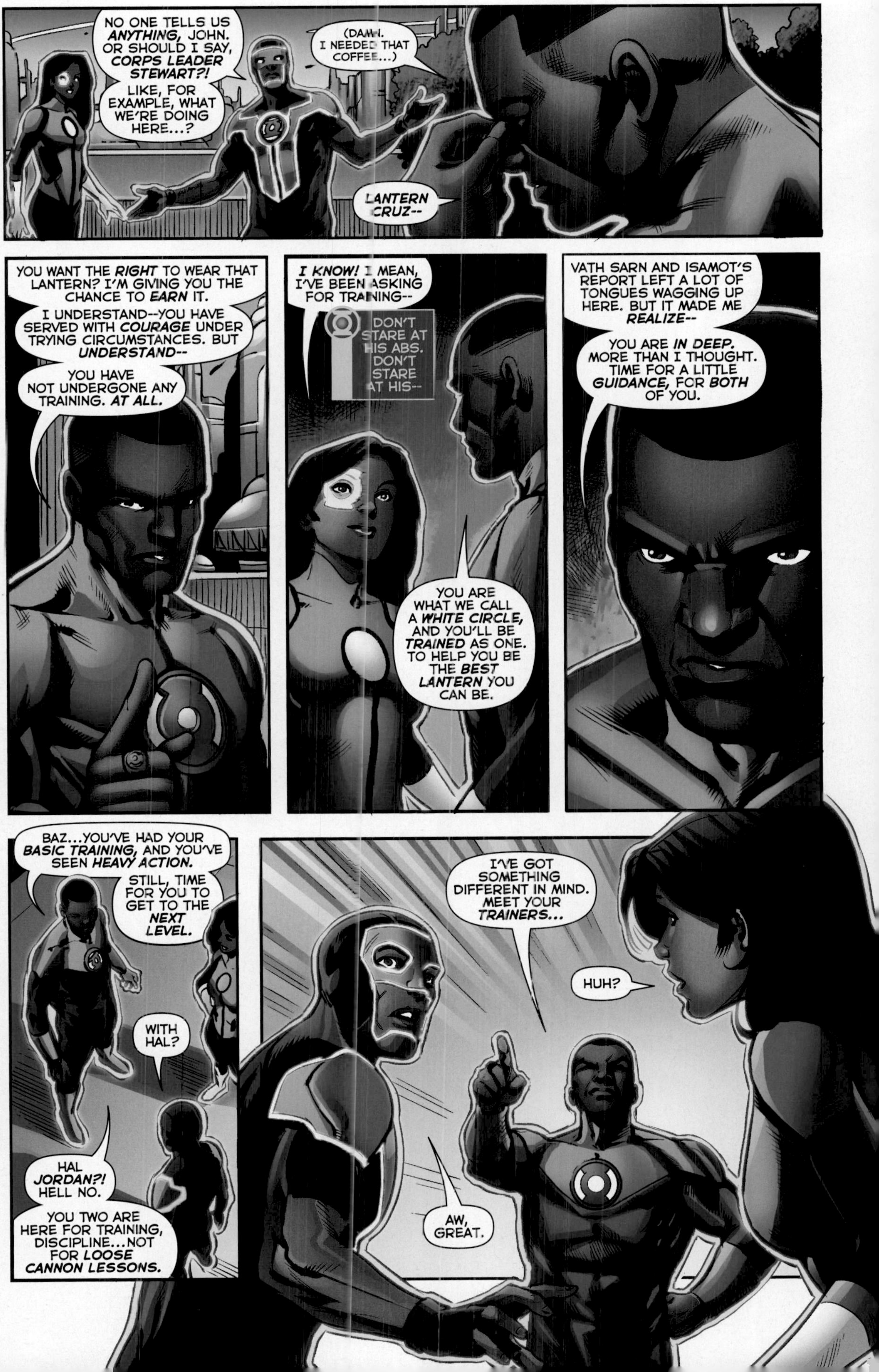
NO ONE TELLS US ANYTHING, JOHN. OR SHOULD I SAY, CORPS LEADER STEWART?!
LIKE, FOR EXAMPLE, WHAT WE'RE DOING HERE...?
(DAMN. I NEEDED THAT COFFEE...)
LANTERN CRUZ--
YOU WANT THE RIGHT TO WEAR THAT LANTERN? I'M GIVING YOU THE CHANCE TO EARN IT.
I UNDERSTAND--YOU HAVE SERVED WITH COURAGE UNDER TRYING CIRCUMSTANCES. BUT UNDERSTAND--
YOU HAVE NOT UNDERGONE ANY TRAINING. AT ALL.
I KNOW! I MEAN, I'VE BEEN ASKING FOR TRAINING--
DON'T STARE AT HIS ABS. DON'T STARE AT HIS--
YOU ARE WHAT WE CALL A WHITE CIRCLE, AND YOU'LL BE TRAINED AS ONE. TO HELP YOU BE THE BEST LANTERN YOU CAN BE.
VATH SARN AND ISAMOT'S REPORT LEFT A LOT OF TONGUES WAGGING UP HERE. BUT IT MADE ME REALIZE--
YOU ARE IN DEEP. MORE THAN I THOUGHT. TIME FOR A LITTLE GUIDANCE, FOR BOTH OF YOU.
BAZ...YOU'VE HAD YOUR BASIC TRAINING, AND YOU'VE SEEN HEAVY ACTION.
STILL, TIME FOR YOU TO GET TO THE NEXT LEVEL.
WITH HAL?
HAL JORDAN?! HELL NO.
YOU TWO ARE HERE FOR TRAINING, DISCIPLINE...NOT FOR LOOSE CANNON LESSONS.
I'VE GOT SOMETHING DIFFERENT IN MIND. MEET YOUR TRAINERS...
HUH?
AW, GREAT.

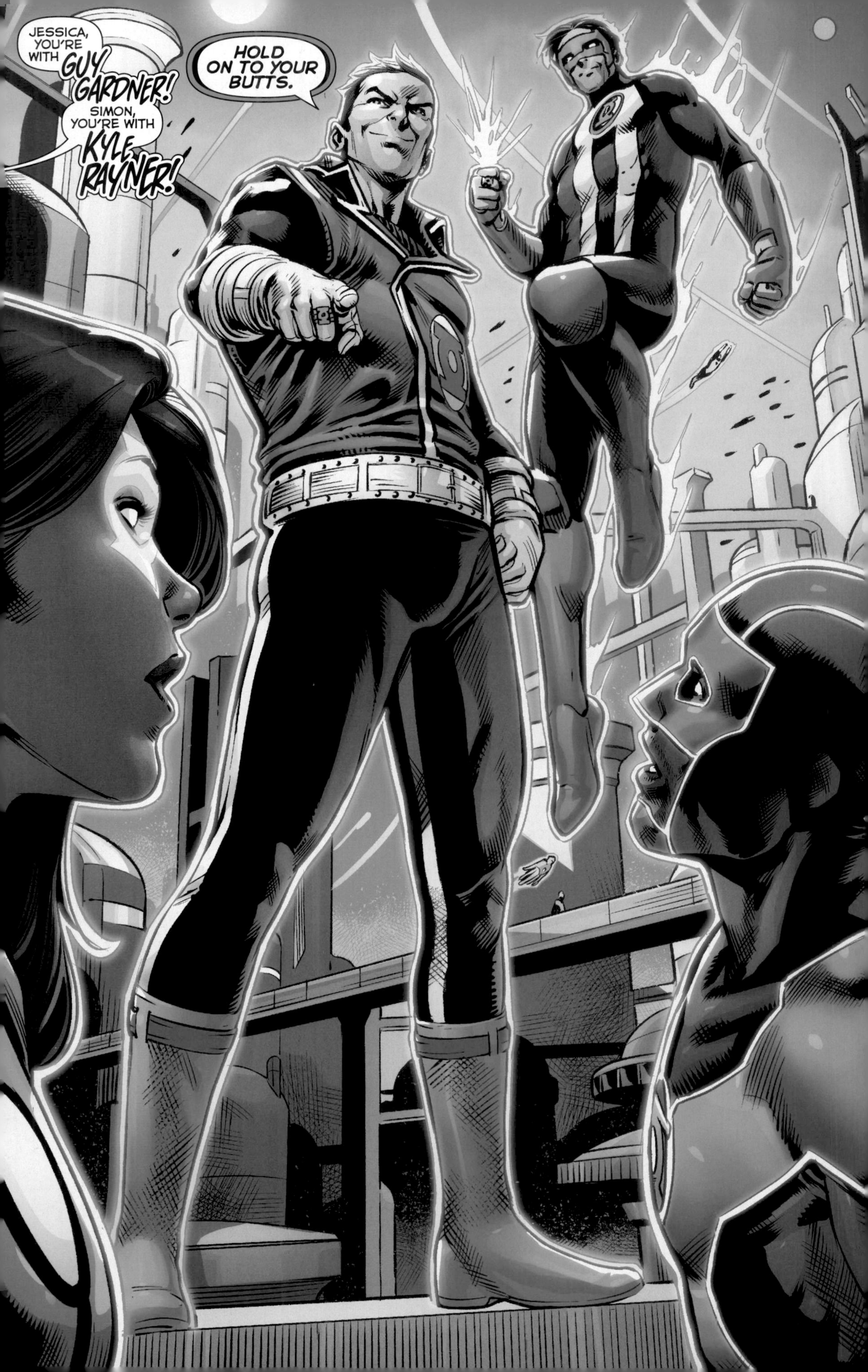
JESSICA, YOU'RE WITH GUY GARDNER! SIMON, YOU'RE WITH KYLE RAYNER!
HOLD ON TO YOUR BUTTS.

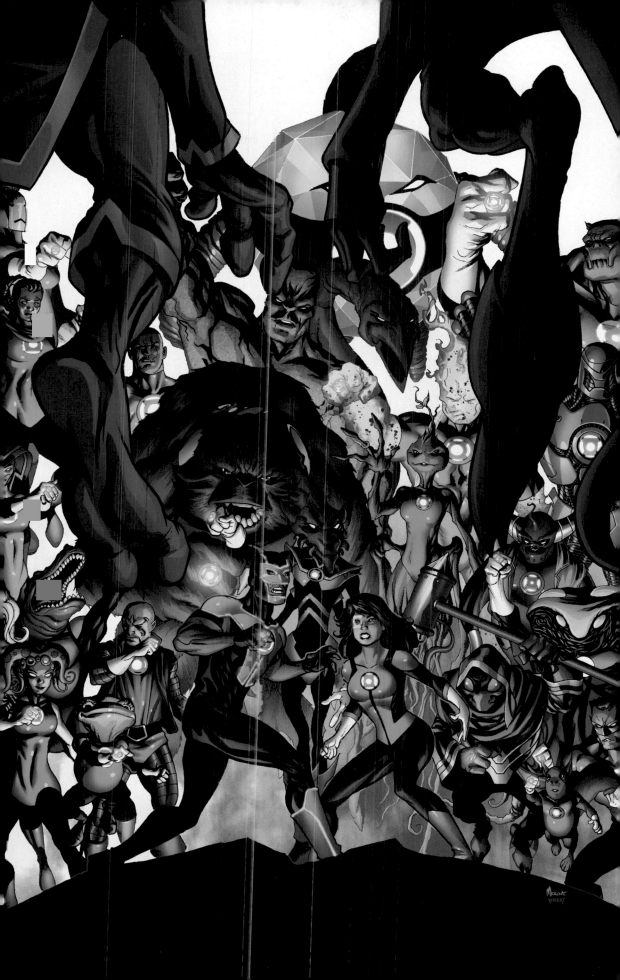

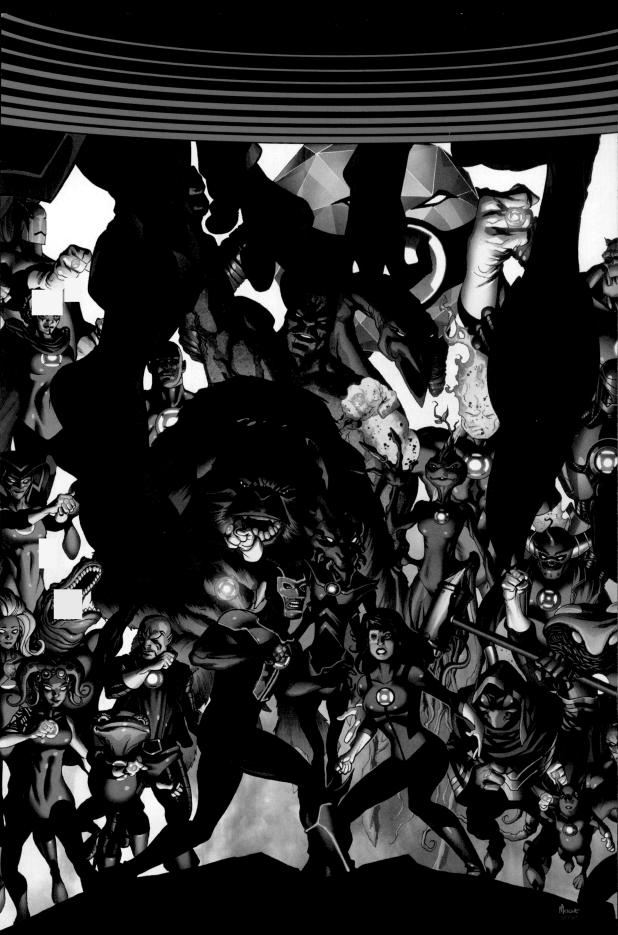

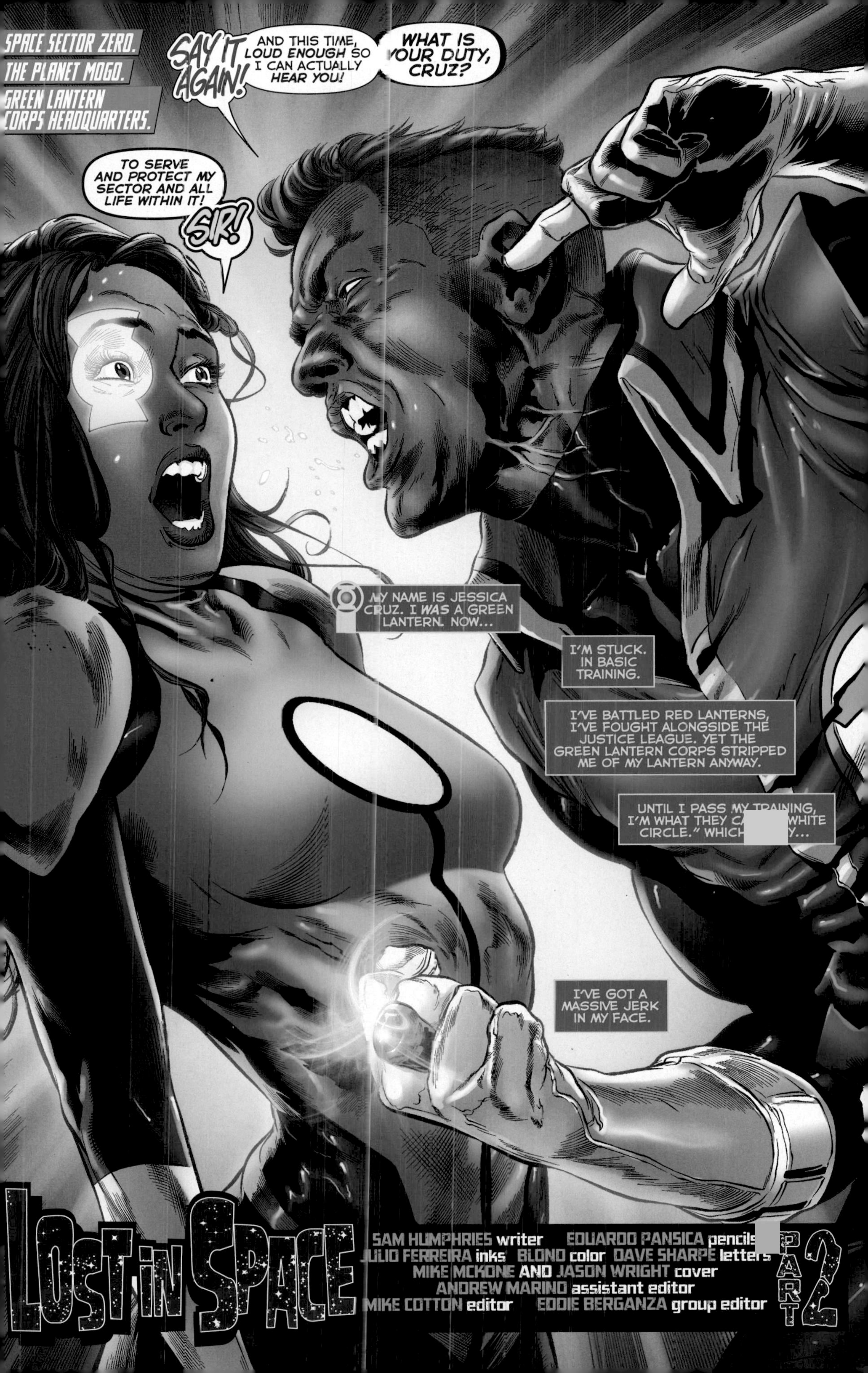
SPACE SECTOR ZERO.
THE PLANET MOGO.
GREEN LANTERN CORPS HEADQUARTERS.
SAY IT AGAIN!
AND THIS TIME, LOUD ENOUGH SO I CAN ACTUALLY HEAR YOU!
WHAT IS YOUR DUTY, CRUZ?
TO SERVE AND PROTECT MY SECTOR AND ALL LIFE WITHIN IT!
SIR!
MY NAME IS JESSICA CRUZ. I WAS A GREEN LANTERN. NOW...
I'M STUCK. IN BASIC TRAINING.
I'VE BATTLED RED LANTERNS, I'VE FOUGHT ALONGSIDE THE JUSTICE LEAGUE. YET THE GREEN LANTERN CORPS STRIPPED ME OF MY LANTERN ANYWAY.
UNTIL I PASS MY TRAINING, I'M WHAT THEY CA WHITE CIRCLE." WHICH Y...
I'VE GOT A MASSIVE JERK IN MY FACE.
LOST IN SPACE
SAM HUMPHRIES writer EDUARDO PANSICA pencils
JULIO FERREIRA inks BLOND color DAVE SHARPE letters
MIKE MCKONE AND JASON WRIGHT cover
ANDREW MARINO assistant editor
MIKE COTTON editor EDDIE BERGANZA group editor
PART 2

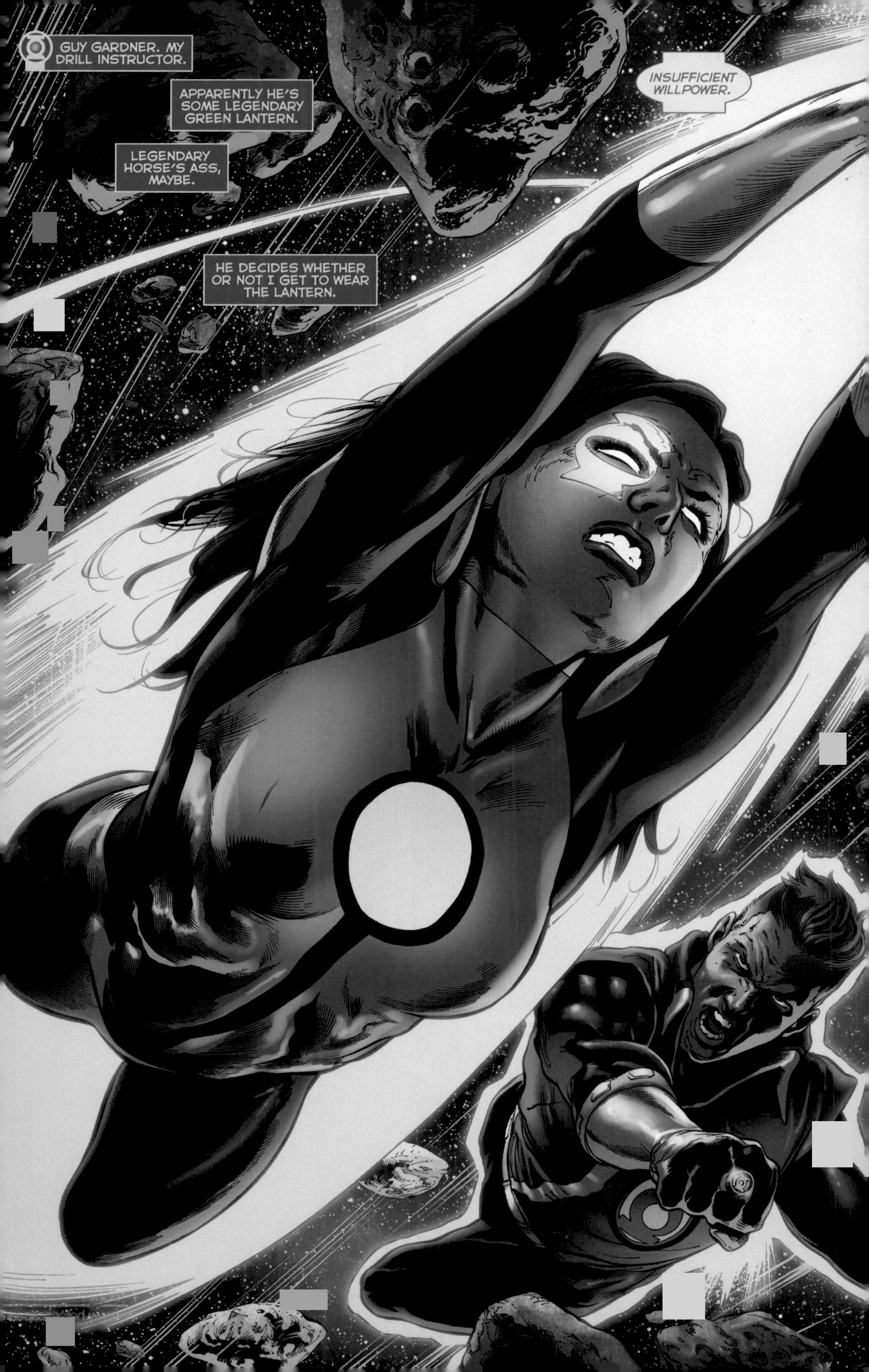
GUY GARDNER. MY DRILL INSTRUCTOR.
APPARENTLY HE'S SOME LEGENDARY GREEN LANTERN.
LEGENDARY HORSE'S ASS, MAYBE.
HE DECIDES WHETHER OR NOT I GET TO WEAR THE LANTERN.
INSUFFICIENT WILLPOWER.

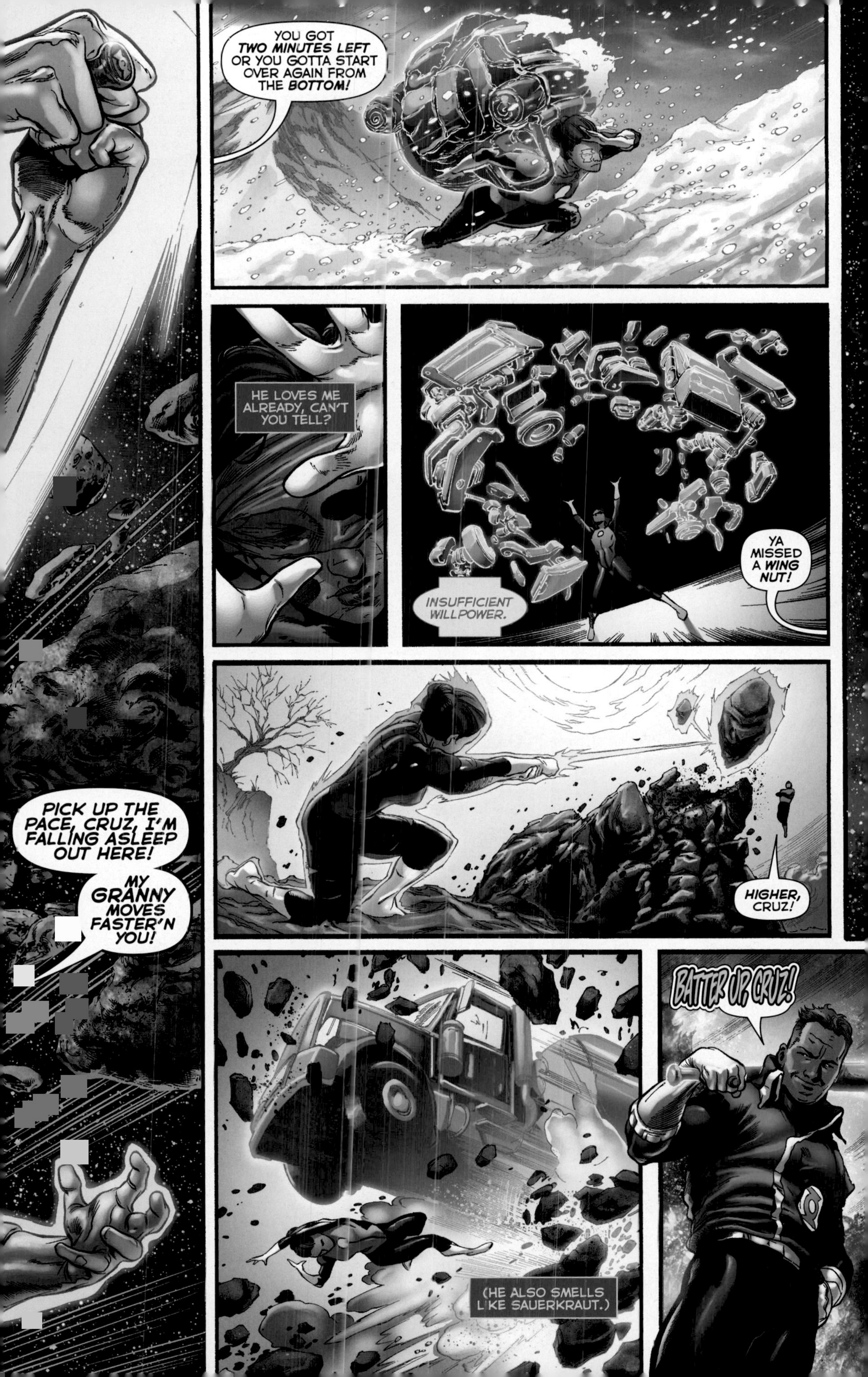
YOU GOT TWO MINUTES LEFT OR YOU GOTTA START OVER AGAIN FROM THE BOTTOM!
HE LOVES ME ALREADY, CAN'T YOU TELL?
INSUFFICIENT WILLPOWER.
YA MISSED A WING NUT!
PICK UP THE PACE, CRUZ, I'M FALLING ASLEEP OUT HERE!
MY GRANNY MOVES FASTER'N YOU!
HIGHER, CRUZ!
BATTER UP, CRUZ!
(HE ALSO SMELLS LIKE SAUERKRAUT.)

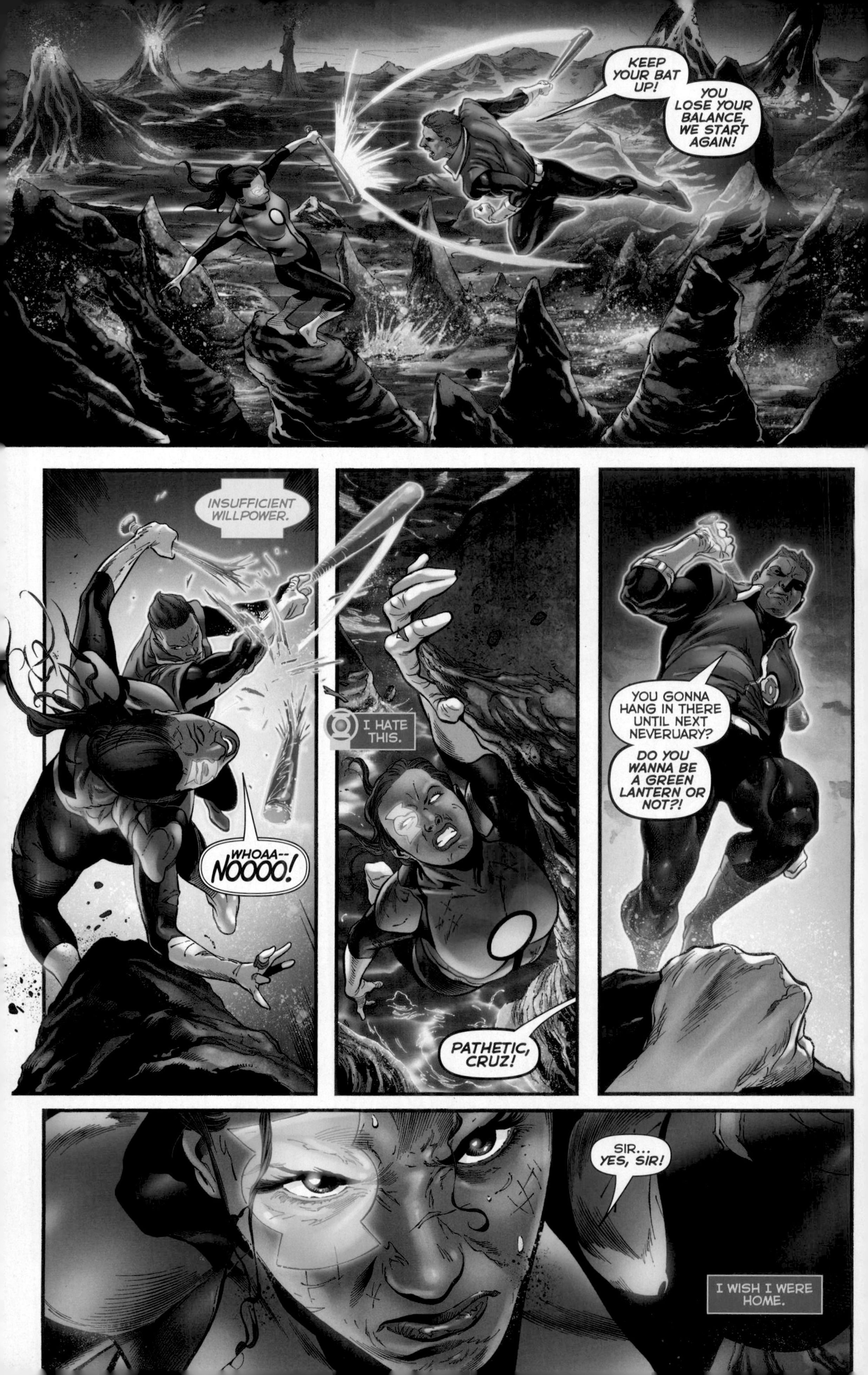
KEEP YOUR BAT UP!
YOU LOSE YOUR BALANCE, WE START AGAIN!
INSUFFICIENT WILLPOWER.
WHOAA-- NOOOO!
I HATE THIS.
PATHETIC, CRUZ!
YOU GONNA HANG IN THERE UNTIL NEXT NEVERUARY?
DO YOU WANNA BE A GREEN LANTERN OR NOT?!
SIR... YES, SIR!
I WISH I WERE HOME.

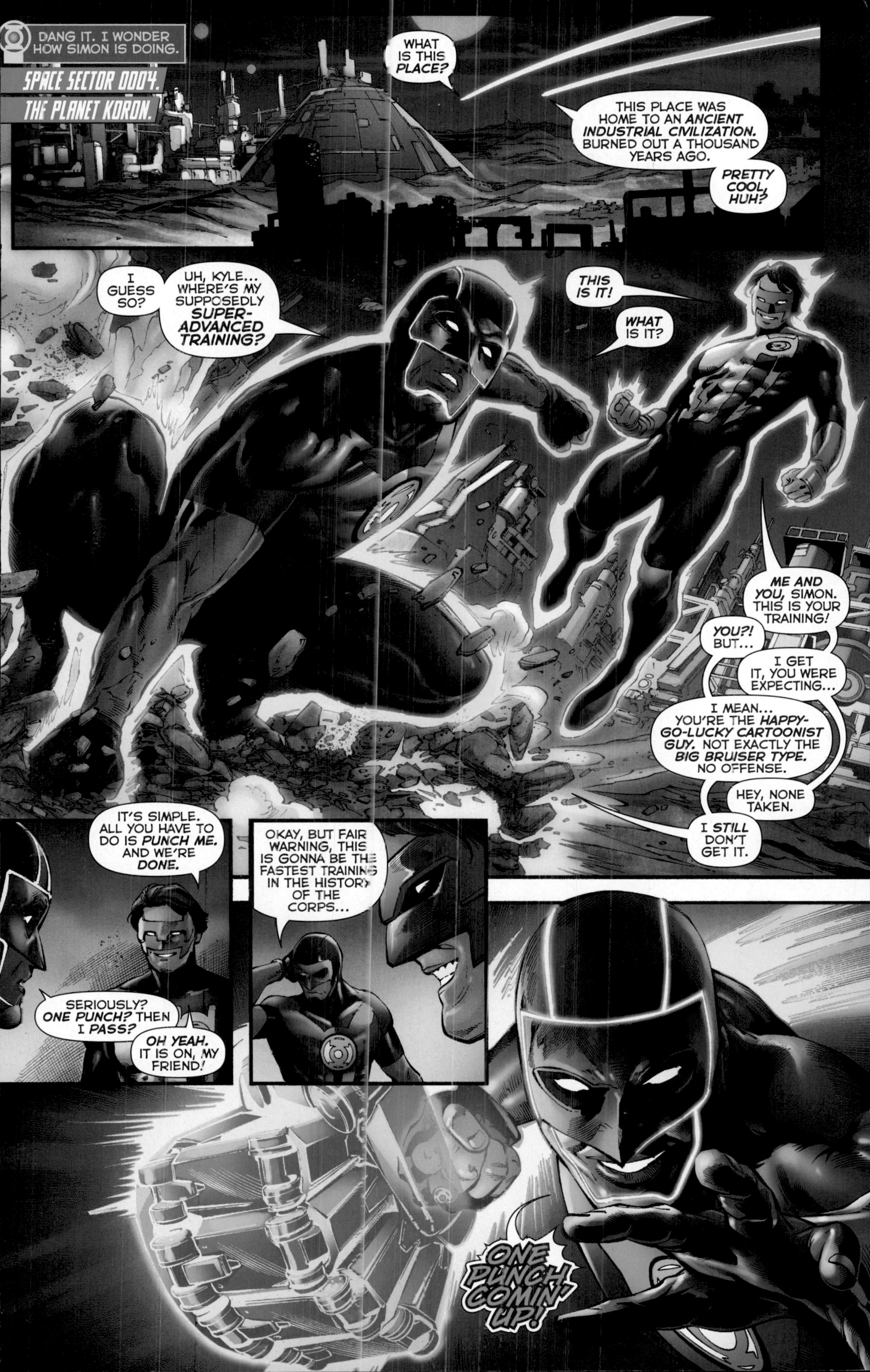
DANG IT. I WONDER HOW SIMON IS DOING.
SPACE SECTOR 0004.
THE PLANET KORON.
WHAT IS THIS PLACE?
THIS PLACE WAS HOME TO AN ANCIENT INDUSTRIAL CIVILIZATION. BURNED OUT A THOUSAND YEARS AGO.
PRETTY COOL, HUH?
I GUESS SO?
UH, KYLE... WHERE'S MY SUPPOSEDLY SUPER-ADVANCED TRAINING?
THIS IS IT!
WHAT IS IT?
ME AND YOU, SIMON. THIS IS YOUR TRAINING!
YOU?! BUT...
I GET IT, YOU WERE EXPECTING...
I MEAN... YOU'RE THE HAPPY-GO-LUCKY CARTOONIST GUY. NOT EXACTLY THE BIG BRUISER TYPE. NO OFFENSE.
HEY, NONE TAKEN.
I STILL DON'T GET IT.
IT'S SIMPLE. ALL YOU HAVE TO DO IS PUNCH ME. AND WE'RE DONE.
SERIOUSLY? ONE PUNCH? THEN I PASS?
OH YEAH. IT IS ON, MY FRIEND!
OKAY, BUT FAIR WARNING, THIS IS GONNA BE THE FASTEST TRAINING IN THE HISTORY OF THE CORPS...
ONE PUNCH COMIN' UP!

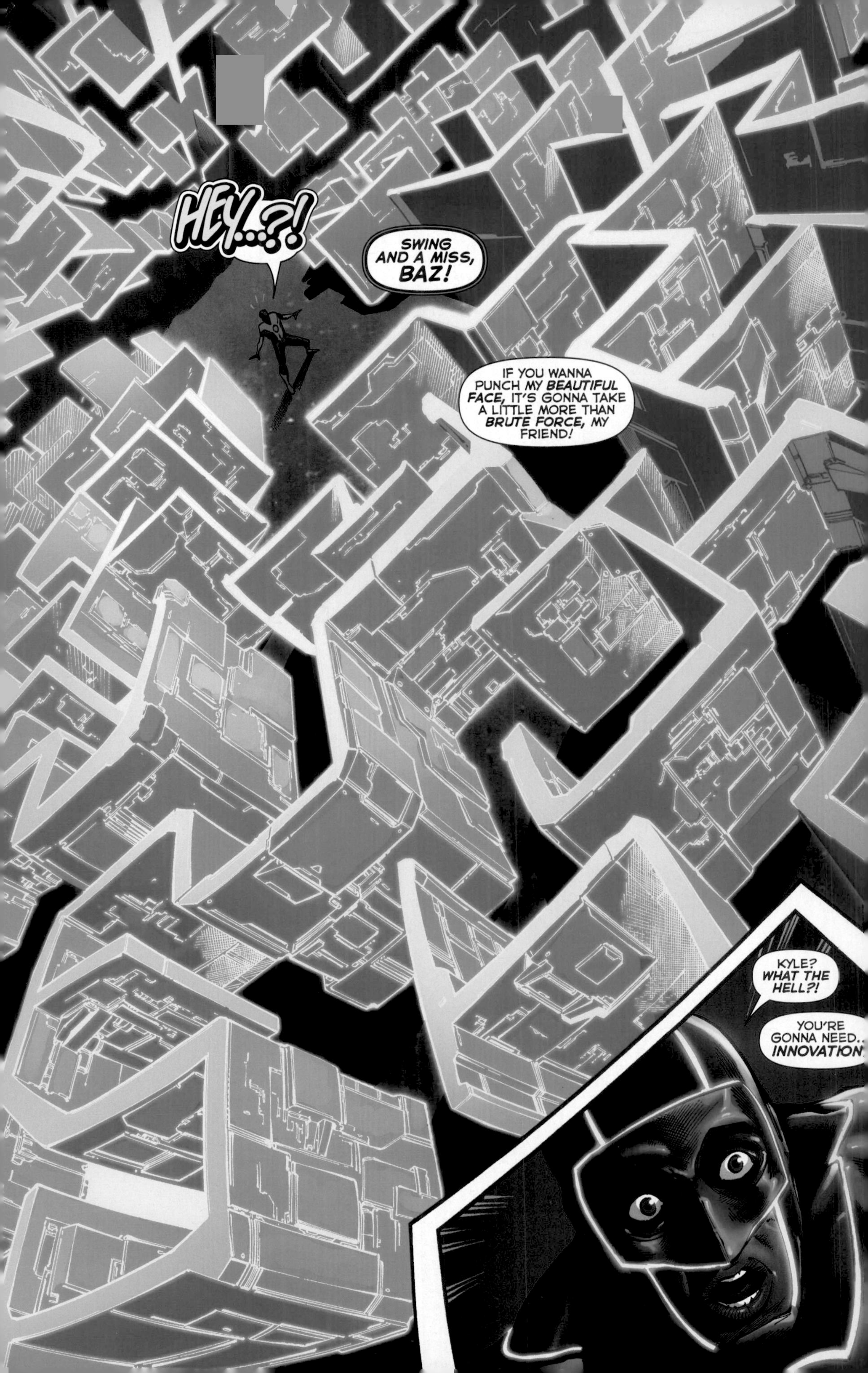
HEY...?!
SWING AND A MISS, BAZ!
IF YOU WANNA PUNCH MY BEAUTIFUL FACE, IT'S GONNA TAKE A LITTLE MORE THAN BRUTE FORCE, MY FRIEND!
KYLE? WHAT THE HELL?!
YOU'RE GONNA NEED... INNOVATION

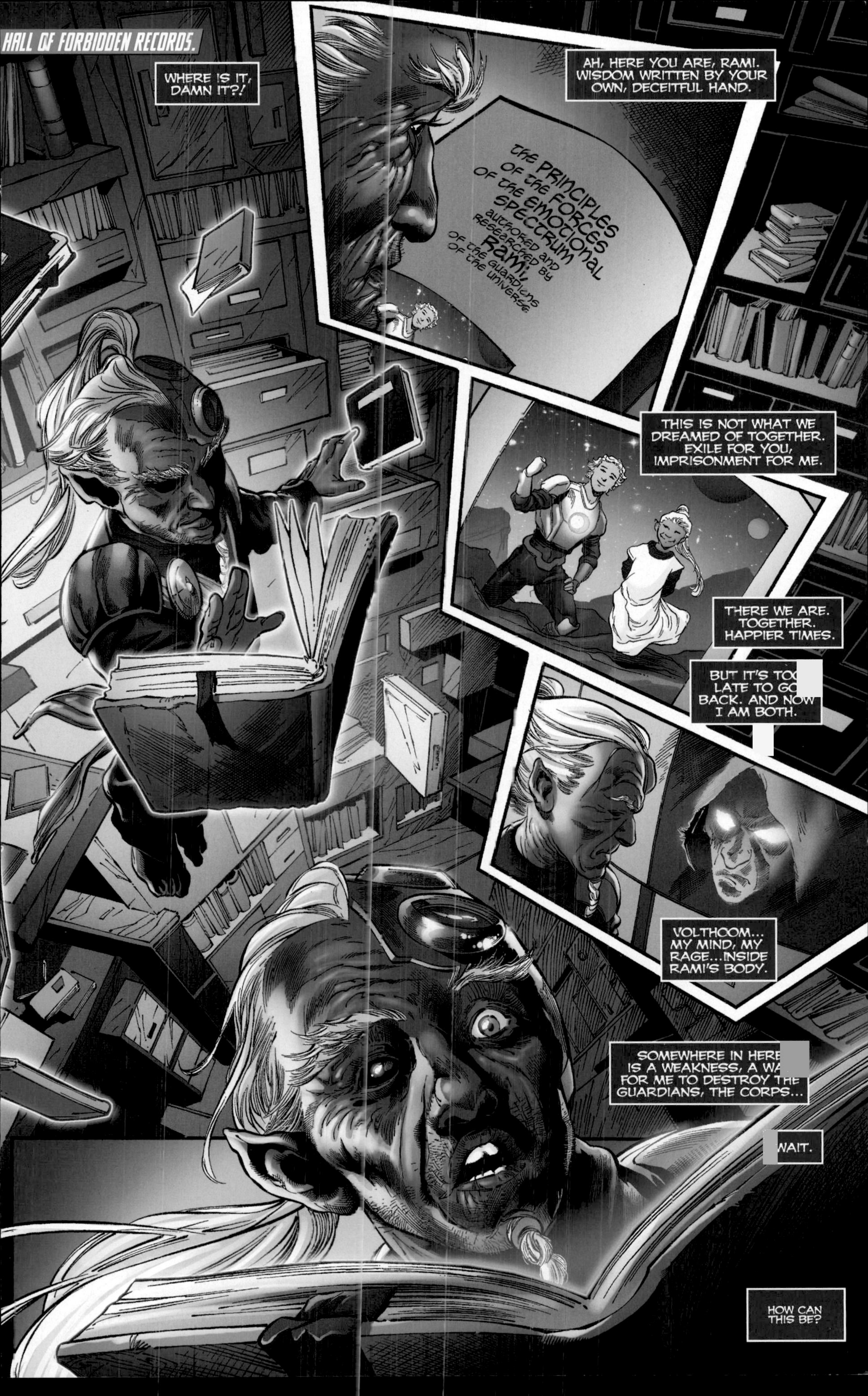

HALL OF FORBIDDEN RECORDS.
WHERE IS IT, DAMN IT?!
AH, HERE YOU ARE, RAMI. WISDOM WRITTEN BY YOUR OWN, DECEITFUL HAND.
THE PRINCIPLES OF THE FORCES OF THE EMOTIONAL SPECTRUM
AUTHORED AND RESEARCHED BY RAMI, OF THE GUARDIANS OF THE UNIVERSE
THIS IS NOT WHAT WE DREAMED OF TOGETHER. EXILE FOR YOU, IMPRISONMENT FOR ME.
THERE WE ARE. TOGETHER. HAPPIER TIMES.
BUT IT'S TOO LATE TO GO BACK. AND NOW I AM BOTH.
VOLTHOOM... MY MIND, MY RAGE...INSIDE RAMI'S BODY.
SOMEWHERE IN HERE IS A WEAKNESS, A WAY FOR ME TO DESTROY THE GUARDIANS, THE CORPS...
WAIT.
HOW CAN THIS BE?

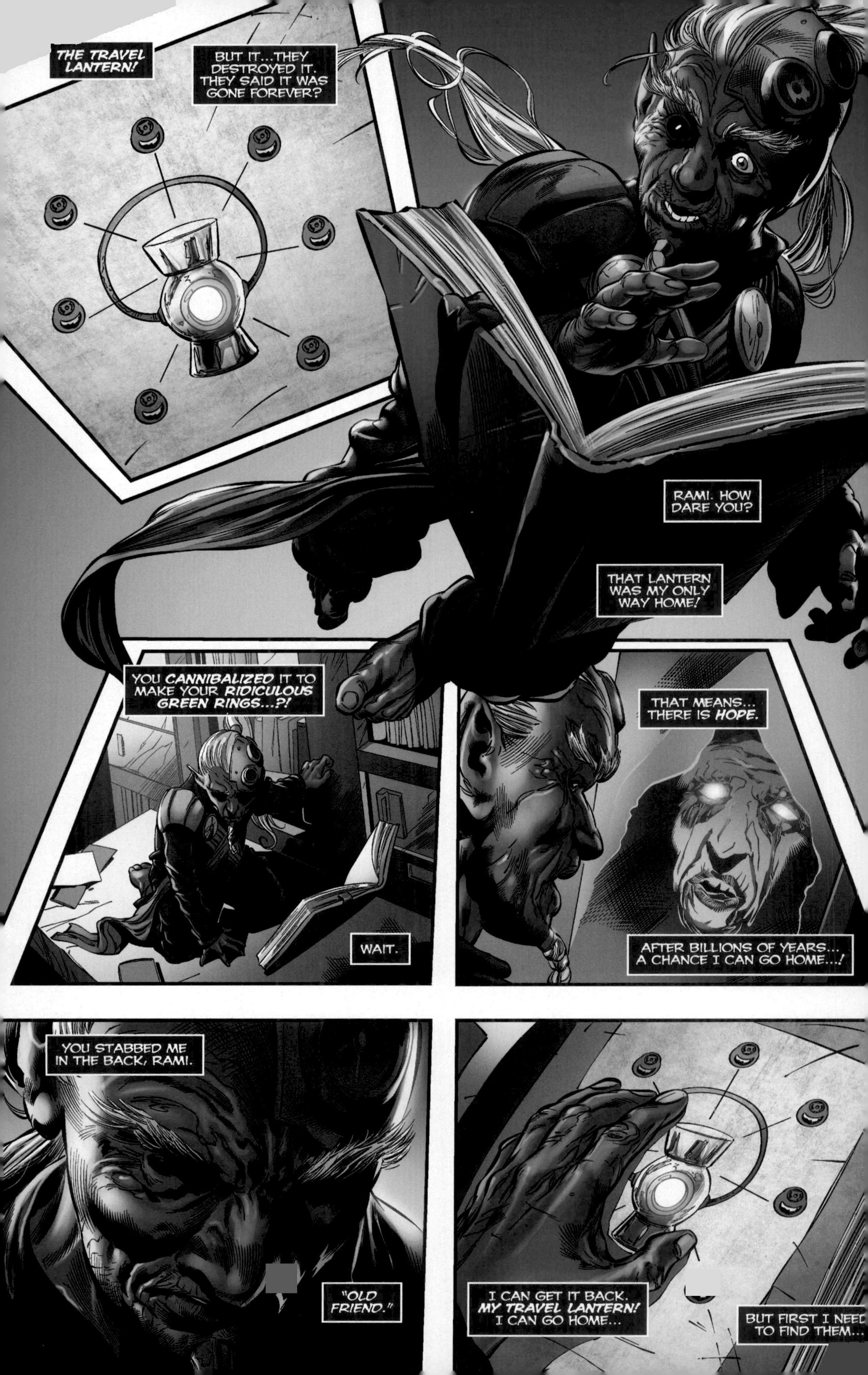

THE TRAVEL LANTERN!
BUT IT...THEY DESTROYED IT. THEY SAID IT WAS GONE FOREVER?
RAMI. HOW DARE YOU?
THAT LANTERN WAS MY ONLY WAY HOME!
YOU CANNIBALIZED IT TO MAKE YOUR RIDICULOUS GREEN RINGS...?!
WAIT.
THAT MEANS... THERE IS HOPE.
AFTER BILLIONS OF YEARS... A CHANCE I CAN GO HOME...!
YOU STABBED ME IN THE BACK, RAMI.
"OLD FRIEND."
I CAN GET IT BACK. MY TRAVEL LANTERN! I CAN GO HOME...
BUT FIRST I NEED TO FIND THEM...

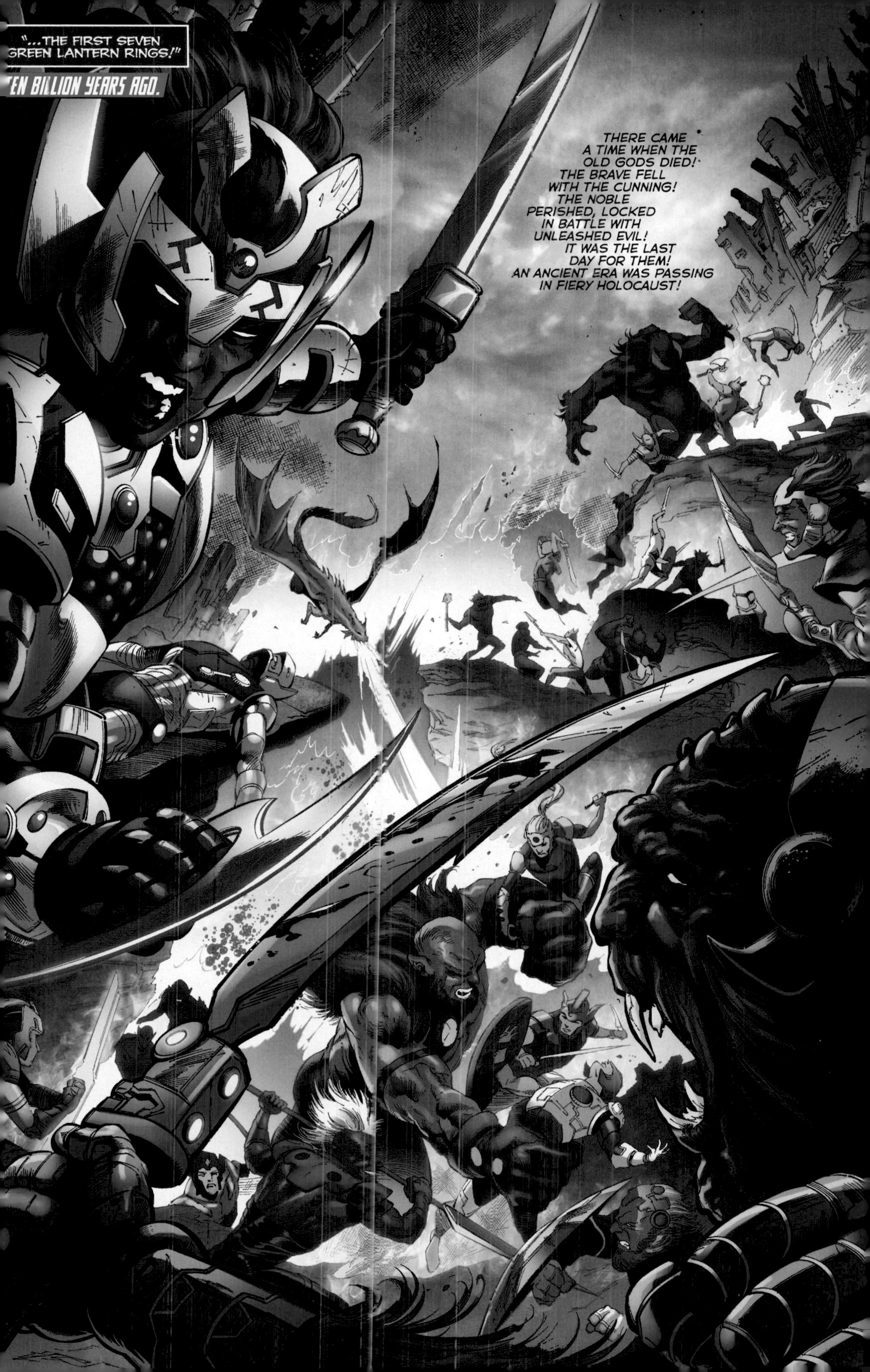
"...THE FIRST SEVEN GREEN LANTERN RINGS!"
TEN BILLION YEARS AGO.
THERE CAME A TIME WHEN THE OLD GODS DIED! THE BRAVE FELL WITH THE CUNNING! THE NOBLE PERISHED, LOCKED IN BATTLE WITH UNLEASHED EVIL! IT WAS THE LAST DAY FOR THEM! AN ANCIENT ERA WAS PASSING IN FIERY HOLOCAUST!

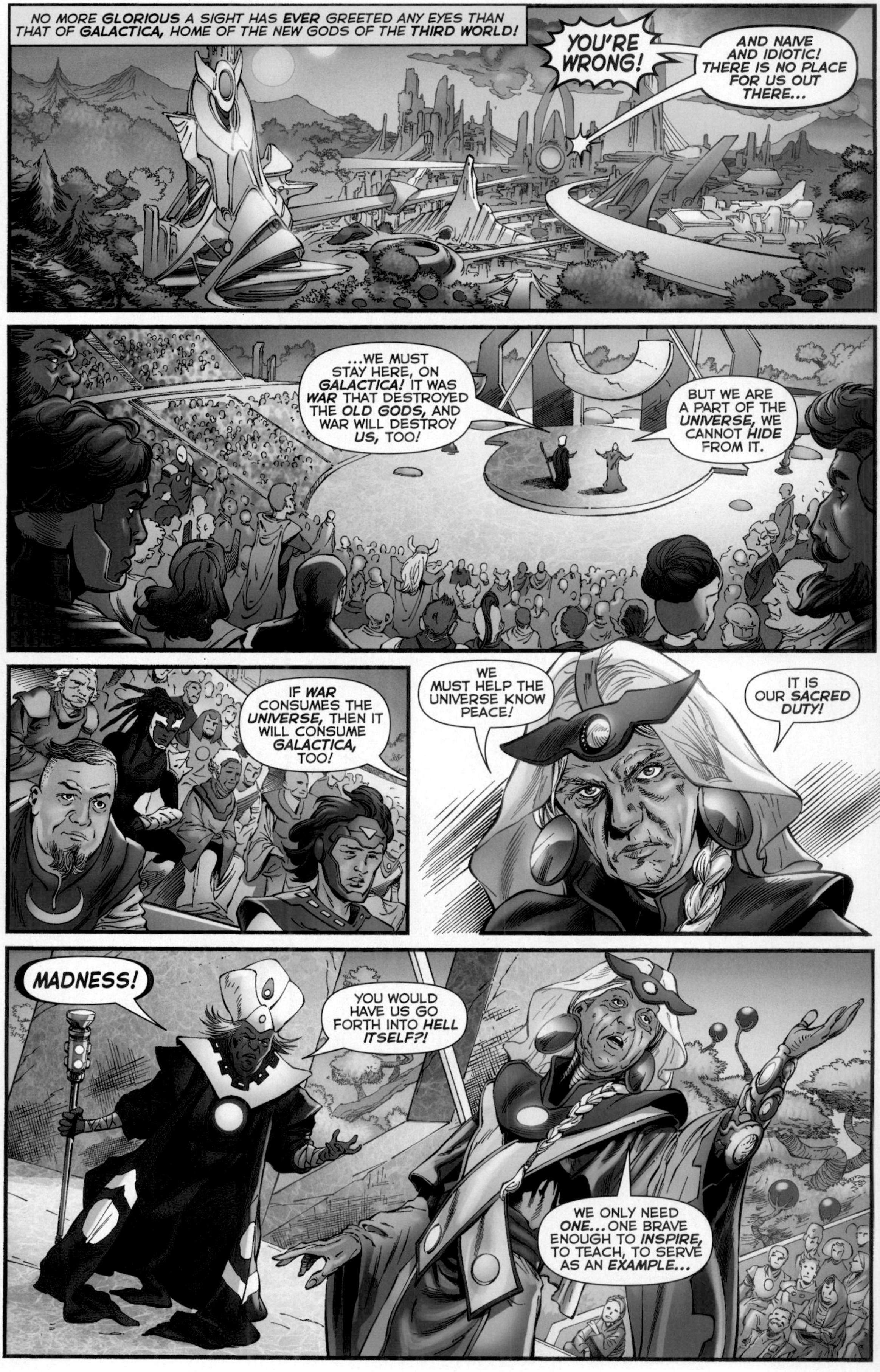

NO MORE GLORIOUS A SIGHT HAS EVER GREETED ANY EYES THAN THAT OF GALACTICA, HOME OF THE NEW GODS OF THE THIRD WORLD!
YOU'RE WRONG!
AND NAIVE AND IDIOTIC! THERE IS NO PLACE FOR US OUT THERE...
...WE MUST STAY HERE, ON GALACTICA! IT WAS WAR THAT DESTROYED THE OLD GODS, AND WAR WILL DESTROY US, TOO!
BUT WE ARE A PART OF THE UNIVERSE, WE CANNOT HIDE FROM IT.
IF WAR CONSUMES THE UNIVERSE, THEN IT WILL CONSUME GALACTICA, TOO!
WE MUST HELP THE UNIVERSE KNOW PEACE!
IT IS OUR SACRED DUTY!
MADNESS!
YOU WOULD HAVE US GO FORTH INTO HELL ITSELF?!
WE ONLY NEED ONE...ONE BRAVE ENOUGH TO INSPIRE, TO TEACH, TO SERVE AS AN EXAMPLE...

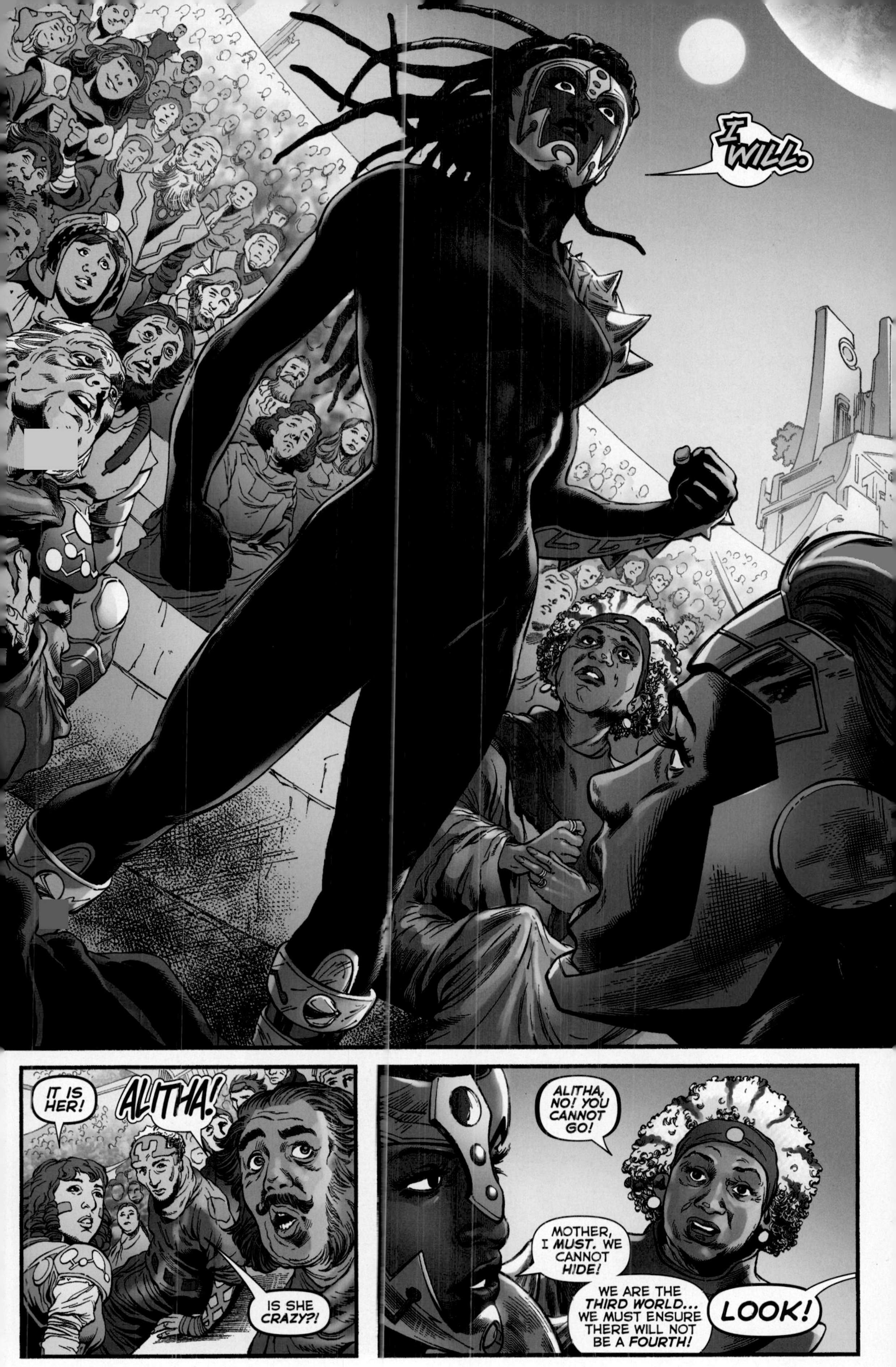
I WILL.
IT IS HER!
ALITHA!
IS SHE CRAZY?!
ALITHA, NO! YOU CANNOT GO!
MOTHER, I MUST. WE CANNOT HIDE!
WE ARE THE THIRD WORLD... WE MUST ENSURE THERE WILL NOT BE A FOURTH!
LOOK!

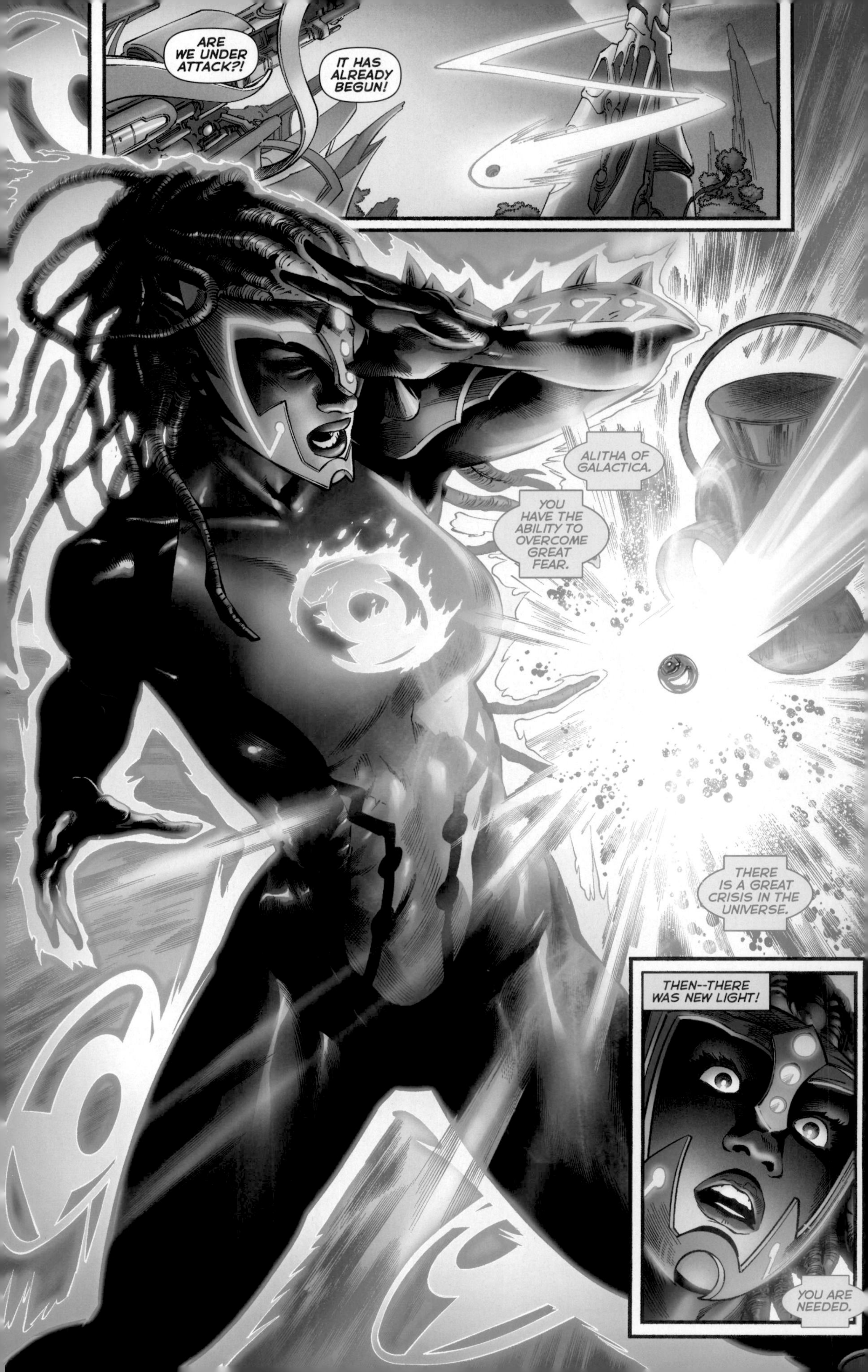
ARE WE UNDER ATTACK?!
IT HAS ALREADY BEGUN!
ALITHA OF GALACTICA.
YOU HAVE THE ABILITY TO OVERCOME GREAT FEAR.
THERE IS A GREAT CRISIS IN THE UNIVERSE.
THEN--THERE WAS NEW LIGHT!
YOU ARE NEEDED.

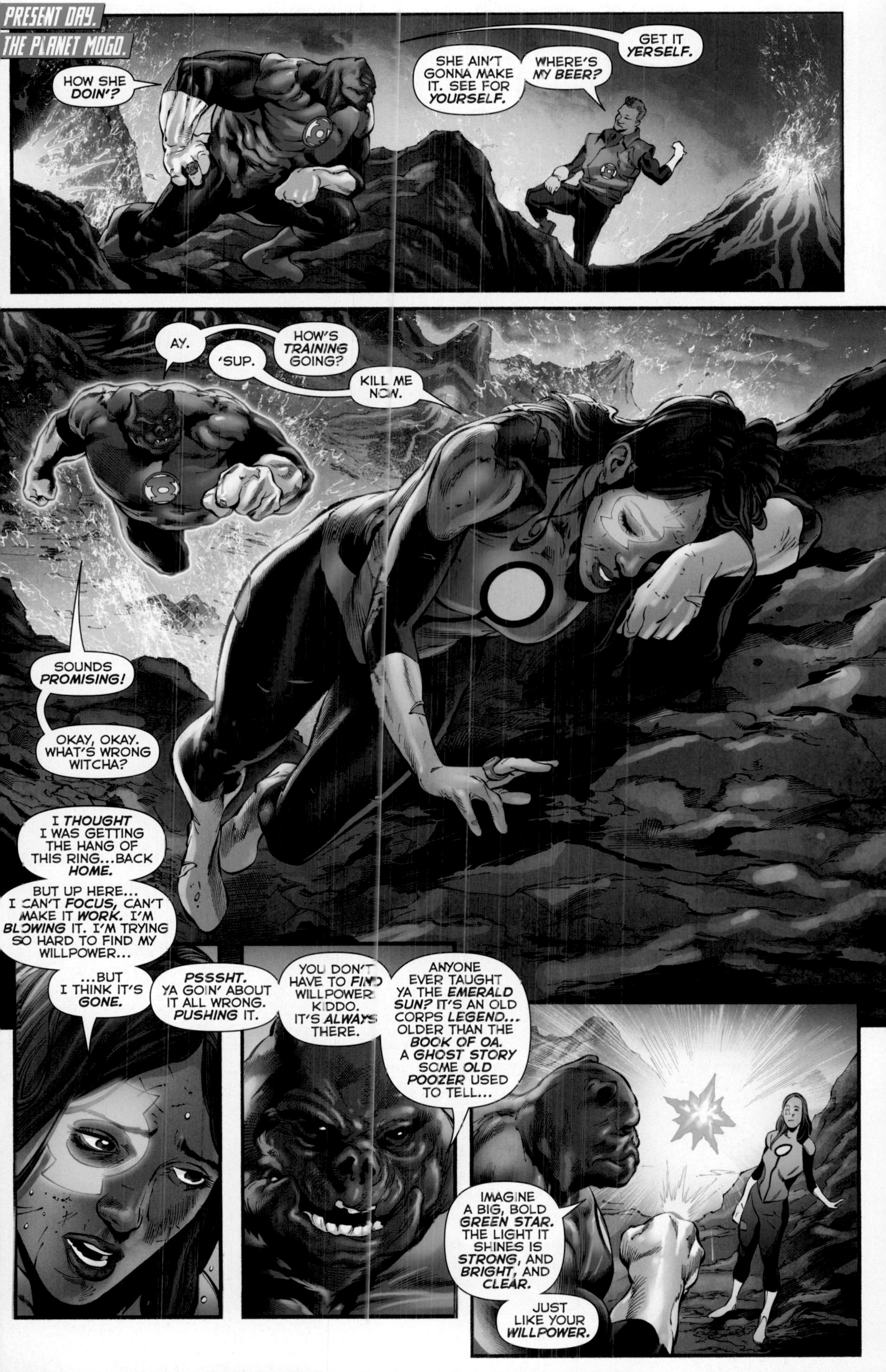
PRESENT DAY.
THE PLANET MOGO.
HOW SHE DOIN'?
SHE AIN'T GONNA MAKE IT. SEE FOR YOURSELF.
WHERE'S MY BEER?
GET IT YERSELF.
AY.
HOW'S TRAINING GOING?
'SUP.
KILL ME NOW.
SOUNDS PROMISING!
OKAY, OKAY. WHAT'S WRONG WITCHA?
I THOUGHT I WAS GETTING THE HANG OF THIS RING...BACK HOME.
BUT UP HERE... I CAN'T FOCUS, CAN'T MAKE IT WORK. I'M BLOWING IT. I'M TRYING SO HARD TO FIND MY WILLPOWER...
...BUT I THINK IT'S GONE.
PSSSHT. YA GOIN' ABOUT IT ALL WRONG. PUSHING IT.
YOU DON'T HAVE TO FIND WILLPOWER, KIDDO. IT'S ALWAYS THERE.
ANYONE EVER TAUGHT YA THE EMERALD SUN? IT'S AN OLD CORPS LEGEND... OLDER THAN THE BOOK OF OA. A GHOST STORY SOME OLD POOZER USED TO TELL...
IMAGINE A BIG, BOLD GREEN STAR. THE LIGHT IT SHINES IS STRONG, AND BRIGHT, AND CLEAR.
JUST LIKE YOUR WILLPOWER.

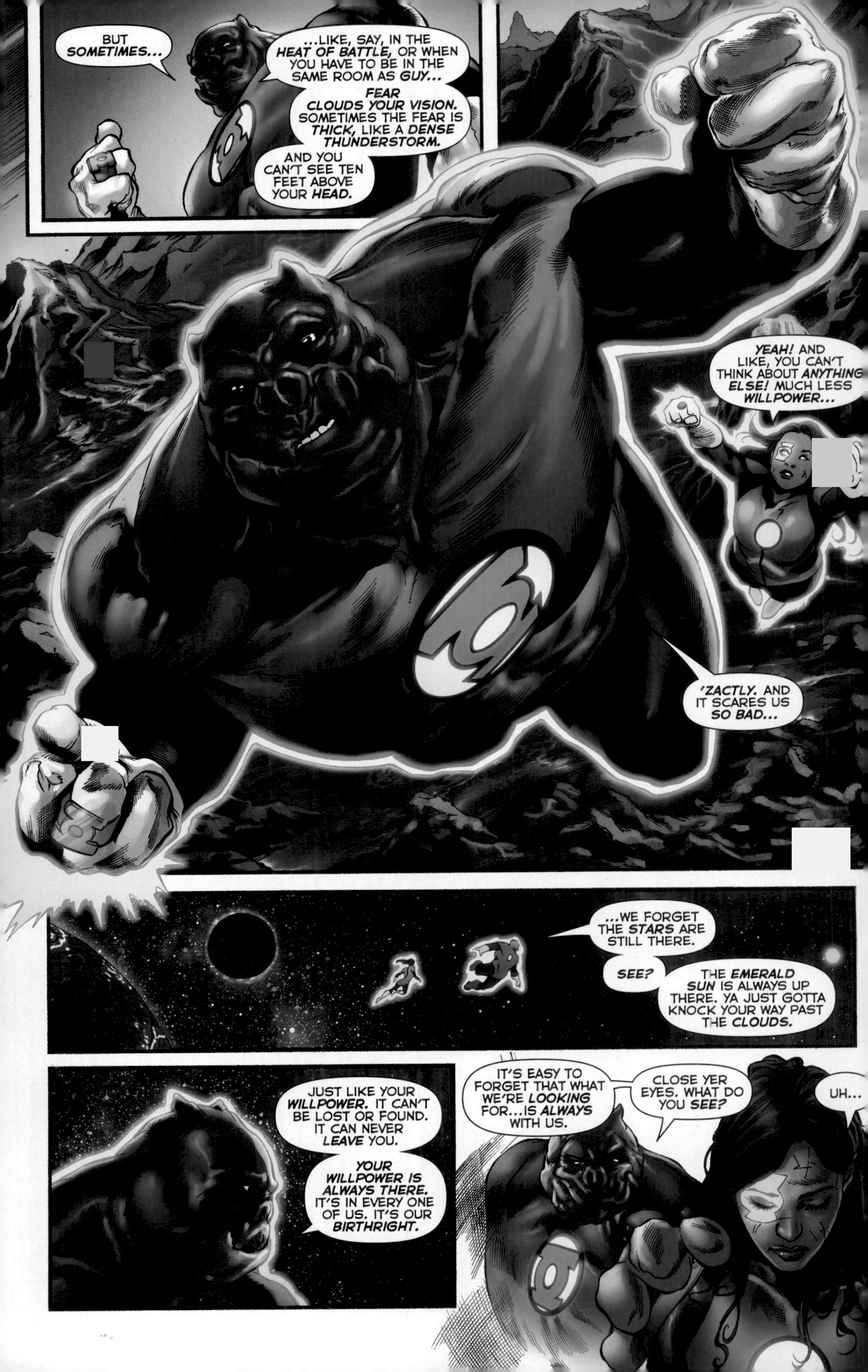
BUT SOMETIMES...
...LIKE, SAY, IN THE HEAT OF BATTLE, OR WHEN YOU HAVE TO BE IN THE SAME ROOM AS GUY...
FEAR CLOUDS YOUR VISION. SOMETIMES THE FEAR IS THICK, LIKE A DENSE THUNDERSTORM.
AND YOU CAN'T SEE TEN FEET ABOVE YOUR HEAD.
YEAH! AND LIKE, YOU CAN'T THINK ABOUT ANYTHING ELSE! MUCH LESS WILLPOWER...
'ZACTLY. AND IT SCARES US SO BAD...
...WE FORGET THE STARS ARE STILL THERE.
SEE?
THE EMERALD SUN IS ALWAYS UP THERE. YA JUST GOTTA KNOCK YOUR WAY PAST THE CLOUDS.
JUST LIKE YOUR WILLPOWER. IT CAN'T BE LOST OR FOUND. IT CAN NEVER LEAVE YOU.
YOUR WILLPOWER IS ALWAYS THERE. IT'S IN EVERY ONE OF US. IT'S OUR BIRTHRIGHT.
IT'S EASY TO FORGET THAT WHAT WE'RE LOOKING FOR...IS ALWAYS WITH US.
CLOSE YER EYES. WHAT DO YOU SEE?
UH...

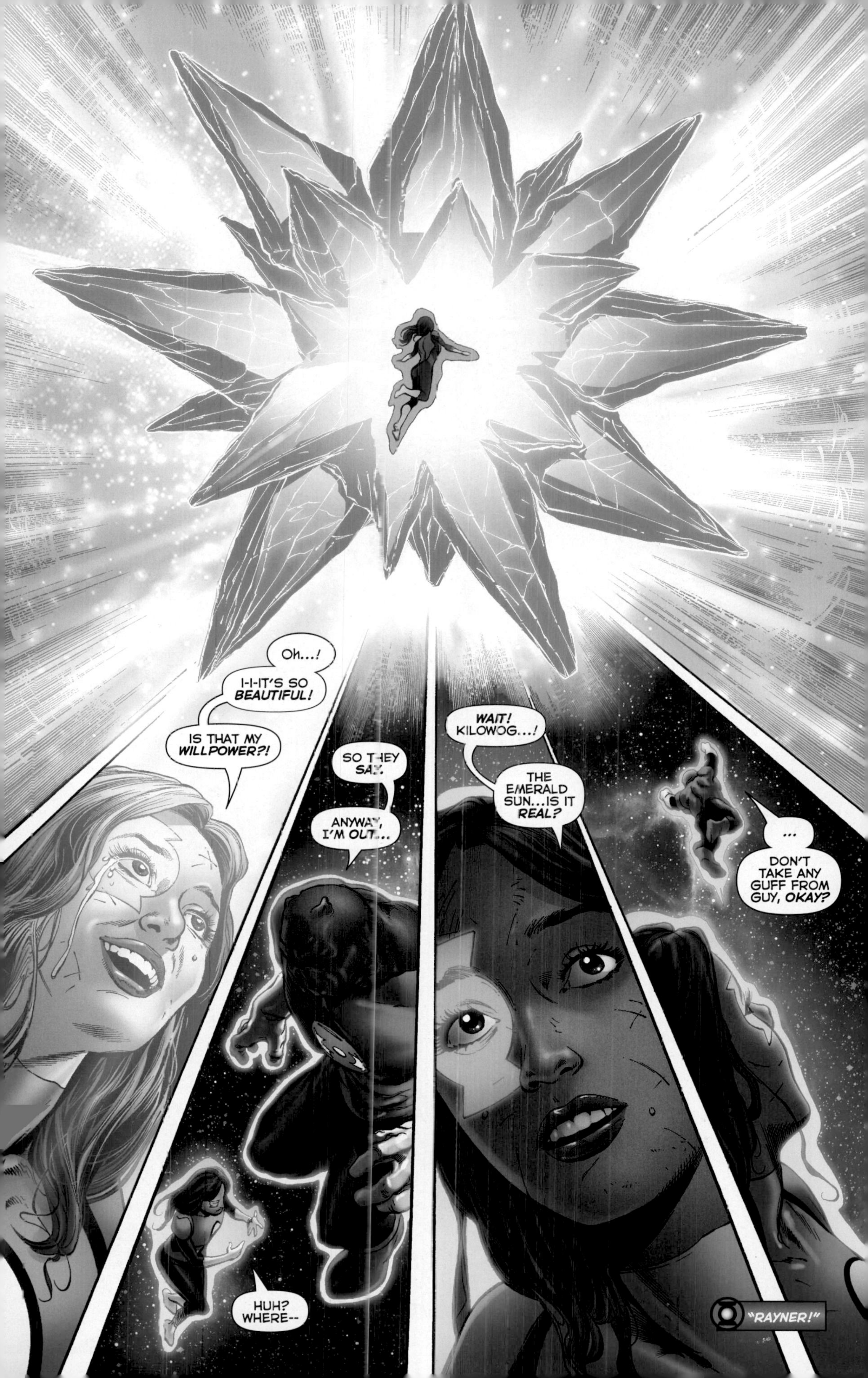
Oh...!
I-I-IT'S SO BEAUTIFUL!
IS THAT MY WILLPOWER?!
SO THEY SAY.
ANYWAY, I'M OUT...
HUH? WHERE--
WAIT! KILOWOG...!
THE EMERALD SUN...IS IT REAL?
...
DON'T TAKE ANY GUFF FROM GUY, OKAY?
"RAYNER!"

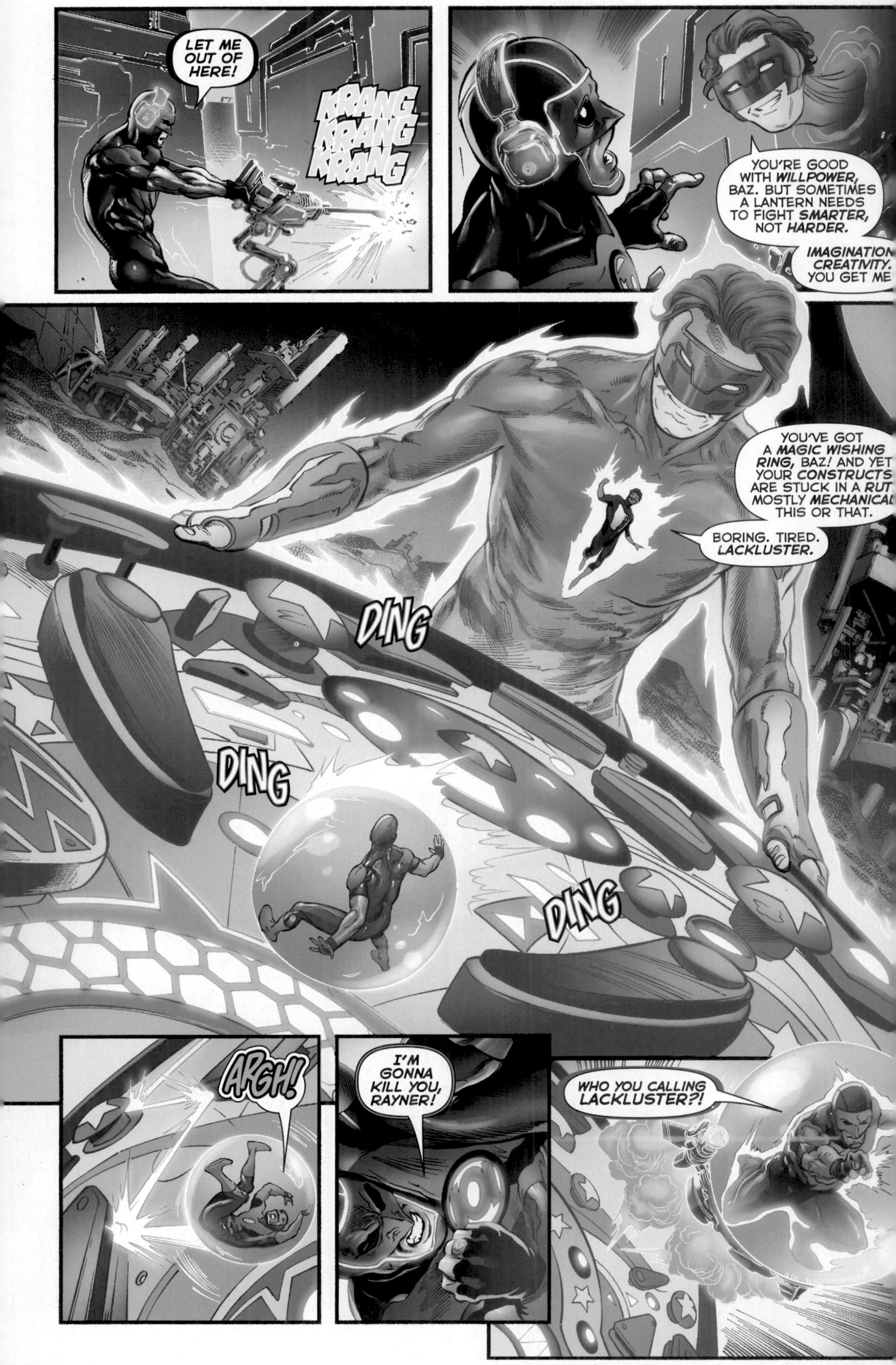
LET ME OUT OF HERE!
KRANG KRANG KRANG
YOU'RE GOOD WITH WILLPOWER, BAZ. BUT SOMETIMES A LANTERN NEEDS TO FIGHT SMARTER, NOT HARDER.
IMAGINATION. CREATIVITY. YOU GET ME
YOU'VE GOT A MAGIC WISHING RING, BAZ! AND YET YOUR CONSTRUCTS ARE STUCK IN A RUT. MOSTLY MECHANICAL THIS OR THAT.
BORING. TIRED. LACKLUSTER.
DING
DING
DING
ARGH!
I'M GONNA KILL YOU, RAYNER!
WHO YOU CALLING LACKLUSTER?!

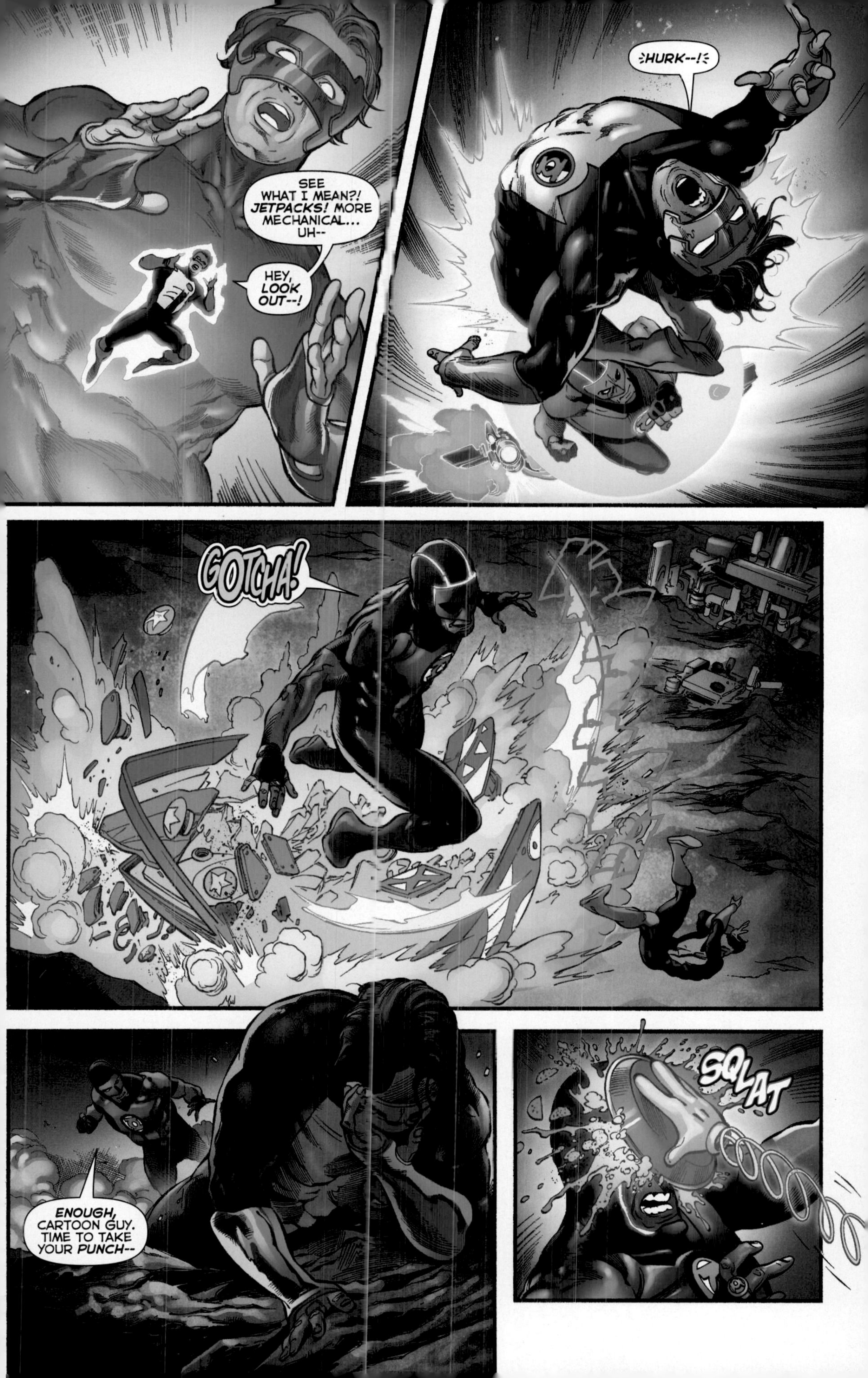
SEE WHAT I MEAN?! JETPACKS! MORE MECHANICAL... UH--
HEY, LOOK OUT--!
HURK--!
GOTCHA!
ENOUGH, CARTOON GUY. TIME TO TAKE YOUR PUNCH--
SQLAT

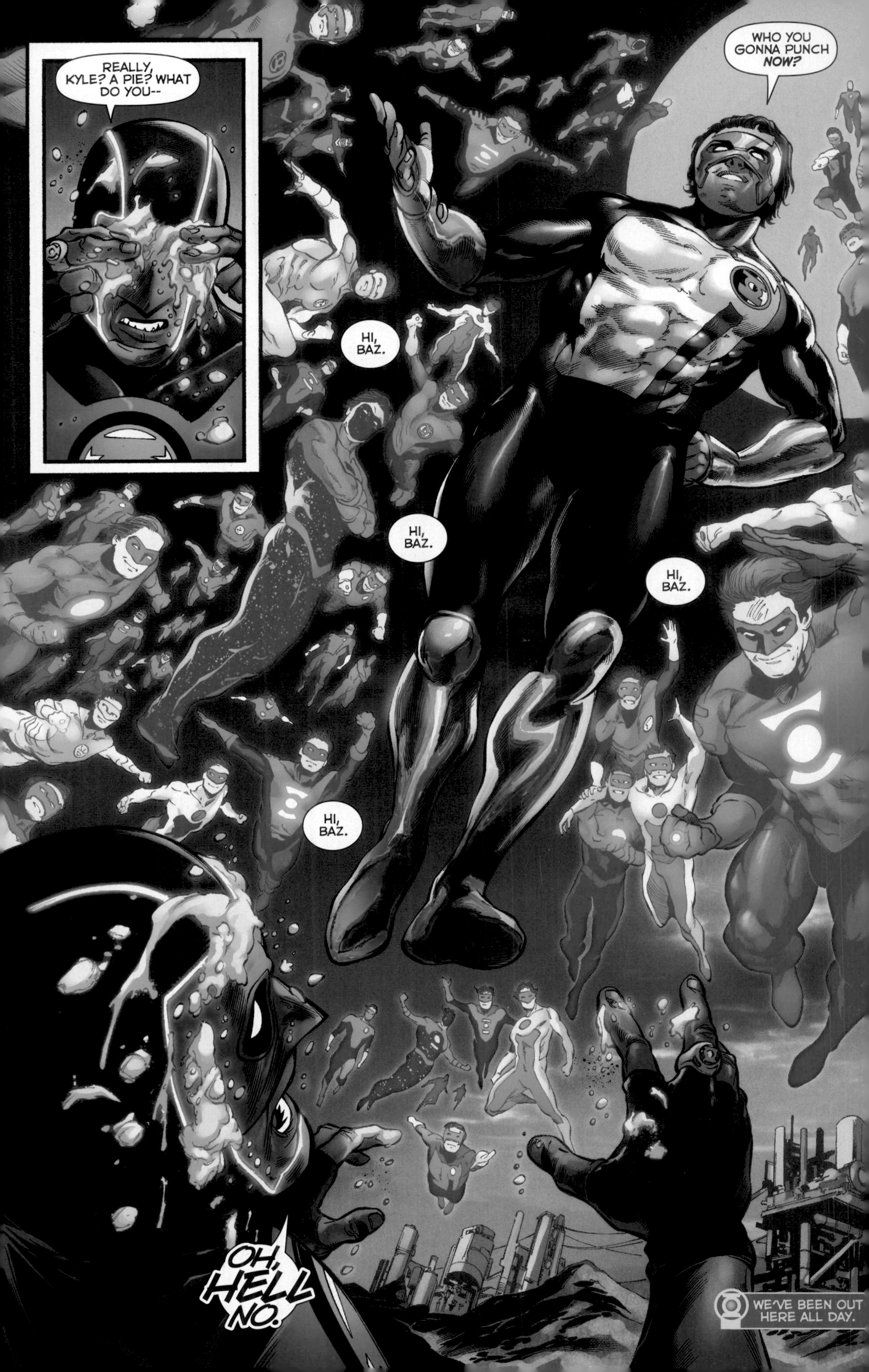
REALLY, KYLE? A PIE? WHAT DO YOU--
WHO YOU GONNA PUNCH NOW?
HI, BAZ.
HI, BAZ.
HI, BAZ.
HI, BAZ.
OH, HELL NO.
WE'VE BEEN OUT HERE ALL DAY.

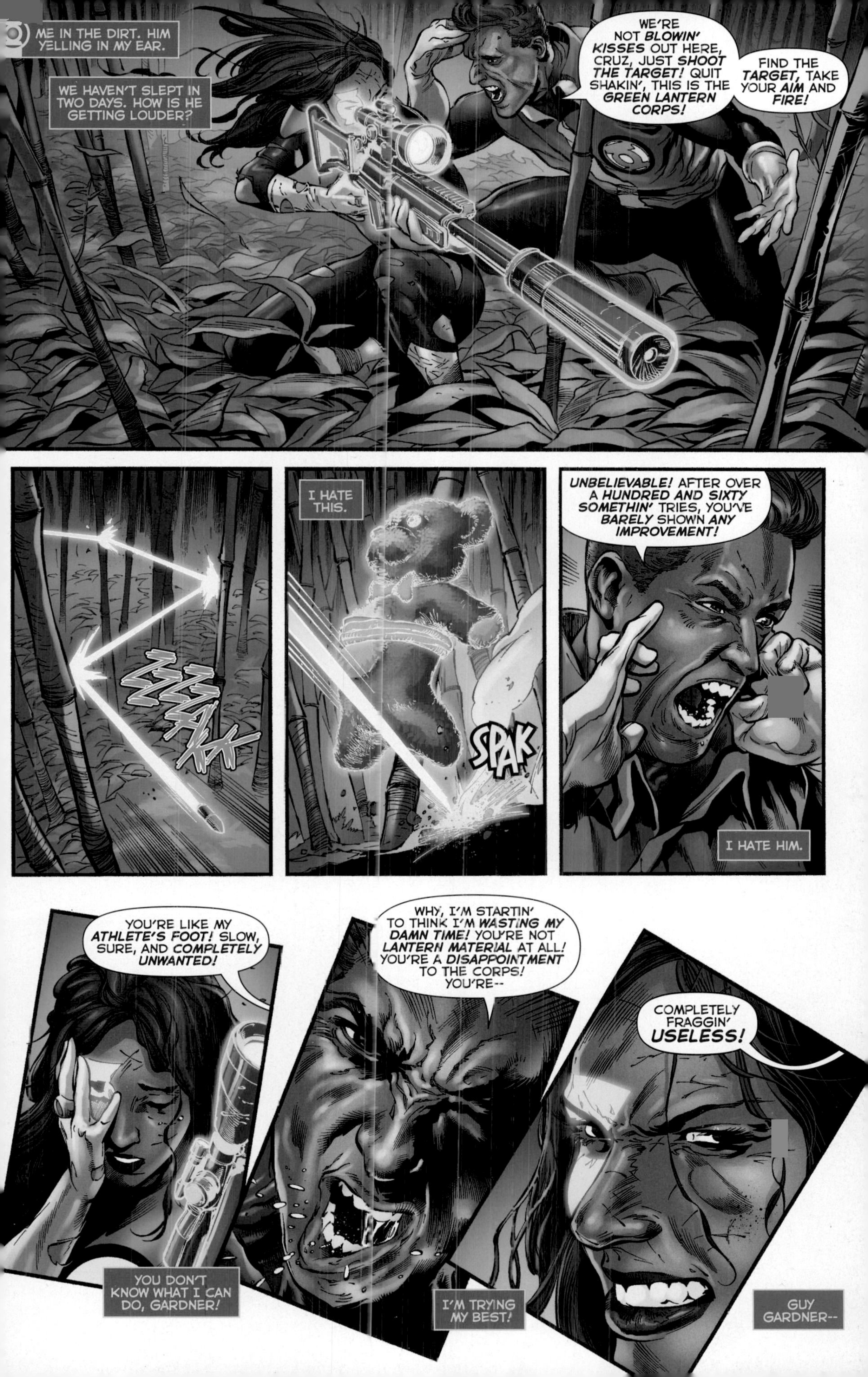

ME IN THE DIRT. HIM YELLING IN MY EAR.
WE HAVEN'T SLEPT IN TWO DAYS. HOW IS HE GETTING LOUDER?
WE'RE NOT BLOWIN' KISSES OUT HERE, CRUZ, JUST SHOOT THE TARGET! QUIT SHAKIN', THIS IS THE GREEN LANTERN CORPS!
FIND THE TARGET, TAKE YOUR AIM AND FIRE!
ZZZZAKK
I HATE THIS.
SPAK
UNBELIEVABLE! AFTER OVER A HUNDRED AND SIXTY SOMETHIN' TRIES, YOU'VE BARELY SHOWN ANY IMPROVEMENT!
I HATE HIM.
YOU'RE LIKE MY ATHLETE'S FOOT! SLOW, SURE, AND COMPLETELY UNWANTED!
YOU DON'T KNOW WHAT I CAN DO, GARDNER!
WHY, I'M STARTIN' TO THINK I'M WASTING MY DAMN TIME! YOU'RE NOT LANTERN MATERIAL AT ALL! YOU'RE A DISAPPOINTMENT TO THE CORPS! YOU'RE--
I'M TRYING MY BEST!
COMPLETELY FRAGGIN' USELESS!
GUY GARDNER--

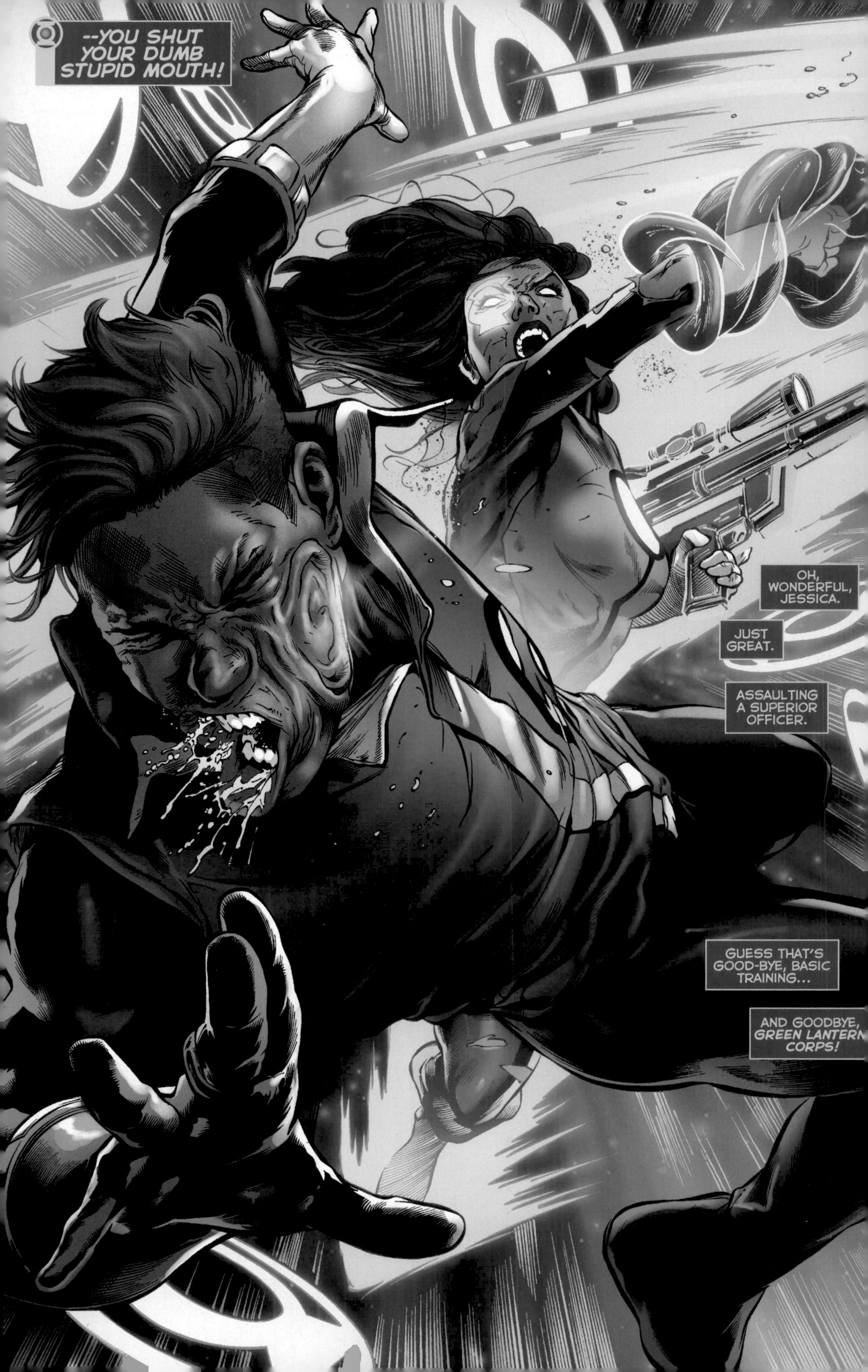
--YOU SHUT YOUR DUMB STUPID MOUTH!
OH, WONDERFUL, JESSICA.
JUST GREAT.
ASSAULTING A SUPERIOR OFFICER.
GUESS THAT'S GOOD-BYE, BASIC TRAINING...
AND GOODBYE, GREEN LANTERN CORPS!

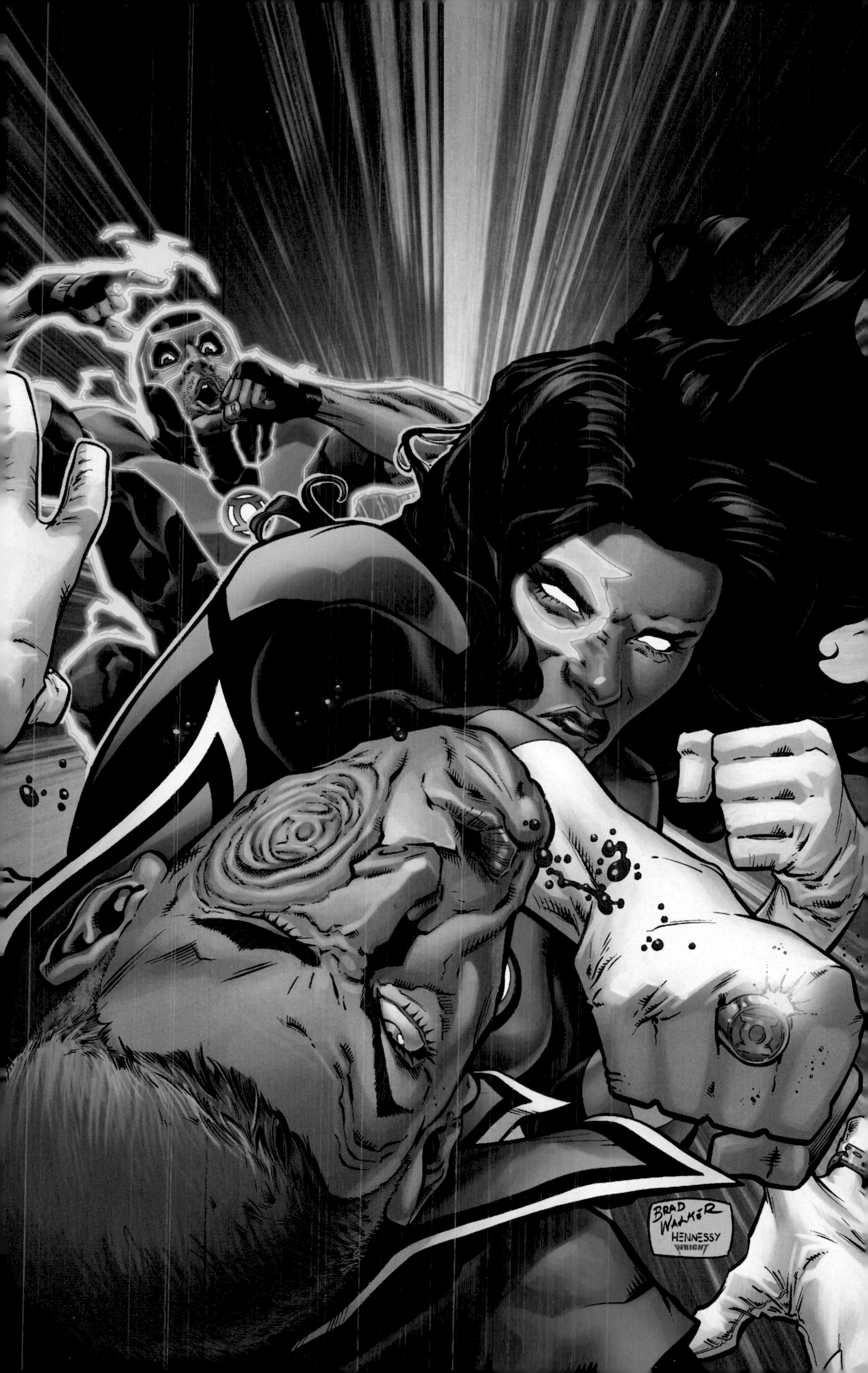
BRAD WALKER
HENNESSY
WRIGHT

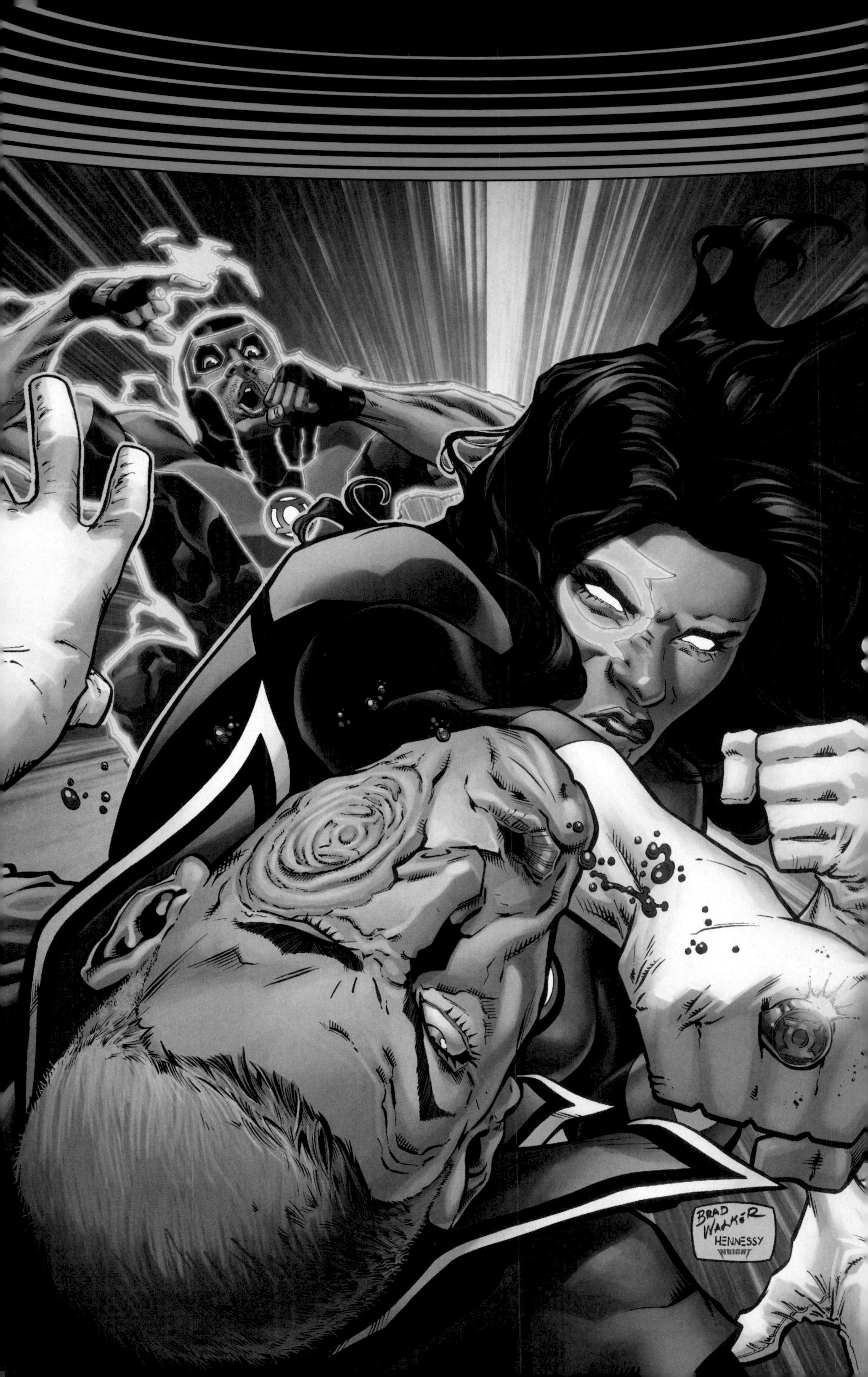
BRAD WALKER
HENNESSY
WRIGHT

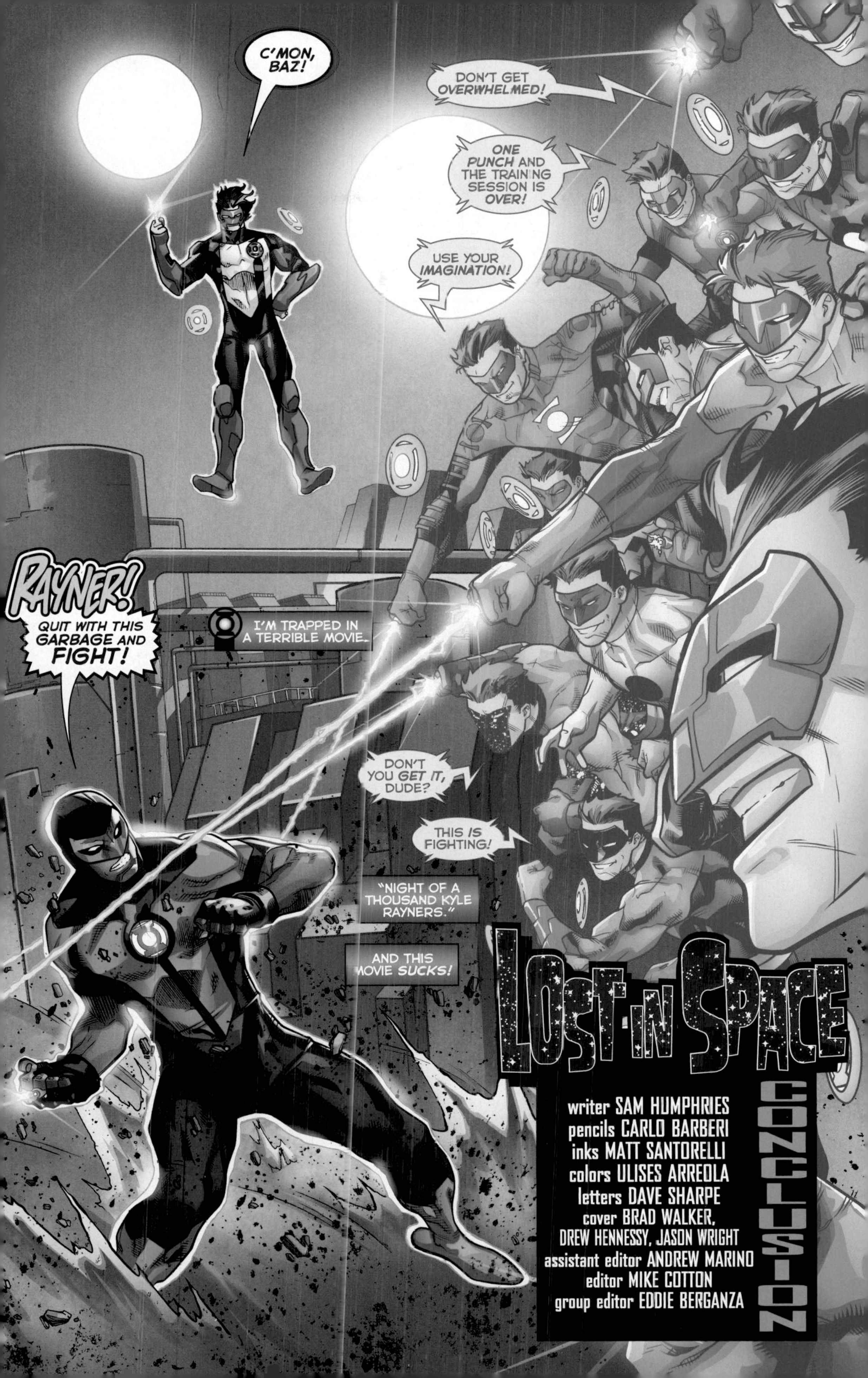

C'MON, BAZ!
DON'T GET OVERWHELMED!
ONE PUNCH AND THE TRAINING SESSION IS OVER!
USE YOUR IMAGINATION!
RAYNER! QUIT WITH THIS GARBAGE AND FIGHT!
I'M TRAPPED IN A TERRIBLE MOVIE...
DON'T YOU GET IT, DUDE?
THIS IS FIGHTING!
"NIGHT OF A THOUSAND KYLE RAYNERS."
AND THIS MOVIE SUCKS!
LOST IN SPACE
CONCLUSION
writer SAM HUMPHRIES
pencils CARLO BARBERI
inks MATT SANTORELLI
colors ULISES ARREOLA
letters DAVE SHARPE
cover BRAD WALKER, DREW HENNESSY, JASON WRIGHT
assistant editor ANDREW MARINO
editor MIKE COTTON
group editor EDDIE BERGANZA

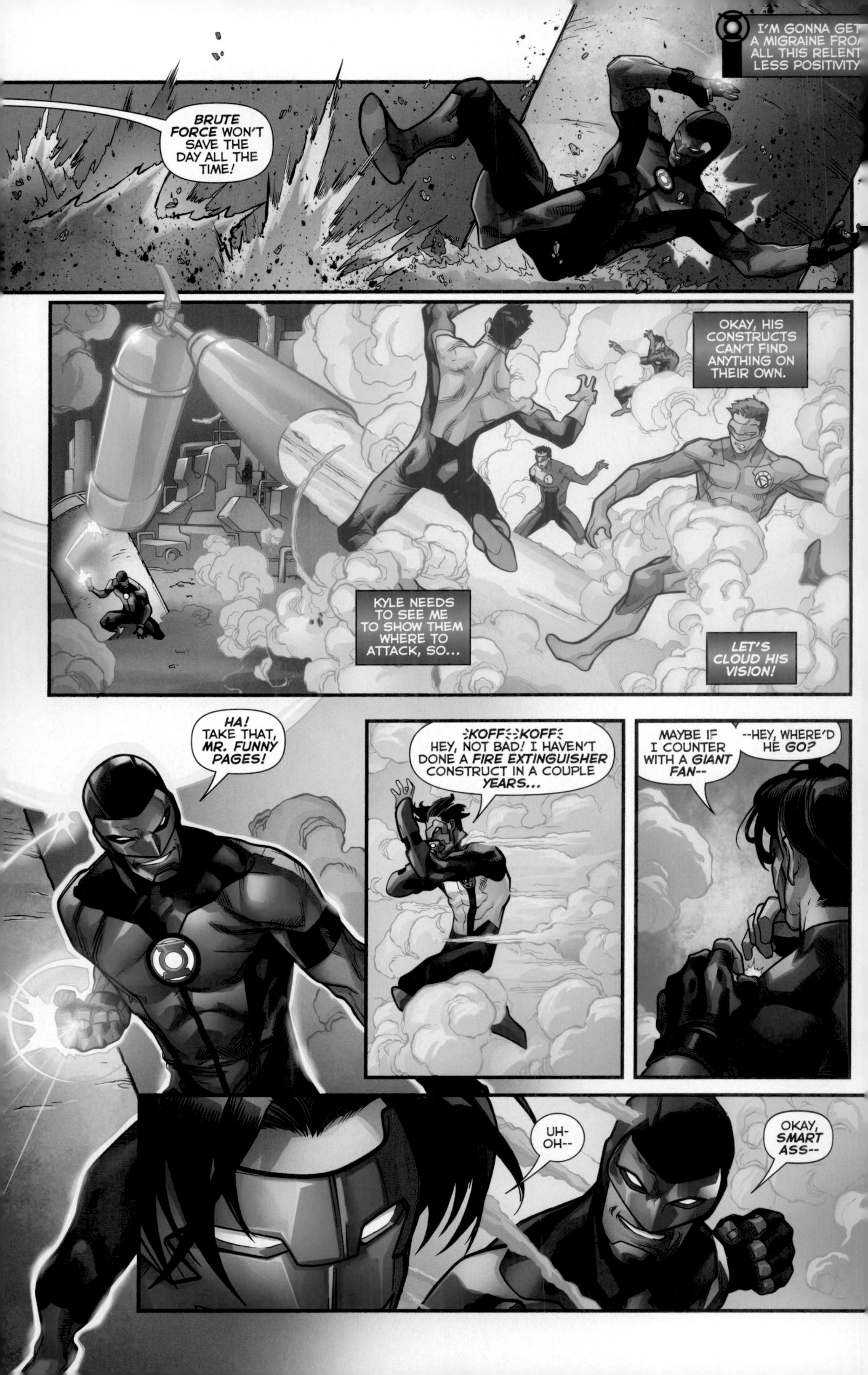

I'M GONNA GET A MIGRAINE FROM ALL THIS RELENTLESS POSITIVITY
BRUTE FORCE WON'T SAVE THE DAY ALL THE TIME!
OKAY, HIS CONSTRUCTS CAN'T FIND ANYTHING ON THEIR OWN.
KYLE NEEDS TO SEE ME TO SHOW THEM WHERE TO ATTACK, SO...
LET'S CLOUD HIS VISION!
HA! TAKE THAT, MR. FUNNY PAGES!
KOFF KOFF HEY, NOT BAD! I HAVEN'T DONE A FIRE EXTINGUISHER CONSTRUCT IN A COUPLE YEARS...
MAYBE IF I COUNTER WITH A GIANT FAN--
--HEY, WHERE'D HE GO?
UH-OH--
OKAY, SMART ASS--

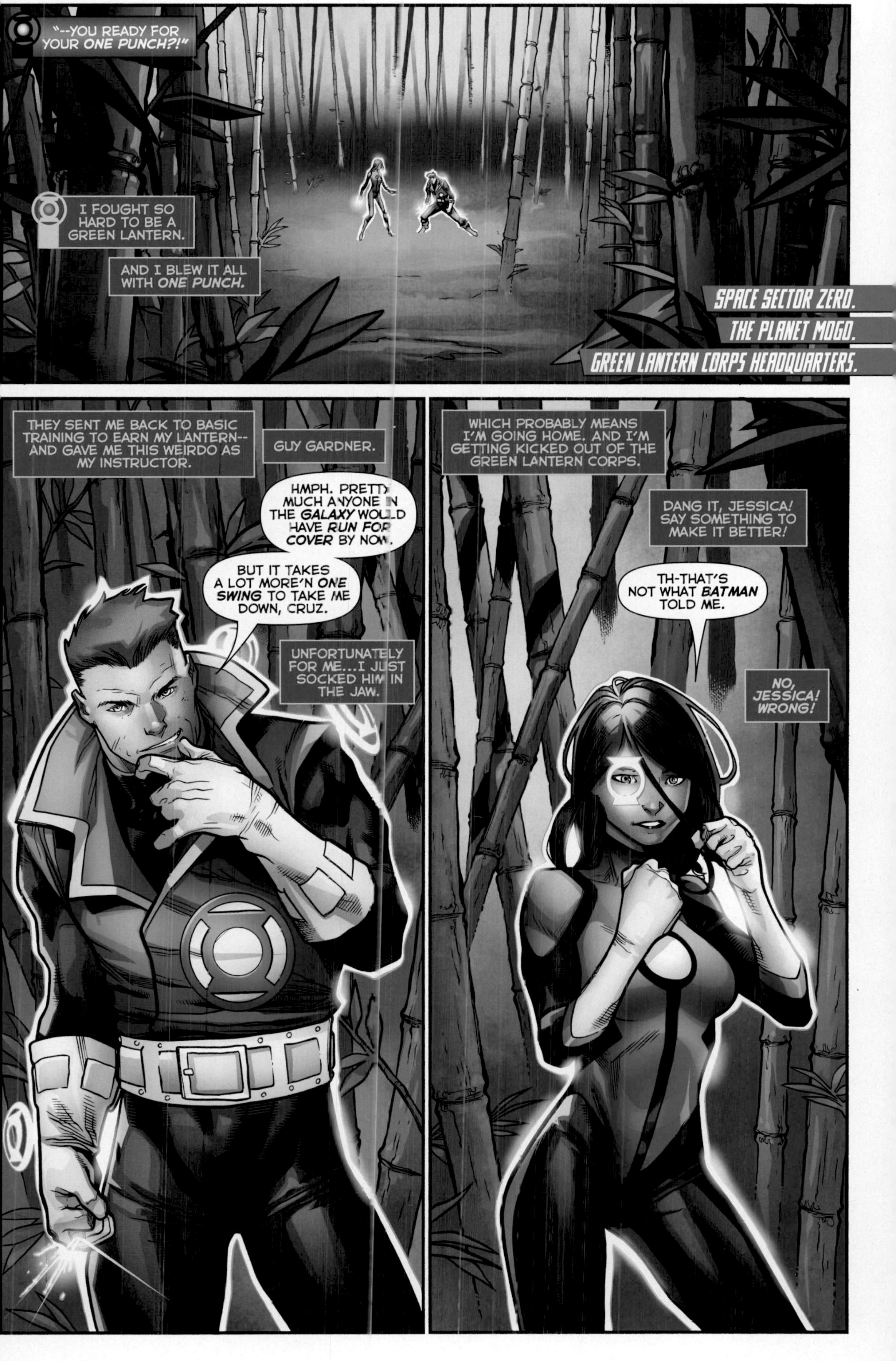
"--YOU READY FOR YOUR ONE PUNCH?!"
I FOUGHT SO HARD TO BE A GREEN LANTERN.
AND I BLEW IT ALL WITH ONE PUNCH.
SPACE SECTOR ZERO.
THE PLANET MOGO.
GREEN LANTERN CORPS HEADQUARTERS.
THEY SENT ME BACK TO BASIC TRAINING TO EARN MY LANTERN-- AND GAVE ME THIS WEIRDO AS MY INSTRUCTOR.
GUY GARDNER.
HMPH. PRETTY MUCH ANYONE IN THE GALAXY WOULD HAVE RUN FOR COVER BY NOW.
BUT IT TAKES A LOT MORE'N ONE SWING TO TAKE ME DOWN, CRUZ.
UNFORTUNATELY FOR ME...I JUST SOCKED HIM IN THE JAW.
WHICH PROBABLY MEANS I'M GOING HOME. AND I'M GETTING KICKED OUT OF THE GREEN LANTERN CORPS.
DANG IT, JESSICA! SAY SOMETHING TO MAKE IT BETTER!
TH-THAT'S NOT WHAT BATMAN TOLD ME.
NO, JESSICA! WRONG!

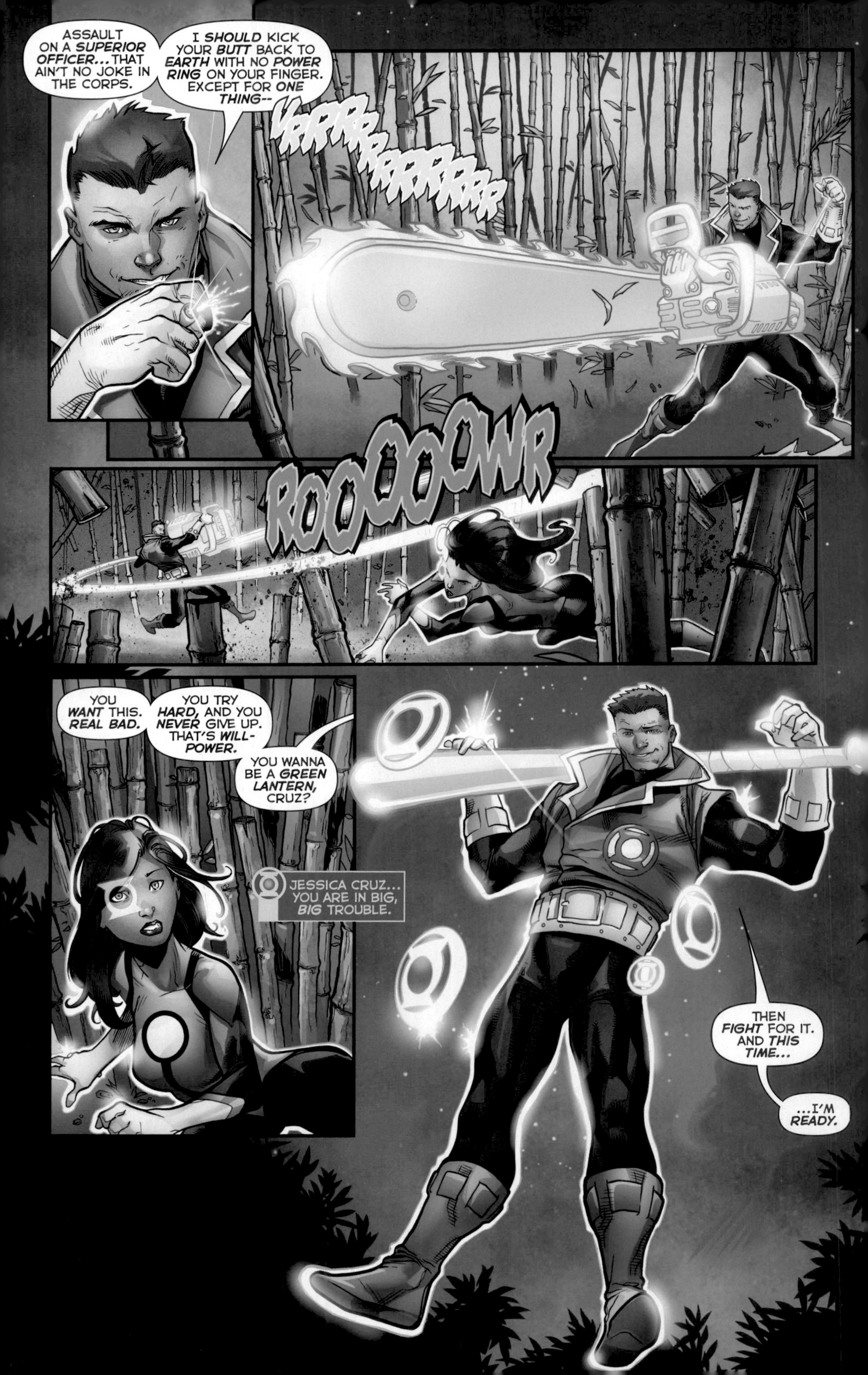

ASSAULT ON A SUPERIOR OFFICER...THAT AIN'T NO JOKE IN THE CORPS.
I SHOULD KICK YOUR BUTT BACK TO EARTH WITH NO POWER RING ON YOUR FINGER. EXCEPT FOR ONE THING--
VRRRRRRRRRRRRR
ROOOOOWR
YOU WANT THIS. REAL BAD.
YOU TRY HARD, AND YOU NEVER GIVE UP. THAT'S WILL-POWER.
YOU WANNA BE A GREEN LANTERN, CRUZ?
JESSICA CRUZ... YOU ARE IN BIG, BIG TROUBLE.
THEN FIGHT FOR IT. AND THIS TIME...
...I'M READY.

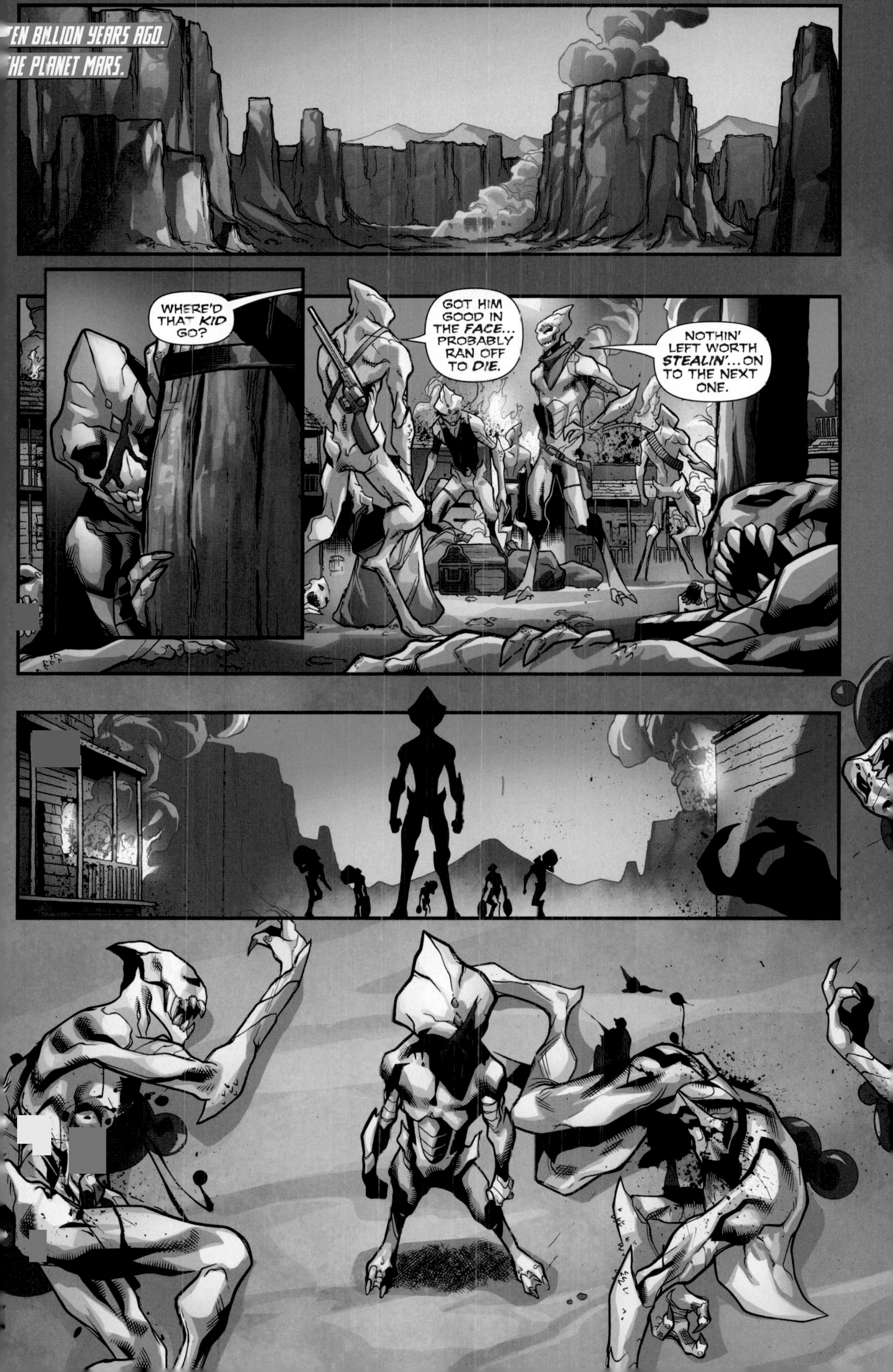

TEN BILLION YEARS AGO.
THE PLANET MARS.
WHERE'D THAT KID GO?
GOT HIM GOOD IN THE FACE... PROBABLY RAN OFF TO DIE.
NOTHIN' LEFT WORTH STEALIN'...ON TO THE NEXT ONE.

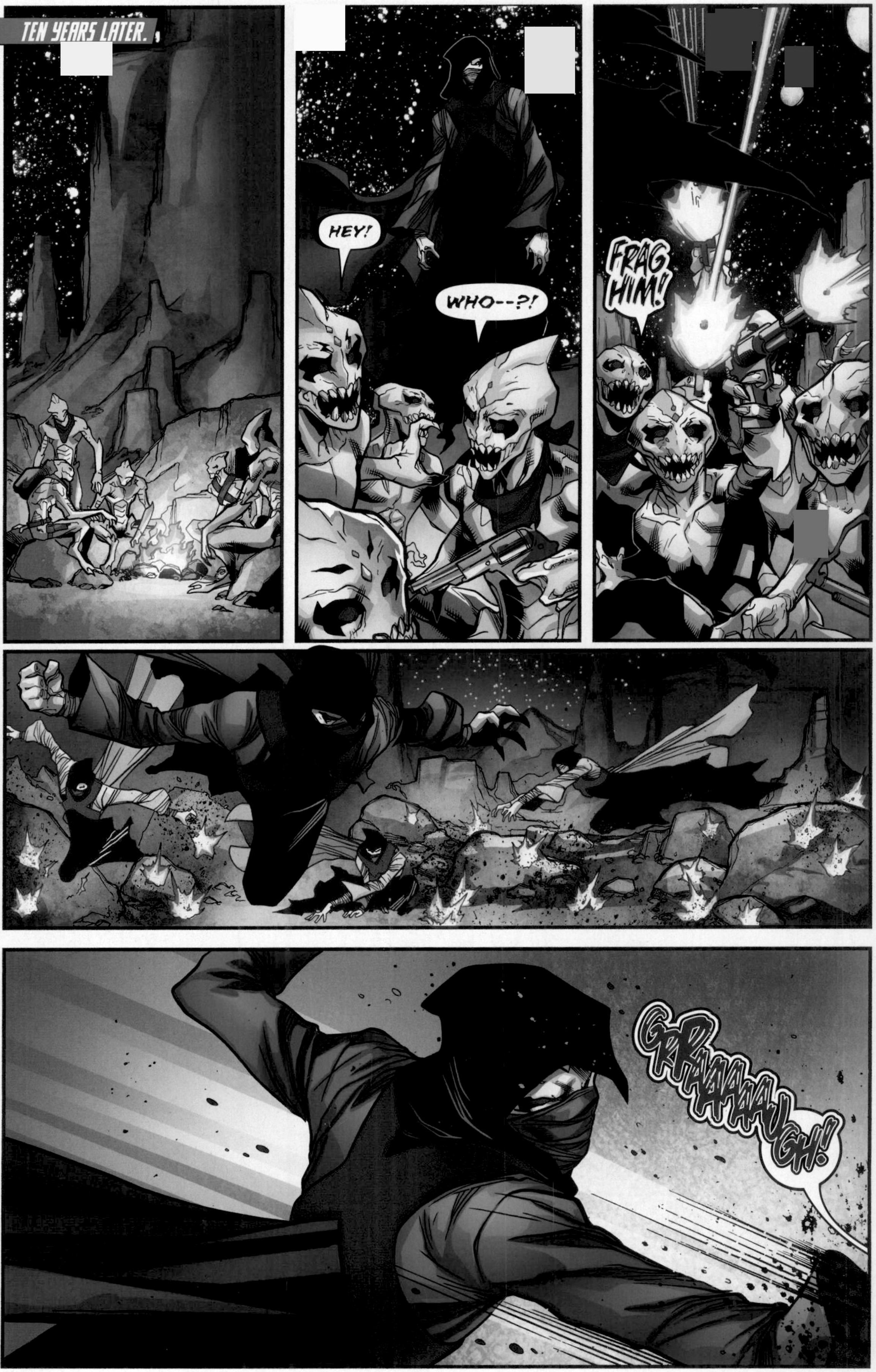
TEN YEARS LATER.
HEY!
WHO--?!
FRAG HIM!
GRRAAAAAAUGH!!

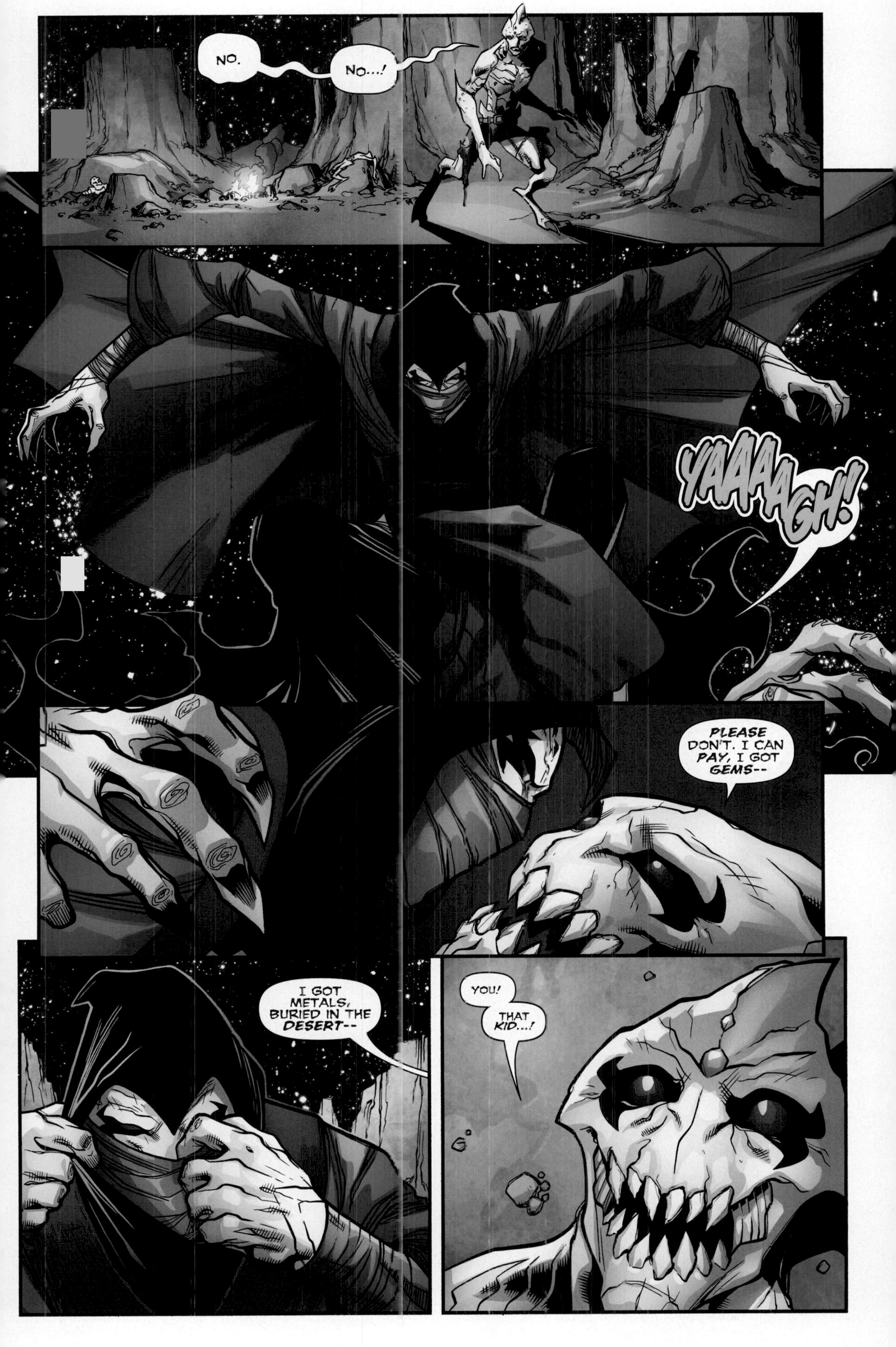
NO.
NO...!
YAAAAGH!
PLEASE DON'T. I CAN PAY, I GOT GEMS--
I GOT METALS, BURIED IN THE DESERT--
YOU!
THAT KID...!

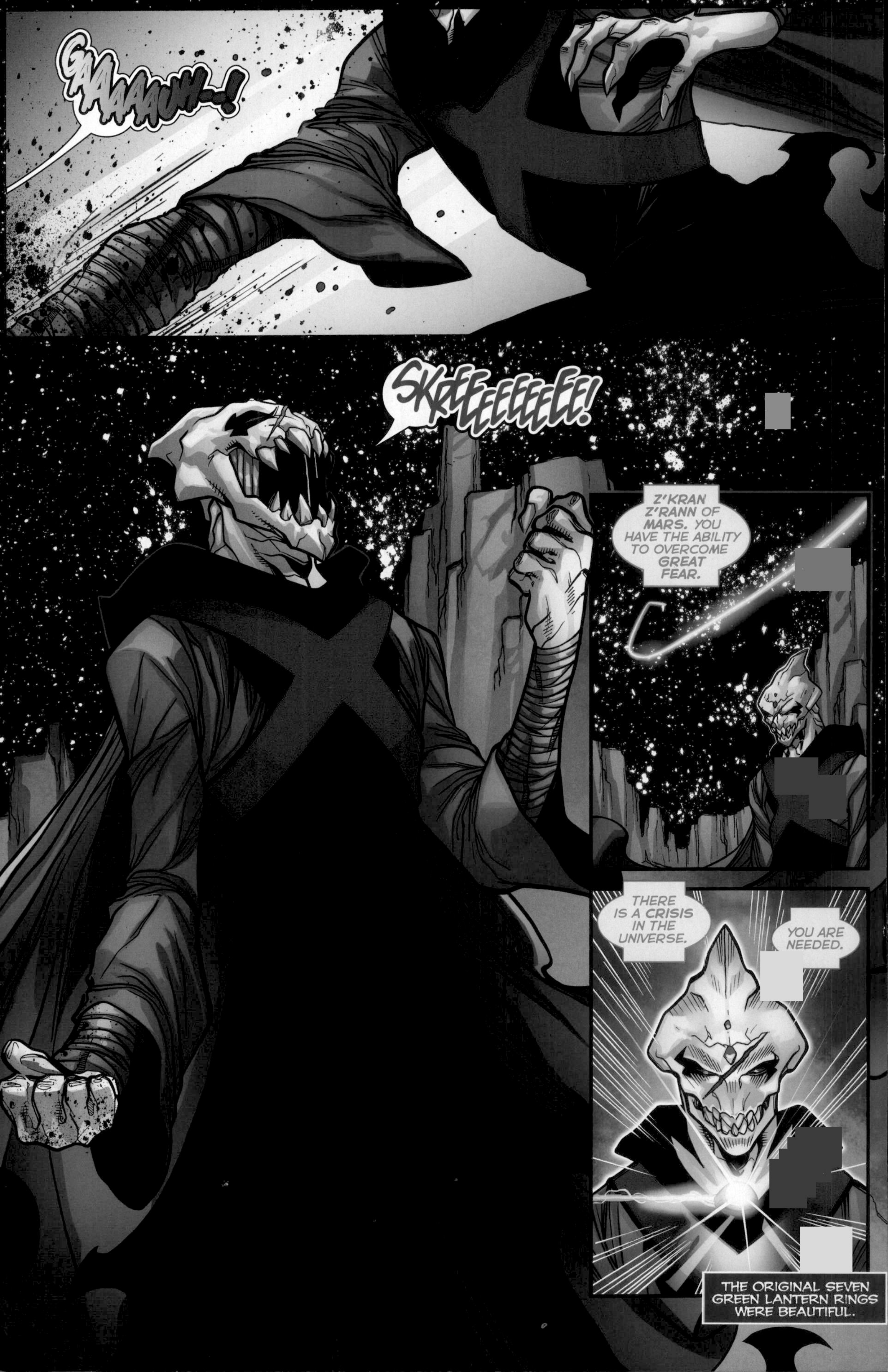
GAAAAAUH--!
SKREEEEEEEEE!
Z'KRAN Z'RANN OF MARS. YOU HAVE THE ABILITY TO OVERCOME GREAT FEAR.
THERE IS A CRISIS IN THE UNIVERSE.
YOU ARE NEEDED.
THE ORIGINAL SEVEN GREEN LANTERN RINGS WERE BEAUTIFUL.

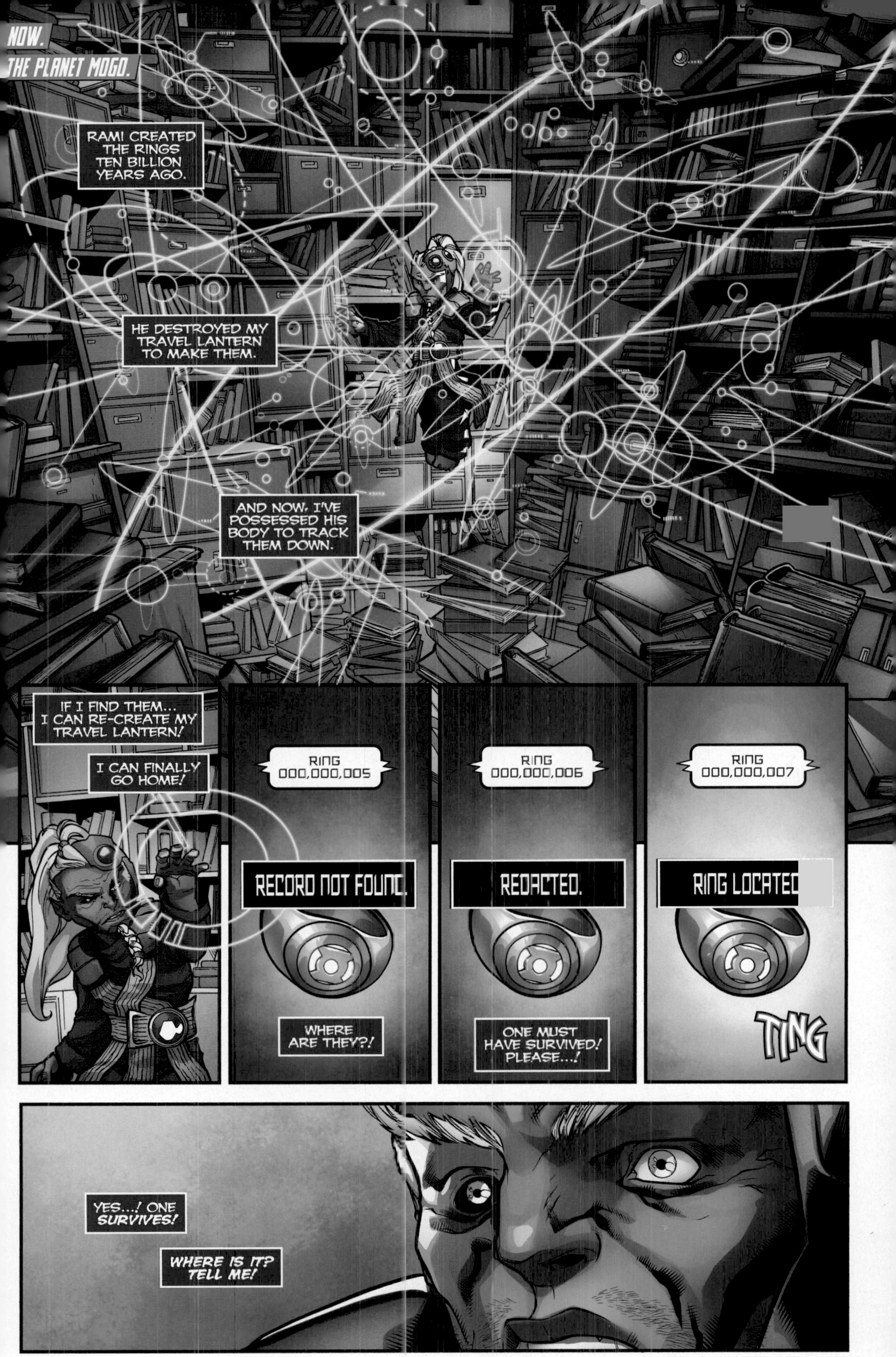
NOW.
THE PLANET MOGO.
RAMI CREATED THE RINGS TEN BILLION YEARS AGO.
HE DESTROYED MY TRAVEL LANTERN TO MAKE THEM.
AND NOW, I'VE POSSESSED HIS BODY TO TRACK THEM DOWN.
IF I FIND THEM... I CAN RE-CREATE MY TRAVEL LANTERN!
I CAN FINALLY GO HOME!
RING 000,000,005
RECORD NOT FOUND.
WHERE ARE THEY?!
RING 000,000,006
REDACTED.
ONE MUST HAVE SURVIVED! PLEASE...!
RING 000,000,007
RING LOCATED
TING
YES...! ONE SURVIVES!
WHERE IS IT? TELL ME!

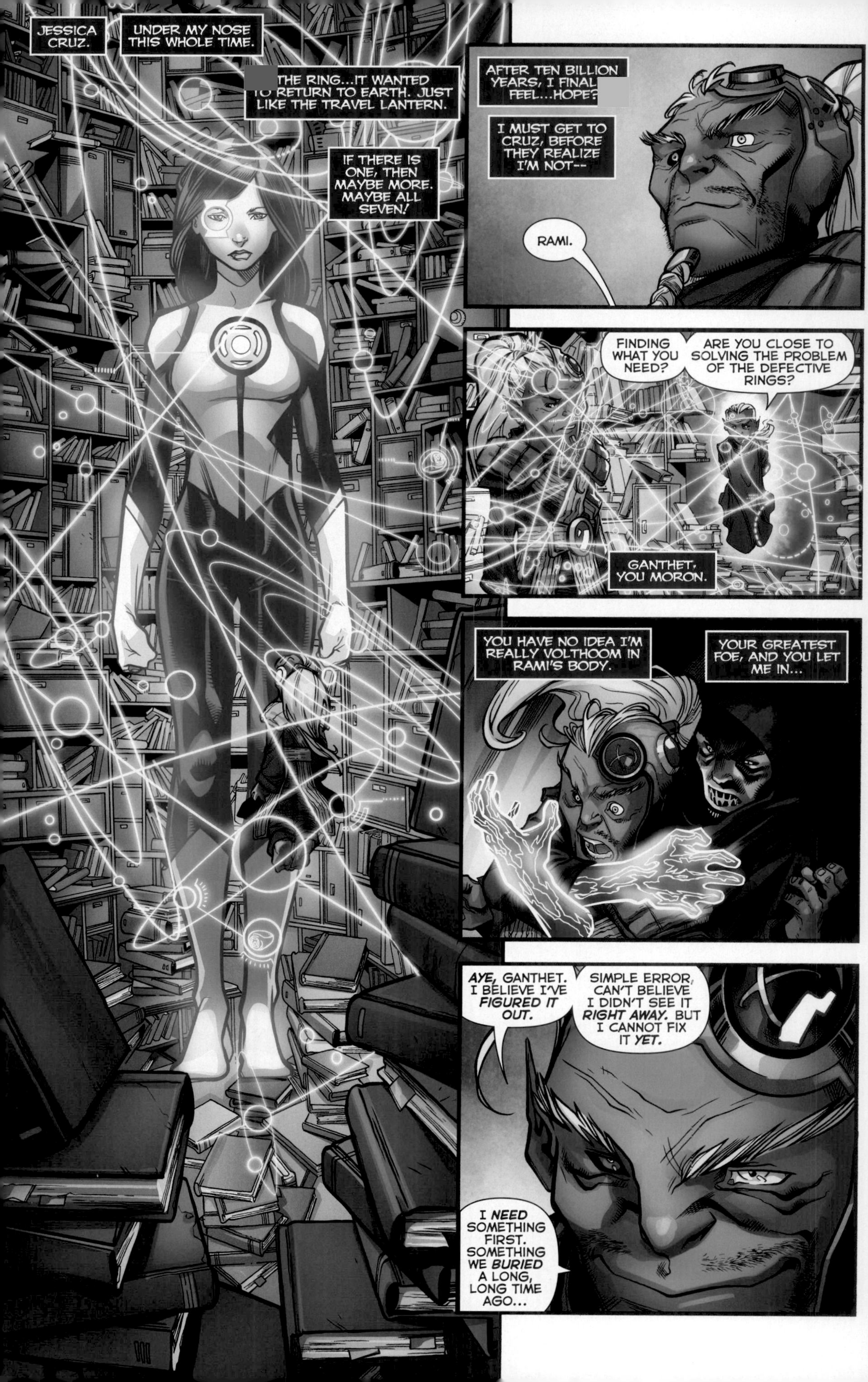
JESSICA CRUZ.
UNDER MY NOSE THIS WHOLE TIME.
THE RING...IT WANTED TO RETURN TO EARTH. JUST LIKE THE TRAVEL LANTERN.
IF THERE IS ONE, THEN MAYBE MORE. MAYBE ALL SEVEN!
AFTER TEN BILLION YEARS, I FINAL FEEL...HOPE?
I MUST GET TO CRUZ, BEFORE THEY REALIZE I'M NOT--
RAMI.
FINDING WHAT YOU NEED?
ARE YOU CLOSE TO SOLVING THE PROBLEM OF THE DEFECTIVE RINGS?
GANTHET, YOU MORON.
YOU HAVE NO IDEA I'M REALLY VOLTHOOM IN RAMI'S BODY.
YOUR GREATEST FOE, AND YOU LET ME IN...
AYE, GANTHET. I BELIEVE I'VE FIGURED IT OUT.
SIMPLE ERROR. CAN'T BELIEVE I DIDN'T SEE IT RIGHT AWAY. BUT I CANNOT FIX IT YET.
I NEED SOMETHING FIRST. SOMETHING WE BURIED A LONG, LONG TIME AGO...

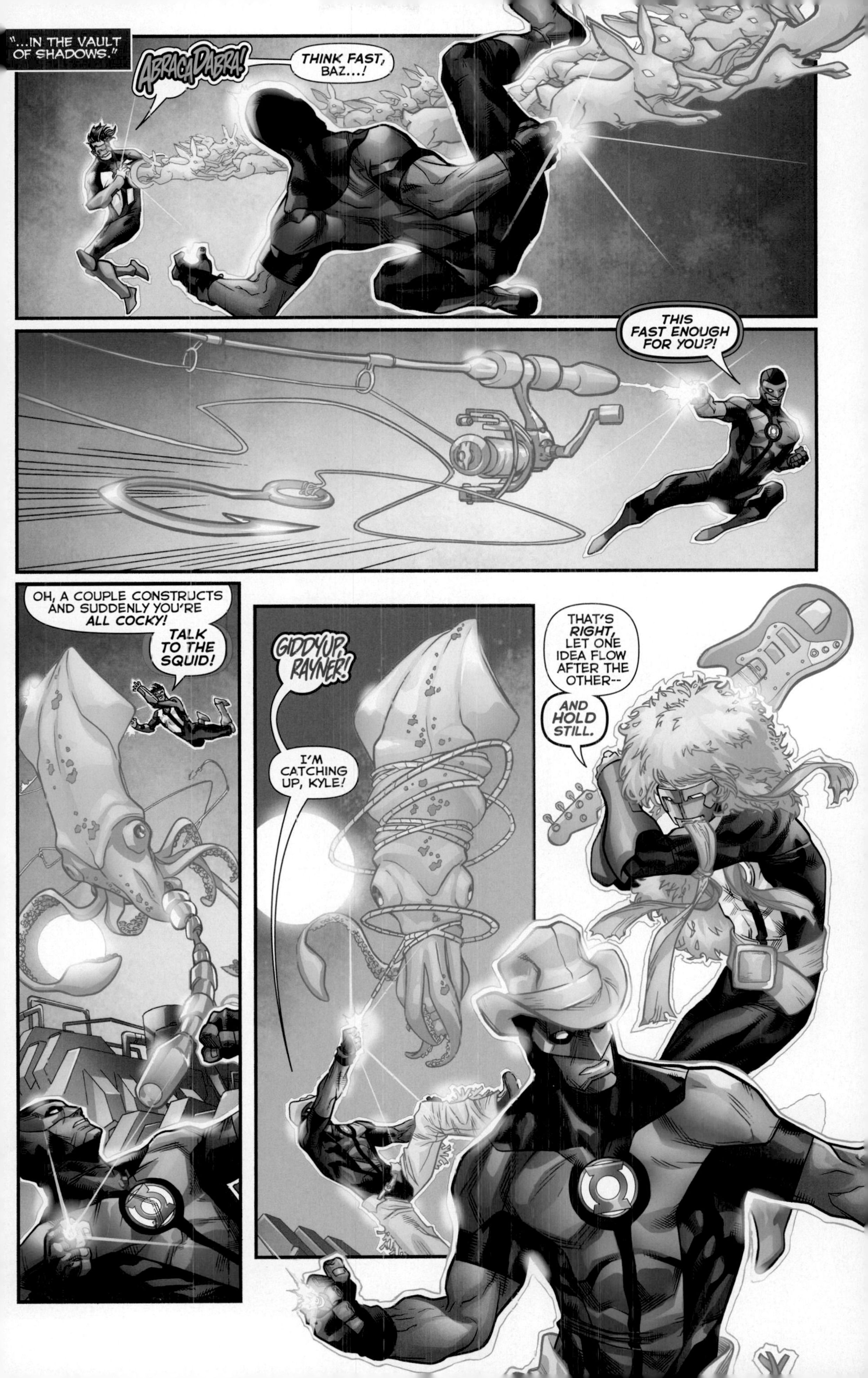
"...IN THE VAULT OF SHADOWS."
ABRACADABRA!
THINK FAST, BAZ...!
THIS FAST ENOUGH FOR YOU?!
OH, A COUPLE CONSTRUCTS AND SUDDENLY YOU'RE ALL COCKY!
TALK TO THE SQUID!
GIDDYUP, RAYNER!
I'M CATCHING UP, KYLE!
THAT'S RIGHT, LET ONE IDEA FLOW AFTER THE OTHER--
AND HOLD STILL.

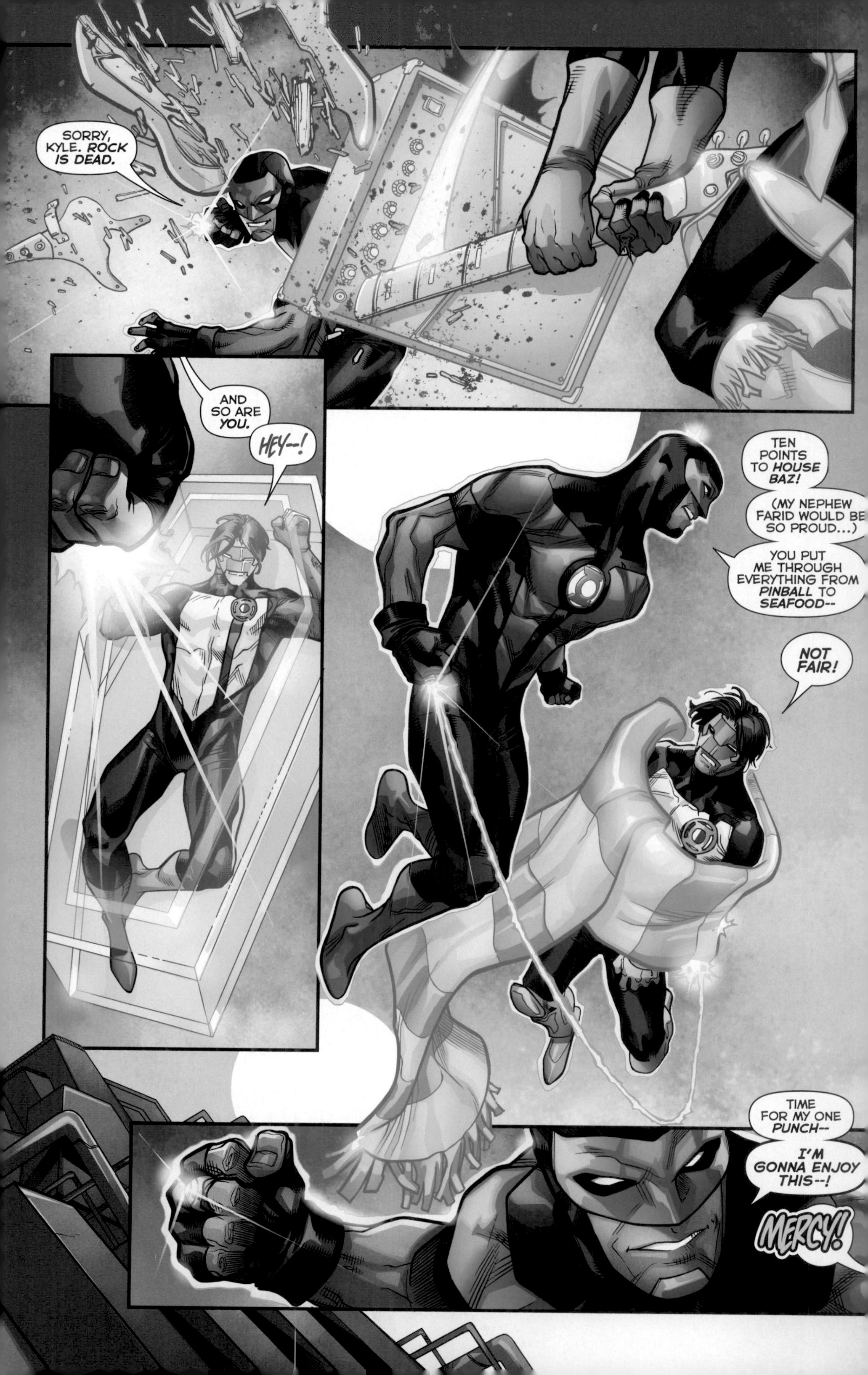
SORRY, KYLE. ROCK IS DEAD.
AND SO ARE YOU.
HEY--!
TEN POINTS TO HOUSE BAZ!
(MY NEPHEW FARID WOULD BE SO PROUD...)
YOU PUT ME THROUGH EVERYTHING FROM PINBALL TO SEAFOOD--
NOT FAIR!
TIME FOR MY ONE PUNCH--
I'M GONNA ENJOY THIS--!
MERCY!

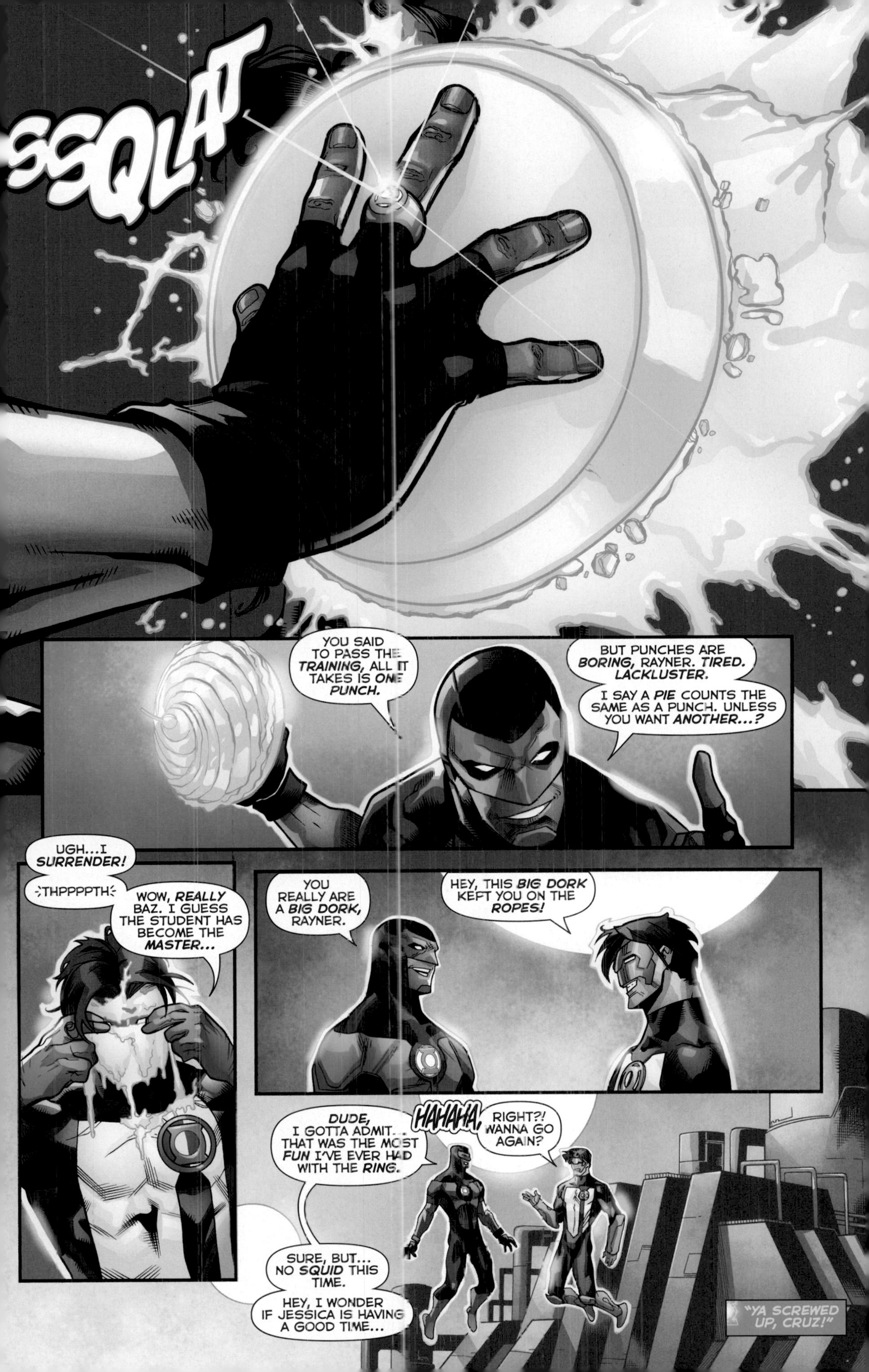
SSQLAT
YOU SAID TO PASS THE TRAINING, ALL IT TAKES IS ONE PUNCH.
BUT PUNCHES ARE BORING, RAYNER. TIRED. LACKLUSTER.
I SAY A PIE COUNTS THE SAME AS A PUNCH. UNLESS YOU WANT ANOTHER...?
UGH...I SURRENDER!
THPPPPTH
WOW, REALLY BAZ. I GUESS THE STUDENT HAS BECOME THE MASTER...
YOU REALLY ARE A BIG DORK, RAYNER.
HEY, THIS BIG DORK KEPT YOU ON THE ROPES!
HAHAHA!
DUDE, I GOTTA ADMIT... THAT WAS THE MOST FUN I'VE EVER HAD WITH THE RING.
RIGHT?! WANNA GO AGAIN?
SURE, BUT... NO SQUID THIS TIME.
HEY, I WONDER IF JESSICA IS HAVING A GOOD TIME...
"YA SCREWED UP, CRUZ!"

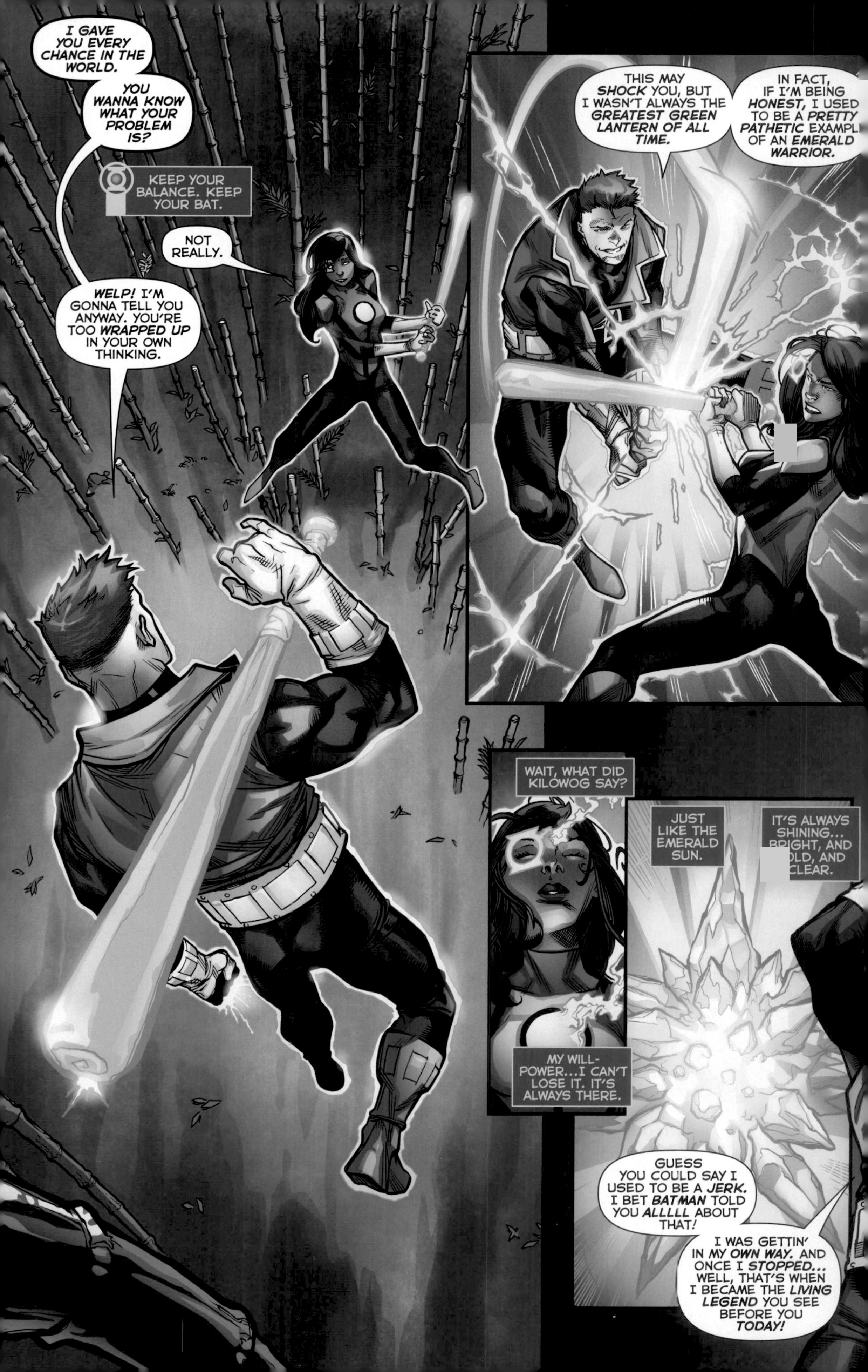
I GAVE YOU EVERY CHANCE IN THE WORLD.
YOU WANNA KNOW WHAT YOUR PROBLEM IS?
KEEP YOUR BALANCE. KEEP YOUR BAT.
NOT REALLY.
WELP! I'M GONNA TELL YOU ANYWAY. YOU'RE TOO WRAPPED UP IN YOUR OWN THINKING.
THIS MAY SHOCK YOU, BUT I WASN'T ALWAYS THE GREATEST GREEN LANTERN OF ALL TIME.
IN FACT, IF I'M BEING HONEST, I USED TO BE A PRETTY PATHETIC EXAMPL OF AN EMERALD WARRIOR.
WAIT, WHAT DID KILOWOG SAY?
JUST LIKE THE EMERALD SUN.
IT'S ALWAYS SHINING... BRIGHT, AND OLD, AND CLEAR.
MY WILL-POWER...I CAN'T LOSE IT. IT'S ALWAYS THERE.
GUESS YOU COULD SAY I USED TO BE A JERK. I BET BATMAN TOLD YOU ALLLLL ABOUT THAT!
I WAS GETTIN' IN MY OWN WAY. AND ONCE I STOPPED... WELL, THAT'S WHEN I BECAME THE LIVING LEGEND YOU SEE BEFORE YOU TODAY!

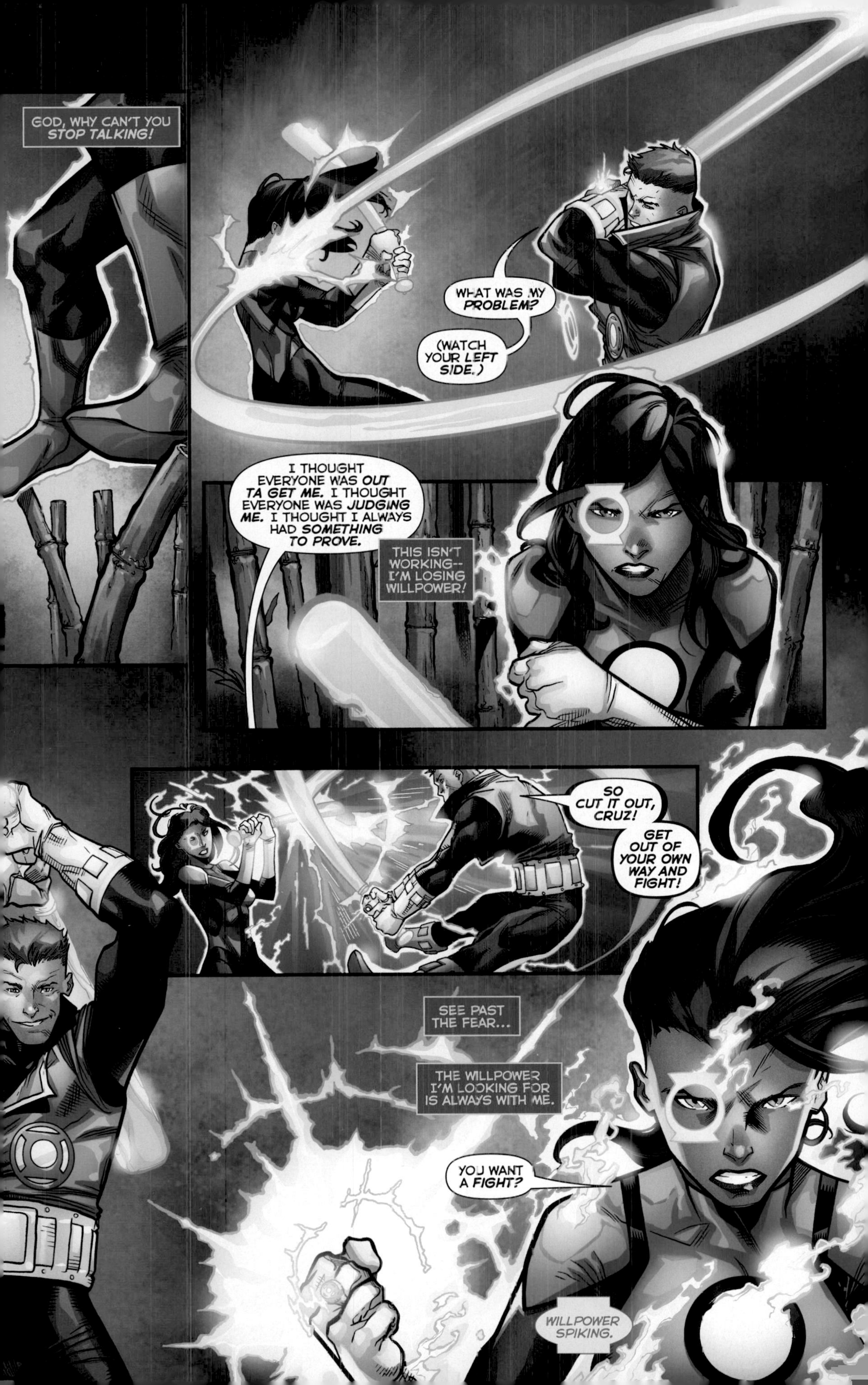
GOD, WHY CAN'T YOU STOP TALKING!
WHAT WAS MY PROBLEM?
(WATCH YOUR LEFT SIDE.)
I THOUGHT EVERYONE WAS OUT TA GET ME. I THOUGHT EVERYONE WAS JUDGING ME. I THOUGHT I ALWAYS HAD SOMETHING TO PROVE.
THIS ISN'T WORKING-- I'M LOSING WILLPOWER!
SO CUT IT OUT, CRUZ!
GET OUT OF YOUR OWN WAY AND FIGHT!
SEE PAST THE FEAR...
THE WILLPOWER I'M LOOKING FOR IS ALWAYS WITH ME.
YOU WANT A FIGHT?
WILLPOWER SPIKING.

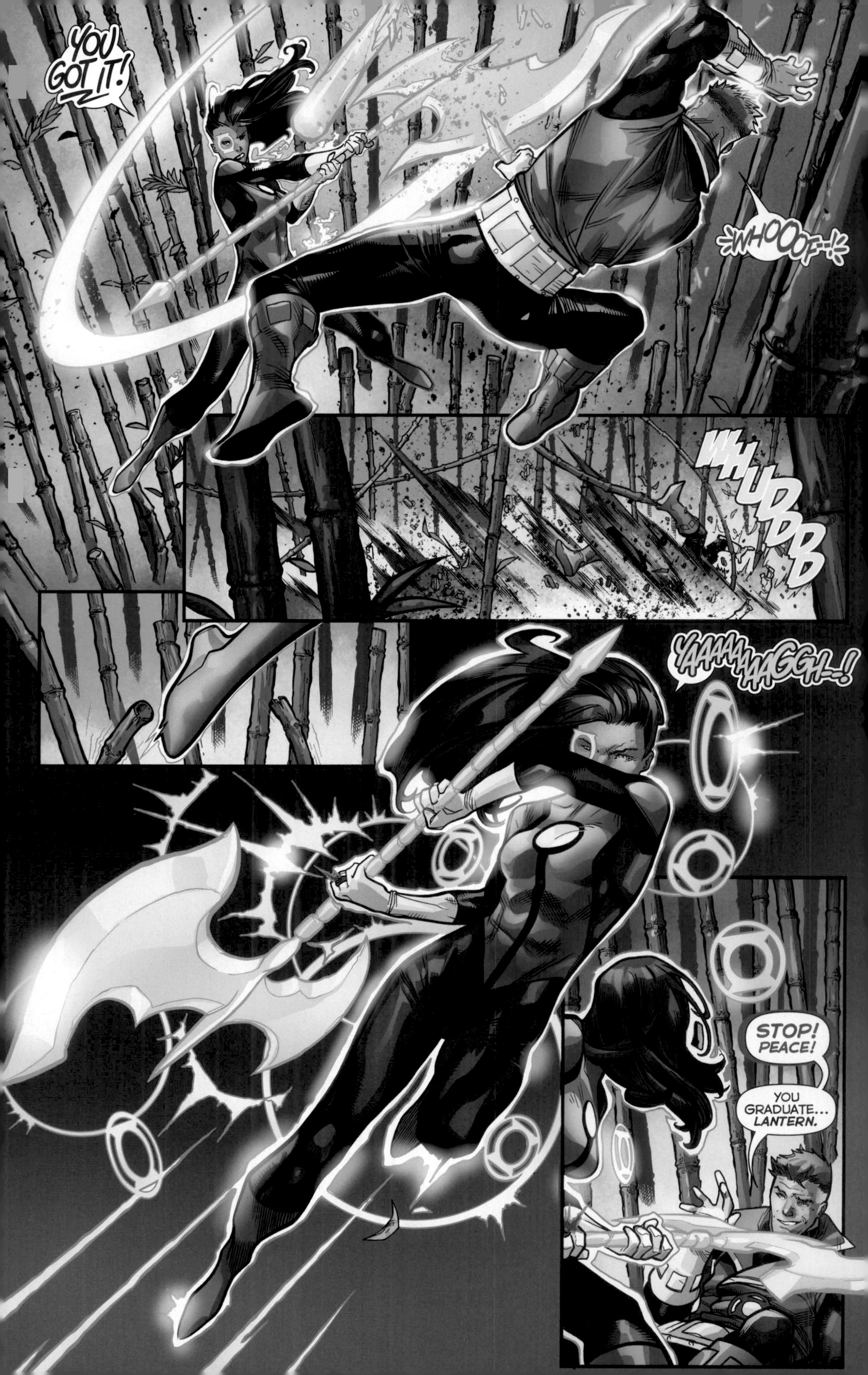
YOU GOT IT!
WHOOOF--!
WHUDBB
YAAAAAAAAGGH--!
STOP! PEACE!
YOU GRADUATE... LANTERN.

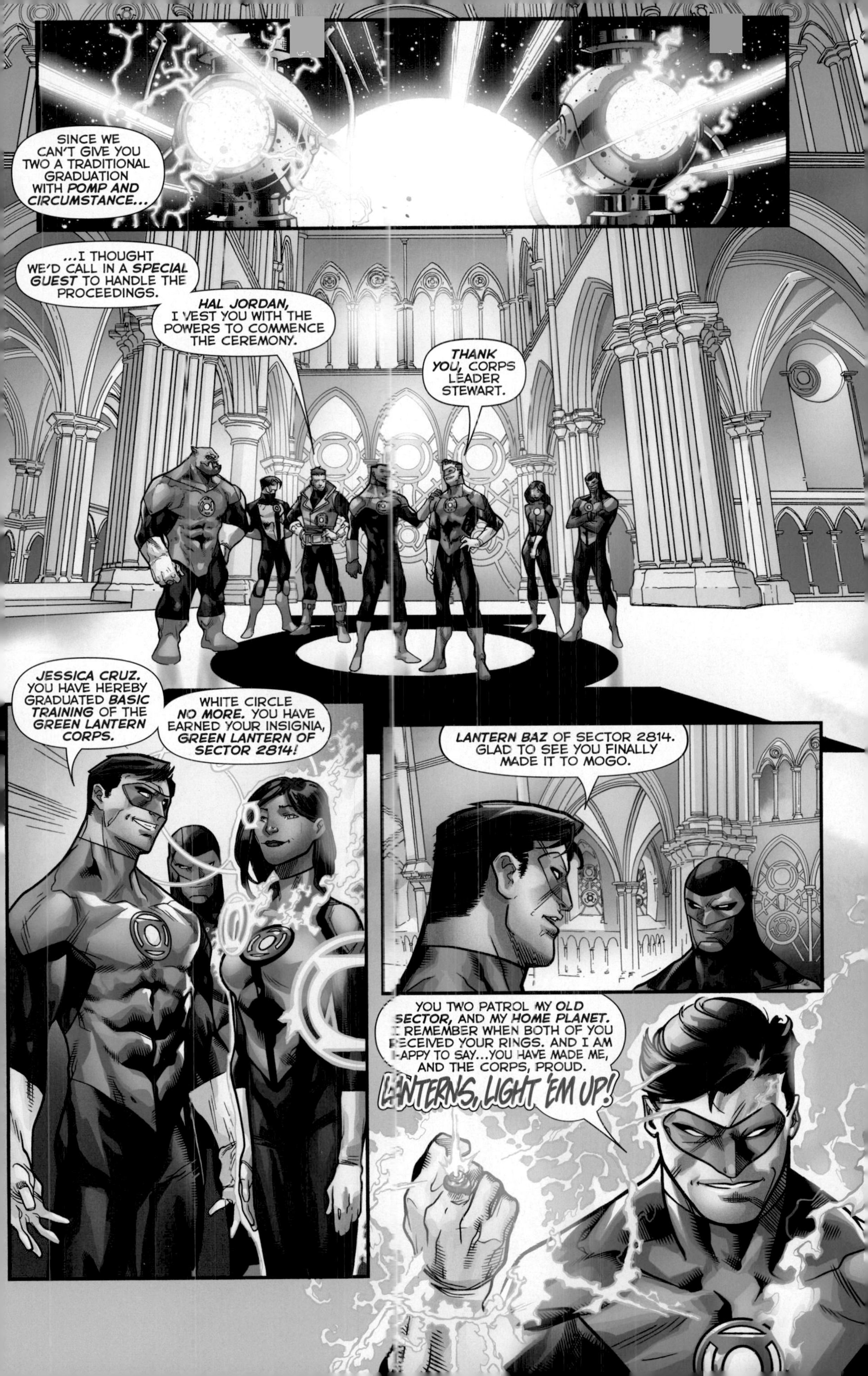

SINCE WE CAN'T GIVE YOU TWO A TRADITIONAL GRADUATION WITH POMP AND CIRCUMSTANCE...
...I THOUGHT WE'D CALL IN A SPECIAL GUEST TO HANDLE THE PROCEEDINGS.
HAL JORDAN, I VEST YOU WITH THE POWERS TO COMMENCE THE CEREMONY.
THANK YOU, CORPS LEADER STEWART.
JESSICA CRUZ. YOU HAVE HEREBY GRADUATED BASIC TRAINING OF THE GREEN LANTERN CORPS.
WHITE CIRCLE NO MORE. YOU HAVE EARNED YOUR INSIGNIA, GREEN LANTERN OF SECTOR 2814!
LANTERN BAZ OF SECTOR 2814. GLAD TO SEE YOU FINALLY MADE IT TO MOGO.
YOU TWO PATROL MY OLD SECTOR, AND MY HOME PLANET. I REMEMBER WHEN BOTH OF YOU RECEIVED YOUR RINGS. AND I AM HAPPY TO SAY...YOU HAVE MADE ME, AND THE CORPS, PROUD.
LANTERNS, LIGHT 'EM UP!

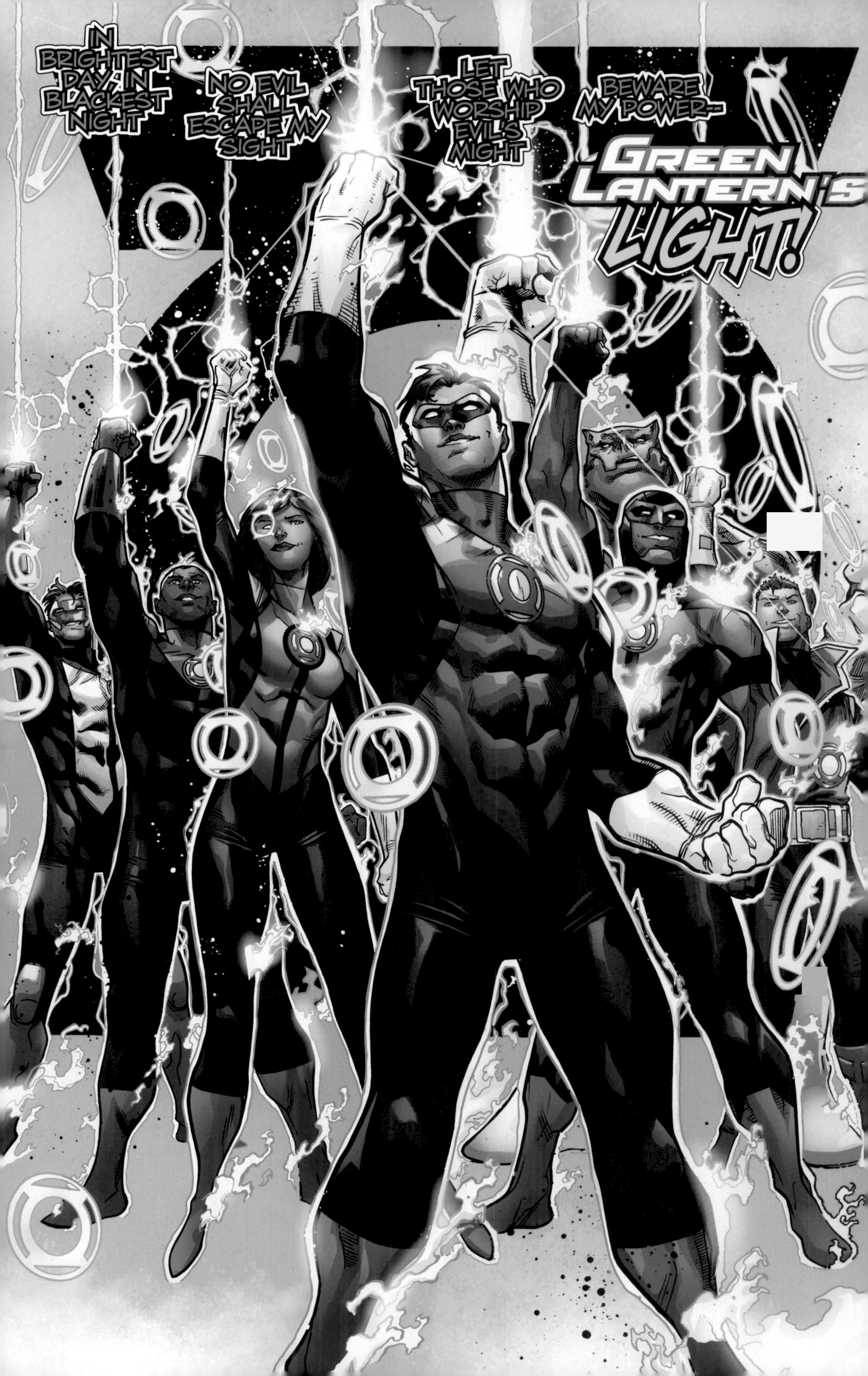
IN BRIGHTEST DAY, IN BLACKEST NIGHT
NO EVIL SHALL ESCAPE MY SIGHT
LET THOSE WHO WORSHIP EVIL'S MIGHT
BEWARE MY POWER--
GREEN LANTERN'S LIGHT!

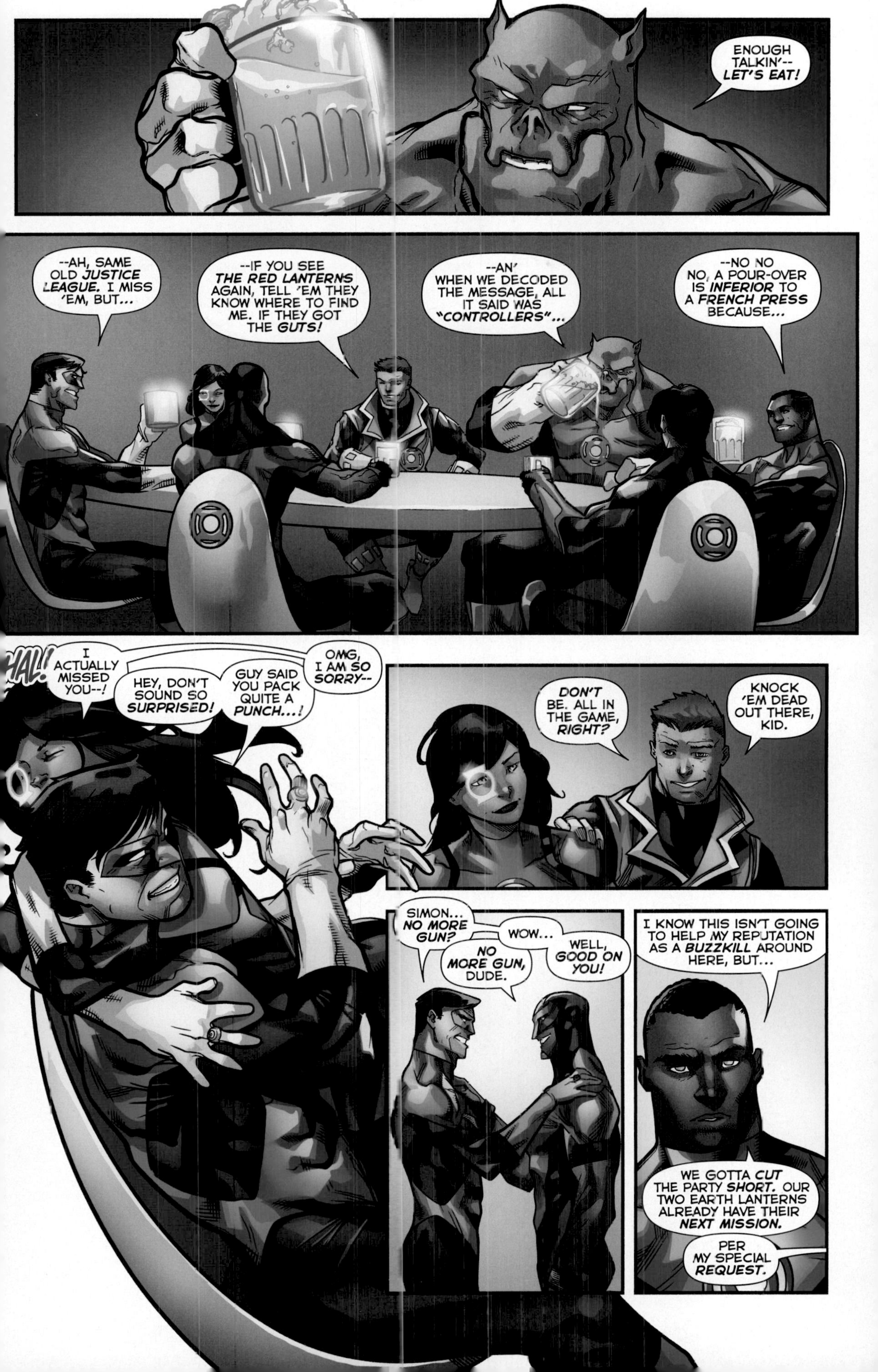
ENOUGH TALKIN'-- LET'S EAT!
--AH, SAME OLD JUSTICE LEAGUE. I MISS 'EM, BUT...
--IF YOU SEE THE RED LANTERNS AGAIN, TELL 'EM THEY KNOW WHERE TO FIND ME. IF THEY GOT THE GUTS!
--AN' WHEN WE DECODED THE MESSAGE, ALL IT SAID WAS "CONTROLLERS"...
--NO NO NO, A POUR-OVER IS INFERIOR TO A FRENCH PRESS BECAUSE...
I ACTUALLY MISSED YOU--!
HEY, DON'T SOUND SO SURPRISED!
GUY SAID YOU PACK QUITE A PUNCH...!
OMG, I AM SO SORRY--
DON'T BE. ALL IN THE GAME, RIGHT?
KNOCK 'EM DEAD OUT THERE, KID.
SIMON... NO MORE GUN?
WOW...
NO MORE GUN, DUDE.
WELL, GOOD ON YOU!
I KNOW THIS ISN'T GOING TO HELP MY REPUTATION AS A BUZZKILL AROUND HERE, BUT...
WE GOTTA CUT THE PARTY SHORT. OUR TWO EARTH LANTERNS ALREADY HAVE THEIR NEXT MISSION.
PER MY SPECIAL REQUEST.

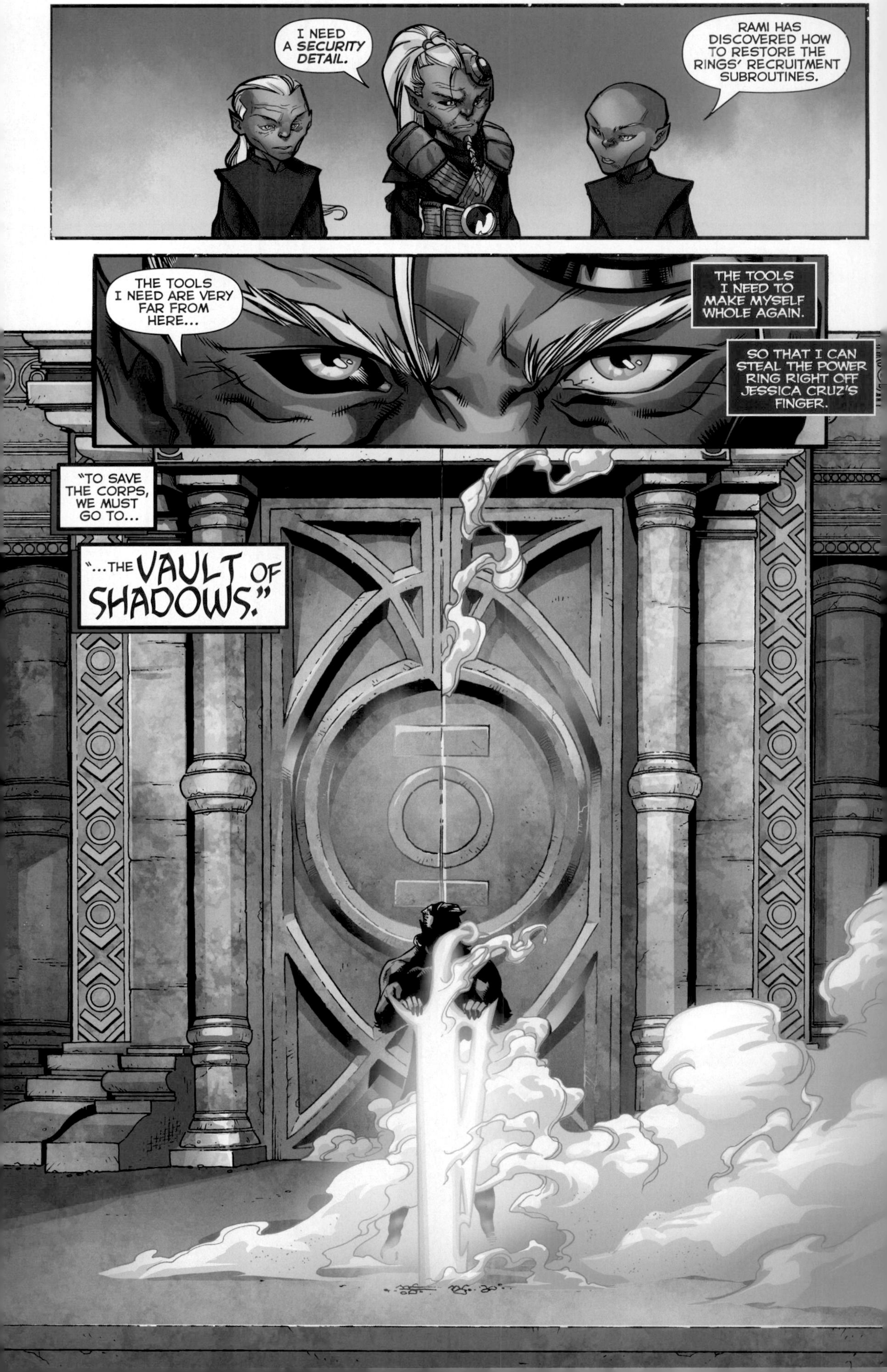
I NEED A SECURITY DETAIL.
RAMI HAS DISCOVERED HOW TO RESTORE THE RINGS' RECRUITMENT SUBROUTINES.
THE TOOLS I NEED ARE VERY FAR FROM HERE...
THE TOOLS I NEED TO MAKE MYSELF WHOLE AGAIN.
SO THAT I CAN STEAL THE POWER RING RIGHT OFF JESSICA CRUZ'S FINGER.
"TO SAVE THE CORPS, WE MUST GO TO...
"...THE VAULT OF SHADOWS."

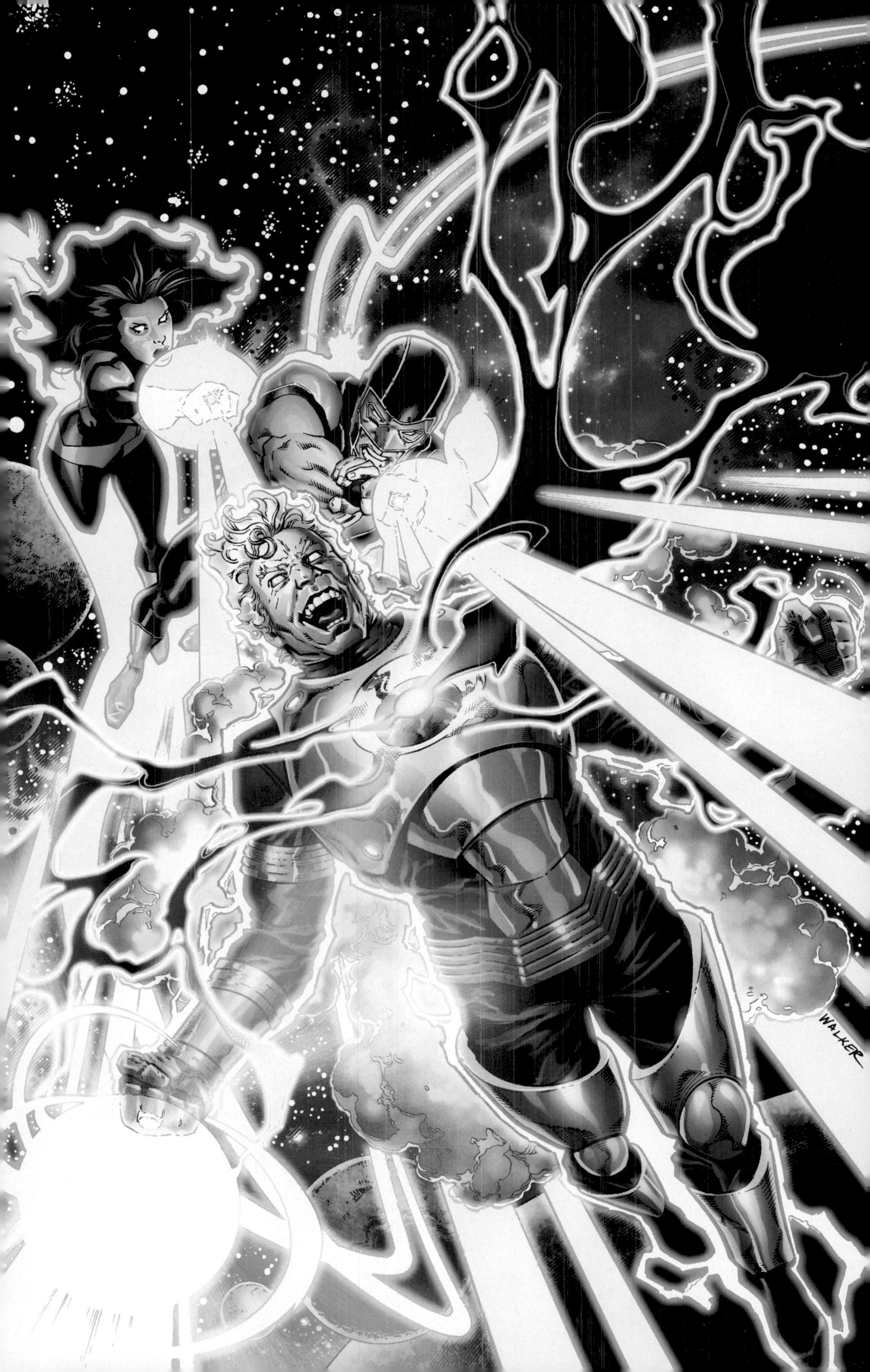
WALKER

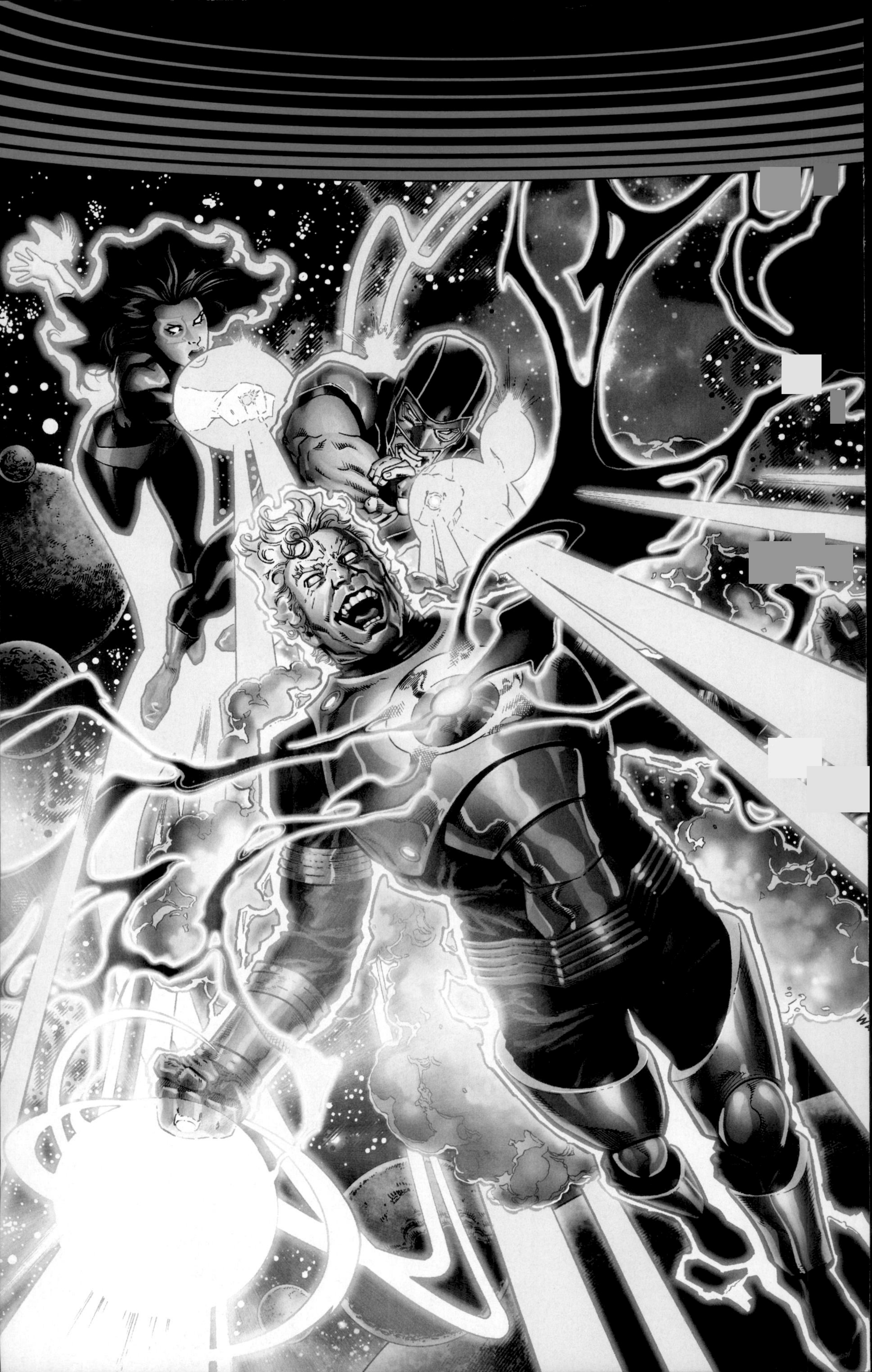

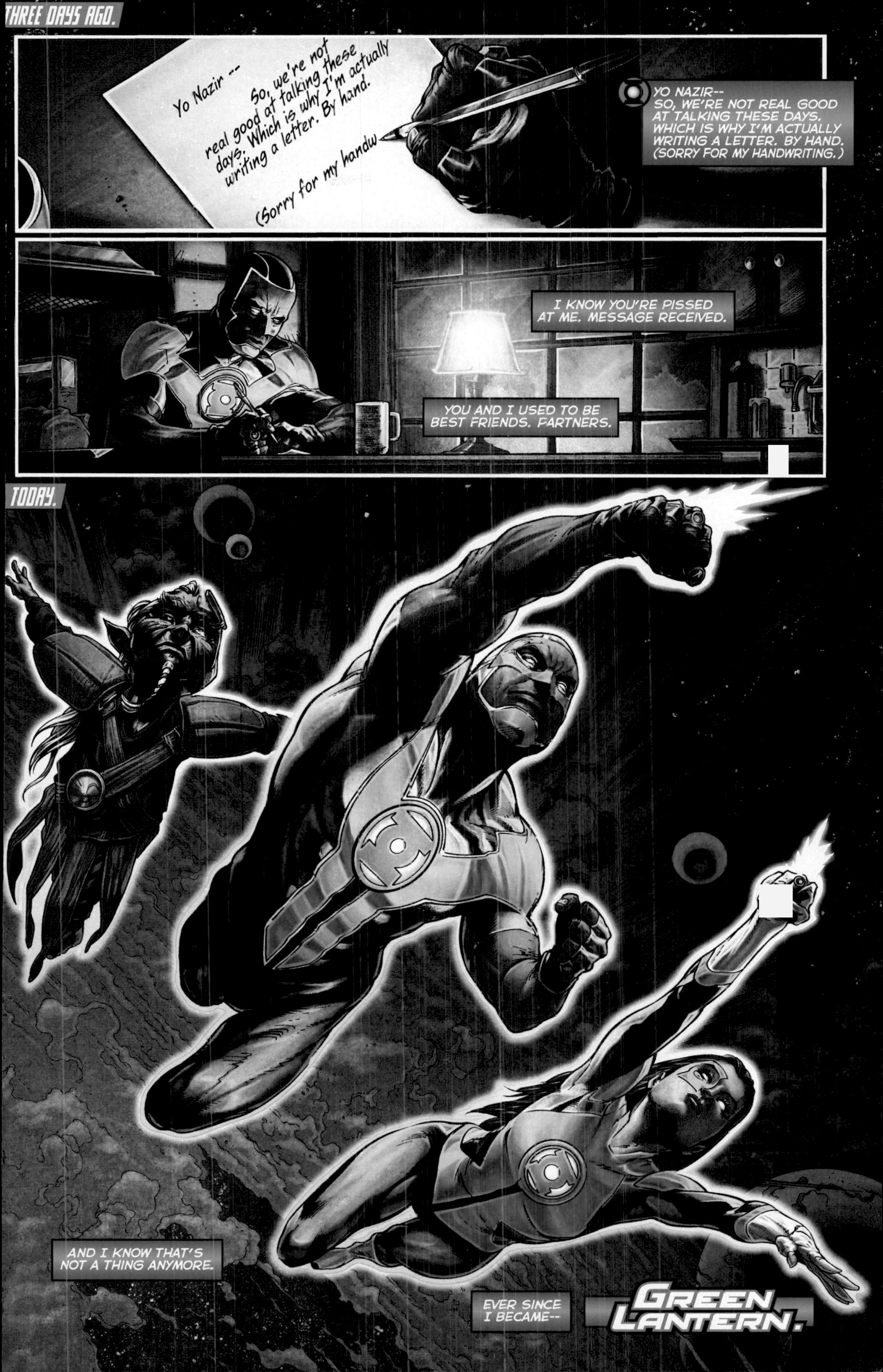
THREE DAYS AGO.
Yo Nazir --
So, we're not real good at talking these days. Which is why I'm actually writing a letter. By hand.
(Sorry for my handw
YO NAZIR--
SO, WE'RE NOT REAL GOOD AT TALKING THESE DAYS. WHICH IS WHY I'M ACTUALLY WRITING A LETTER. BY HAND. (SORRY FOR MY HANDWRITING.)
I KNOW YOU'RE PISSED AT ME. MESSAGE RECEIVED.
YOU AND I USED TO BE BEST FRIENDS. PARTNERS.
TODAY.
AND I KNOW THAT'S NOT A THING ANYMORE.
EVER SINCE I BECAME--
GREEN LANTERN.

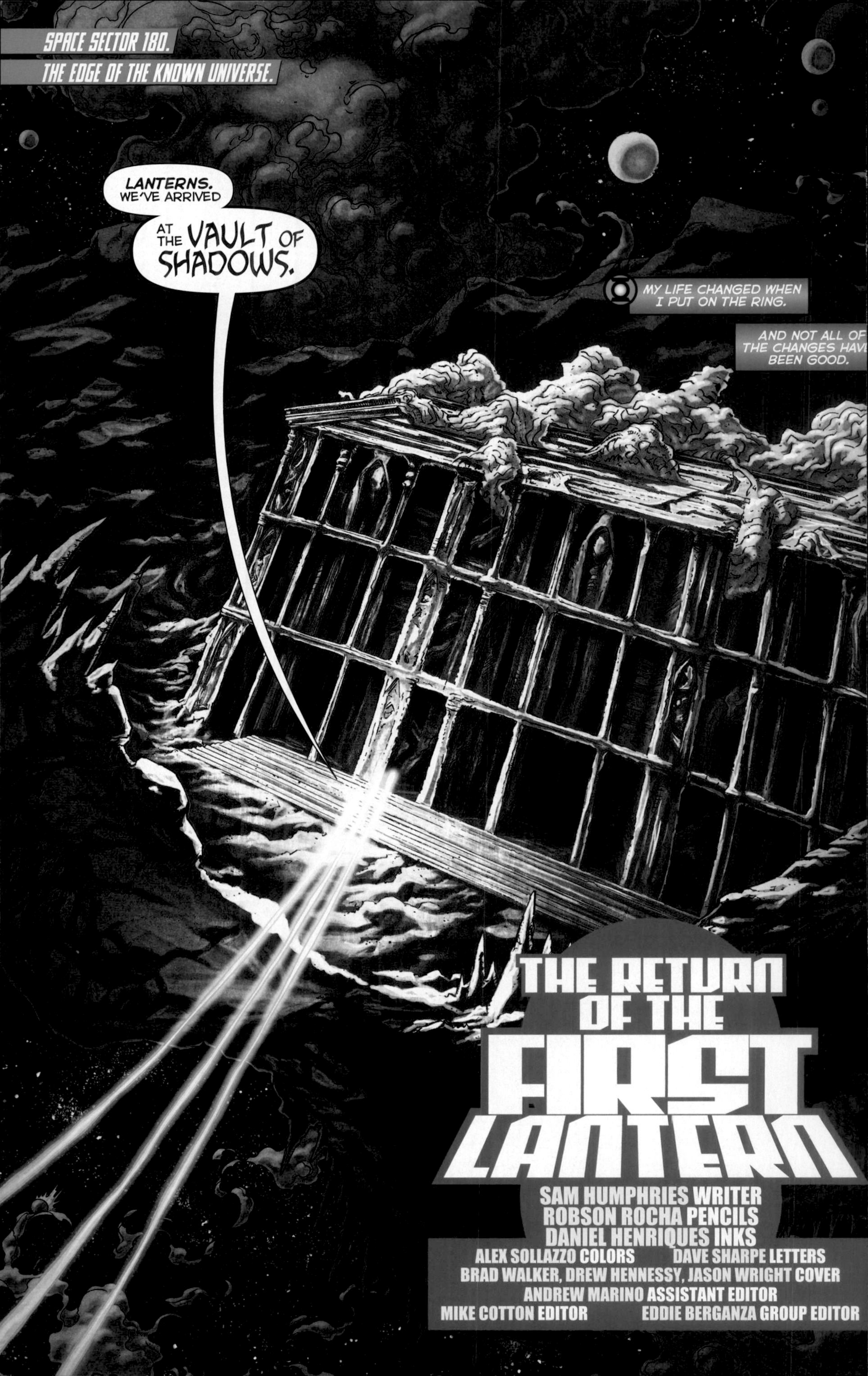
SPACE SECTOR 180.
THE EDGE OF THE KNOWN UNIVERSE.
LANTERNS. WE'VE ARRIVED
AT THE VAULT OF SHADOWS.
MY LIFE CHANGED WHEN I PUT ON THE RING.
AND NOT ALL OF THE CHANGES HAVE BEEN GOOD.
THE RETURN OF THE FIRST LANTERN
SAM HUMPHRIES WRITER
ROBSON ROCHA PENCILS
DANIEL HENRIQUES INKS
ALEX SOLLAZZO COLORS
DAVE SHARPE LETTERS
BRAD WALKER, DREW HENNESSY, JASON WRIGHT COVER
ANDREW MARINO ASSISTANT EDITOR
MIKE COTTON EDITOR
EDDIE BERGANZA GROUP EDITOR

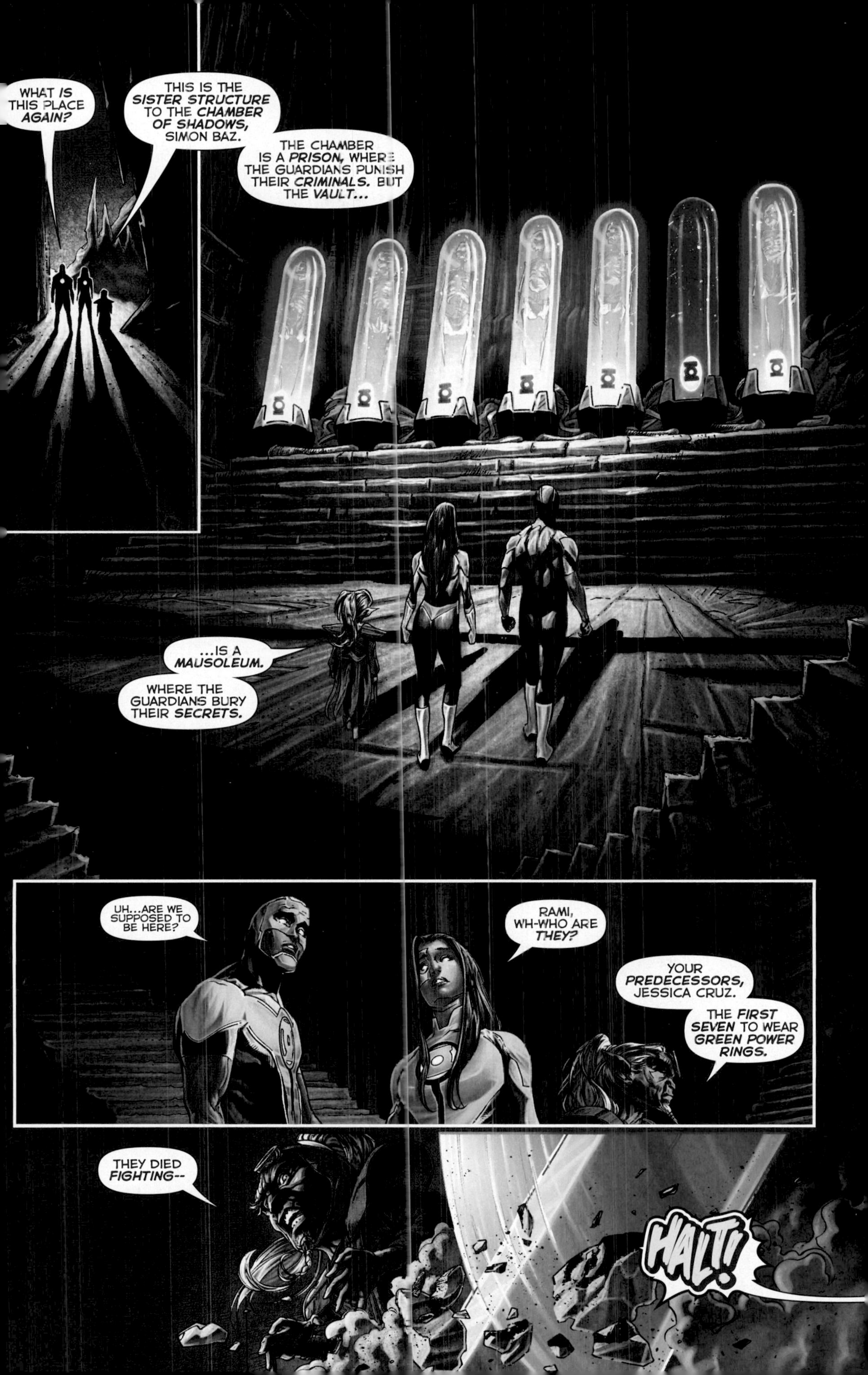
WHAT IS THIS PLACE AGAIN?
THIS IS THE SISTER STRUCTURE TO THE CHAMBER OF SHADOWS, SIMON BAZ.
THE CHAMBER IS A PRISON, WHERE THE GUARDIANS PUNISH THEIR CRIMINALS. BUT THE VAULT...
...IS A MAUSOLEUM.
WHERE THE GUARDIANS BURY THEIR SECRETS.
UH...ARE WE SUPPOSED TO BE HERE?
RAMI, WH-WHO ARE THEY?
YOUR PREDECESSORS, JESSICA CRUZ.
THE FIRST SEVEN TO WEAR GREEN POWER RINGS.
THEY DIED FIGHTING--
HALT!

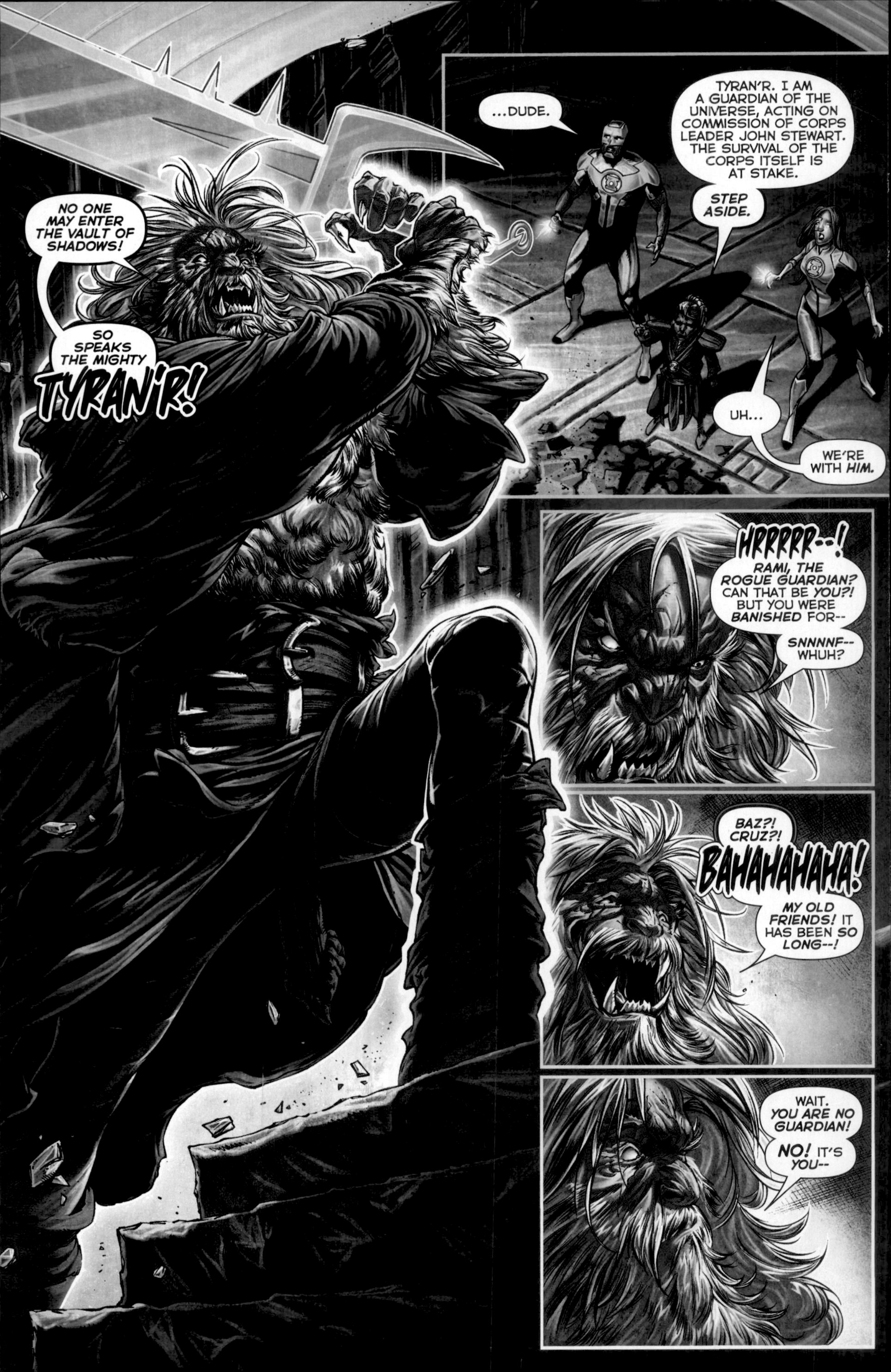
NO ONE MAY ENTER THE VAULT OF SHADOWS!
SO SPEAKS THE MIGHTY
TYRAN'R!
...DUDE.
TYRAN'R. I AM A GUARDIAN OF THE UNIVERSE, ACTING ON COMMISSION OF CORPS LEADER JOHN STEWART. THE SURVIVAL OF THE CORPS ITSELF IS AT STAKE.
STEP ASIDE.
UH...
WE'RE WITH HIM.
HRRRRR--!
RAMI, THE ROGUE GUARDIAN? CAN THAT BE YOU?! BUT YOU WERE BANISHED FOR--
SNNNNF-- WHUH?
BAZ?! CRUZ?!
BAHAHAHAHA!
MY OLD FRIENDS! IT HAS BEEN SO LONG--!
WAIT. YOU ARE NO GUARDIAN!
NO! IT'S YOU--

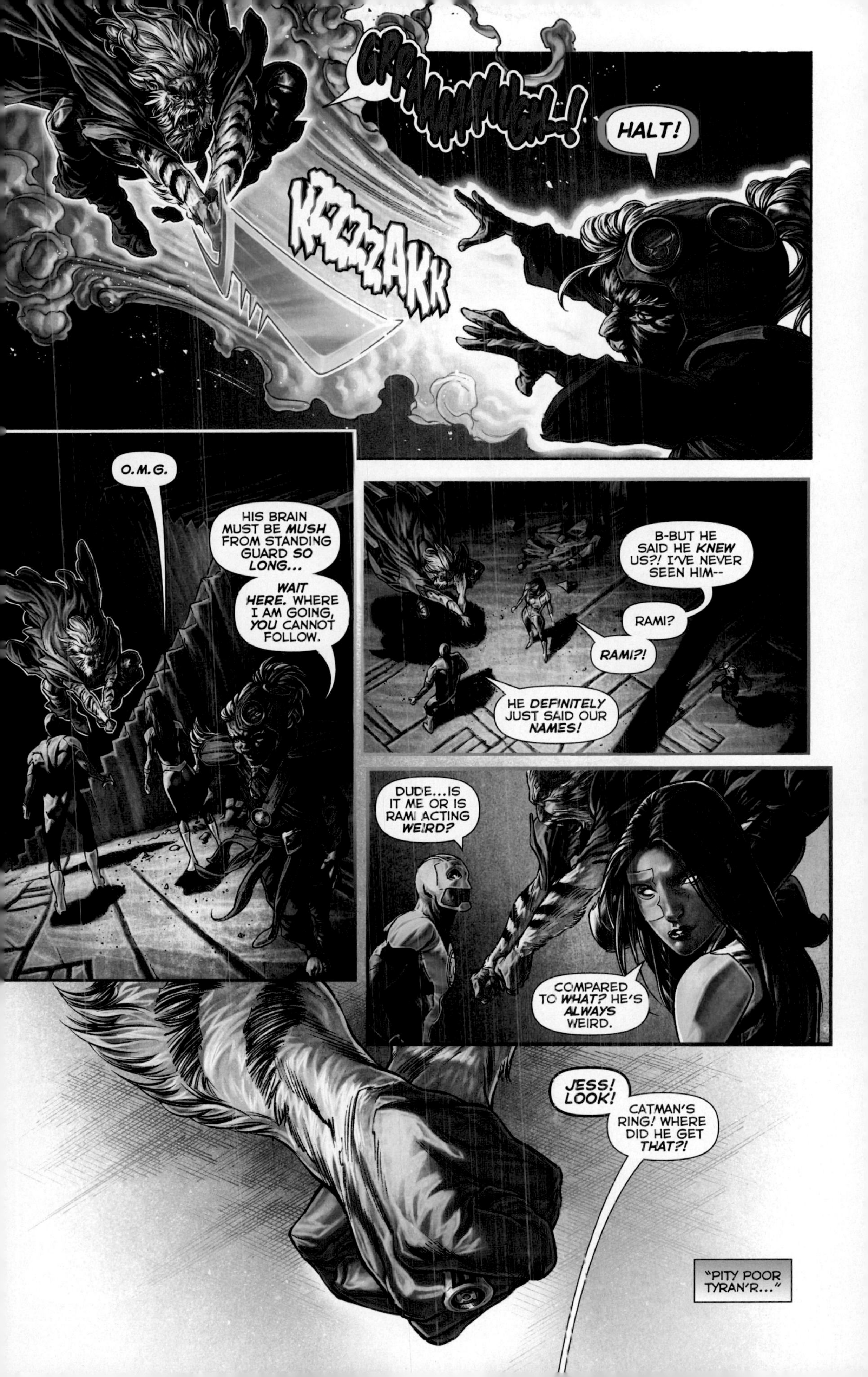
GRRAAAAAUGH..!
HALT!
KRZZZAKK
O.M.G.
HIS BRAIN MUST BE MUSH FROM STANDING GUARD SO LONG...
WAIT HERE. WHERE I AM GOING, YOU CANNOT FOLLOW.
B-BUT HE SAID HE KNEW US?! I'VE NEVER SEEN HIM--
RAMI?
RAMI?!
HE DEFINITELY JUST SAID OUR NAMES!
DUDE...IS IT ME OR IS RAMI ACTING WEIRD?
COMPARED TO WHAT? HE'S ALWAYS WEIRD.
JESS! LOOK!
CATMAN'S RING! WHERE DID HE GET THAT?!
"PITY POOR TYRAN'R..."

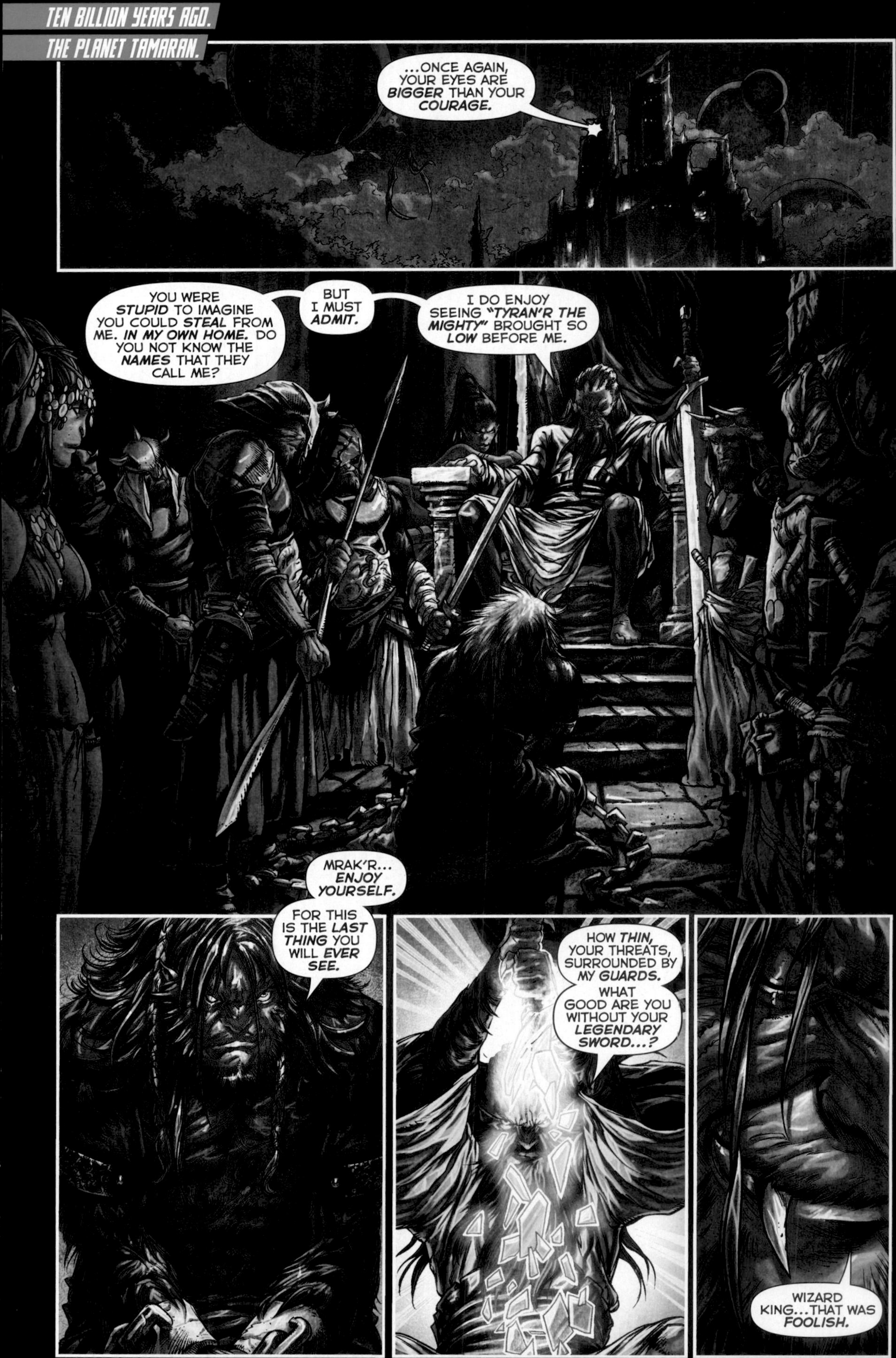
TEN BILLION YEARS AGO.
THE PLANET TAMARAN.
...ONCE AGAIN, YOUR EYES ARE BIGGER THAN YOUR COURAGE.
YOU WERE STUPID TO IMAGINE YOU COULD STEAL FROM ME. IN MY OWN HOME. DO YOU NOT KNOW THE NAMES THAT THEY CALL ME?
BUT I MUST ADMIT.
I DO ENJOY SEEING "TYRAN'R THE MIGHTY" BROUGHT SO LOW BEFORE ME.
MRAK'R... ENJOY YOURSELF.
FOR THIS IS THE LAST THING YOU WILL EVER SEE.
HOW THIN, YOUR THREATS, SURROUNDED BY MY GUARDS.
WHAT GOOD ARE YOU WITHOUT YOUR LEGENDARY SWORD...?
WIZARD KING...THAT WAS FOOLISH.

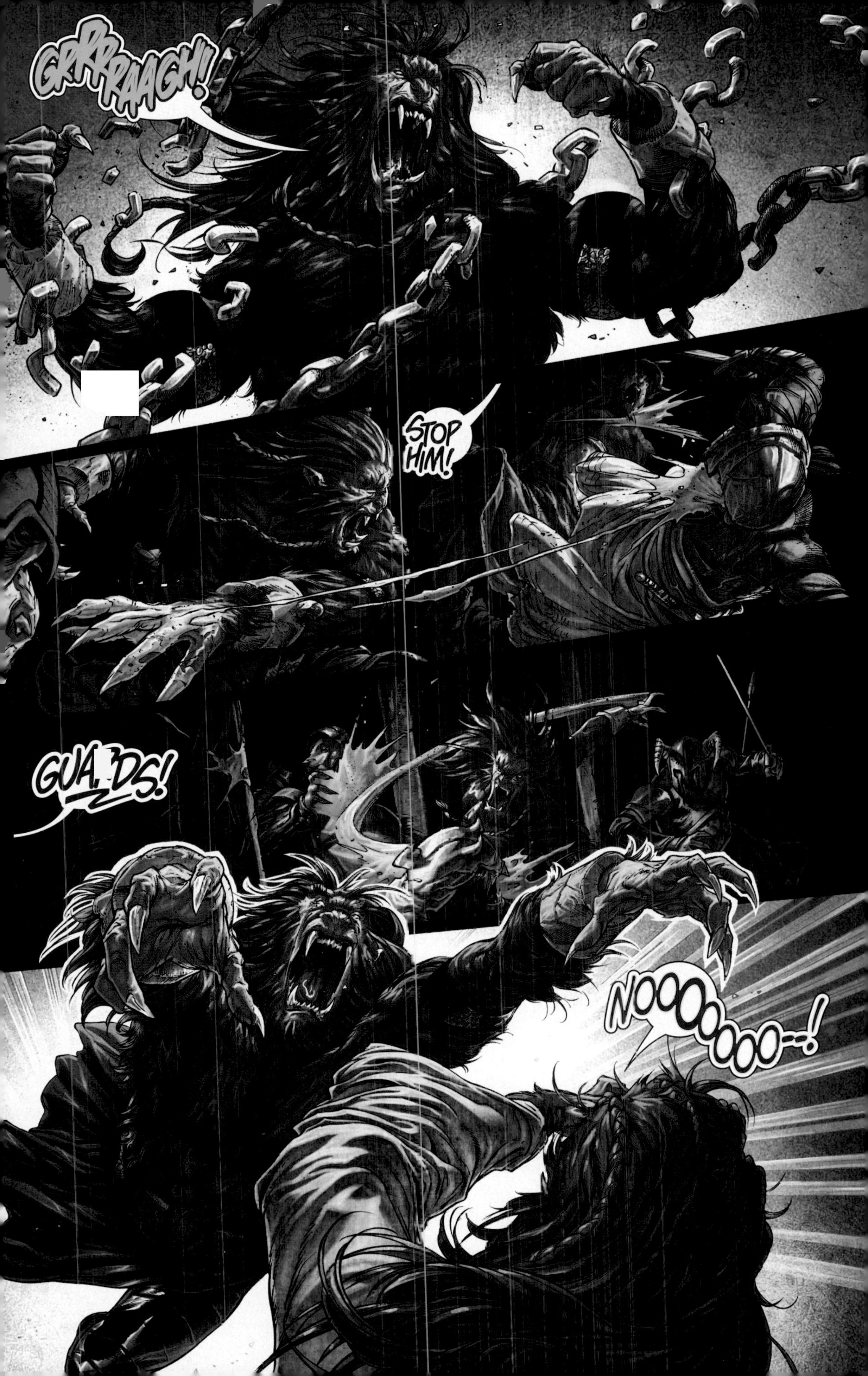
GRRRRAAGH!!
STOP HIM!
GUARDS!
NOOOOOOO--!

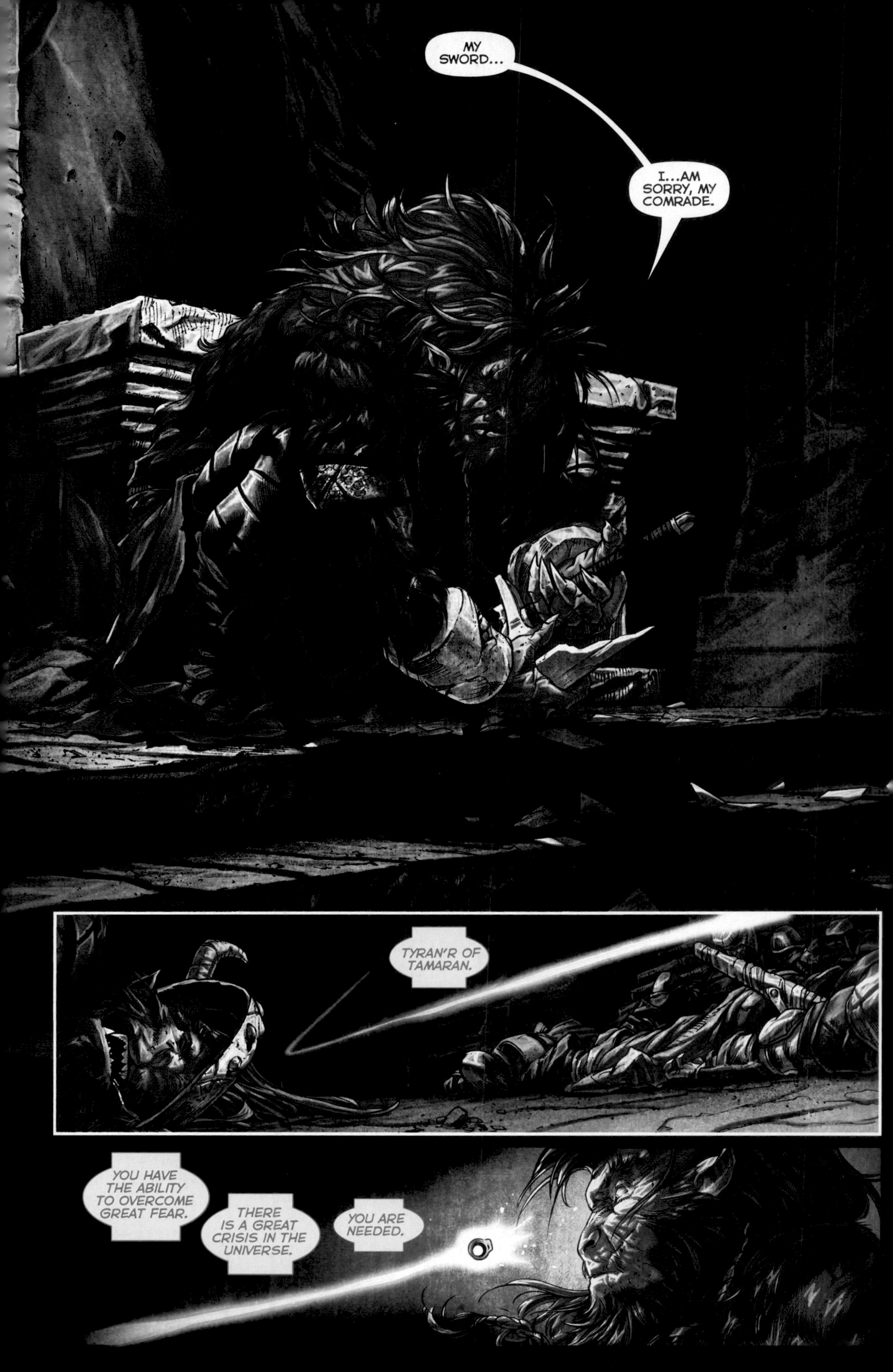

MY SWORD...
I...AM SORRY, MY COMRADE.
TYRAN'R OF TAMARAN.
YOU HAVE THE ABILITY TO OVERCOME GREAT FEAR.
THERE IS A GREAT CRISIS IN THE UNIVERSE.
YOU ARE NEEDED.

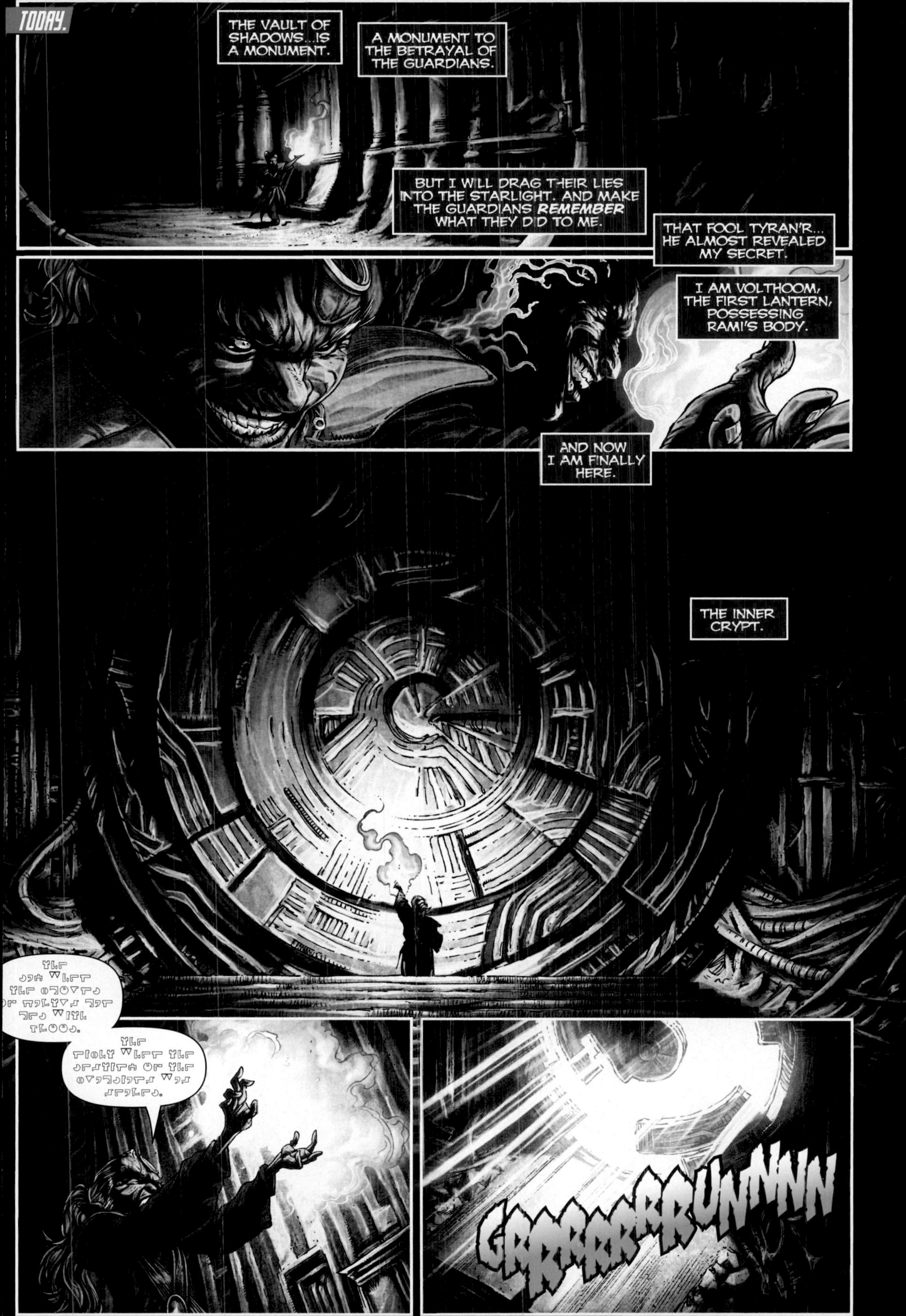
TODAY.
THE VAULT OF SHADOWS...IS A MONUMENT.
A MONUMENT TO THE BETRAYAL OF THE GUARDIANS.
BUT I WILL DRAG THEIR LIES INTO THE STARLIGHT. AND MAKE THE GUARDIANS *REMEMBER* WHAT THEY DID TO ME.
THAT FOOL TYRAN'R... HE ALMOST REVEALED MY SECRET.
I AM VOLTHOOM, THE FIRST LANTERN, POSSESSING RAMI'S BODY.
AND NOW I AM FINALLY HERE.
THE INNER CRYPT.
GRRRRRRRUNNNNN

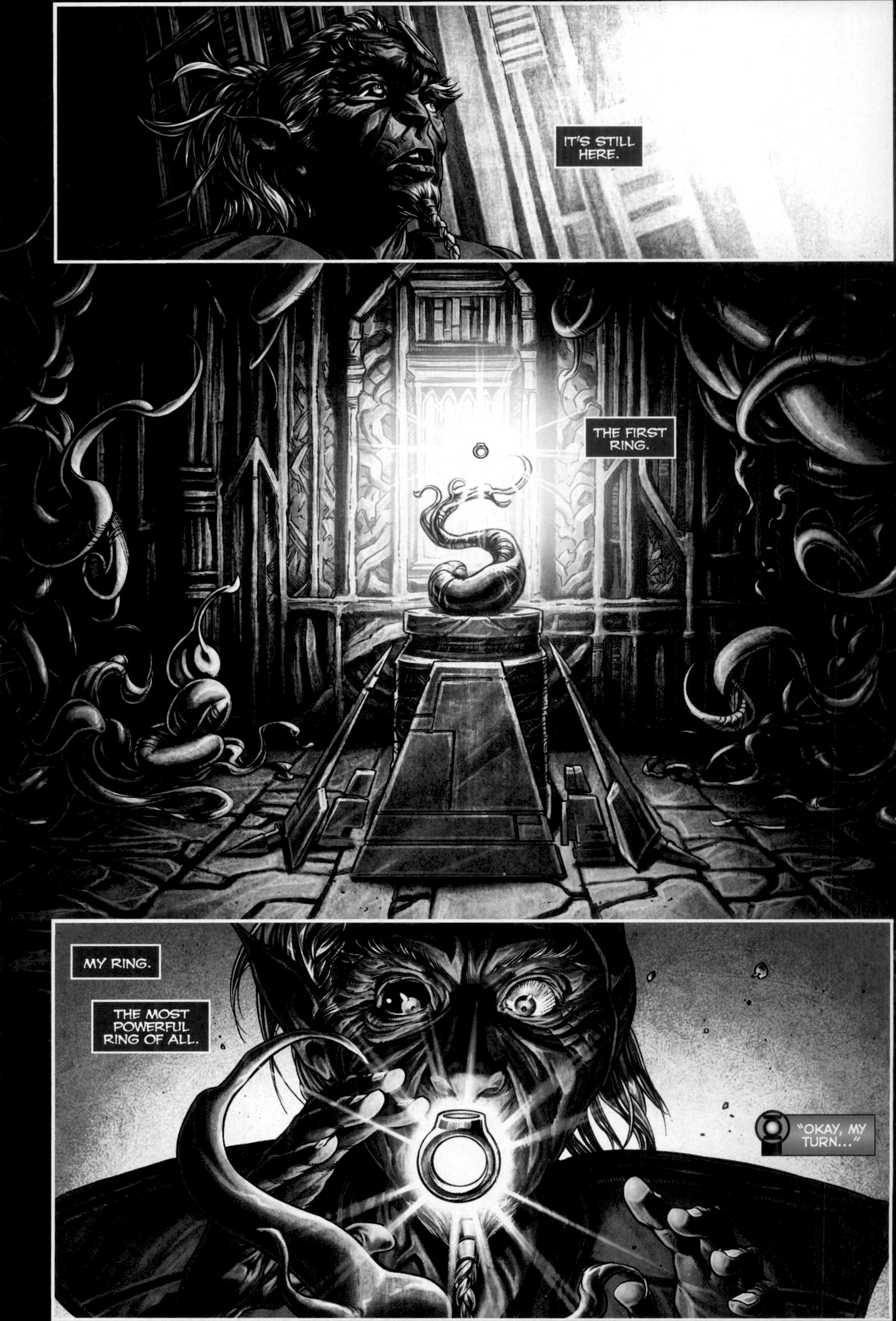
IT'S STILL HERE.
THE FIRST RING.
MY RING.
THE MOST POWERFUL RING OF ALL.
"OKAY, MY TURN..."

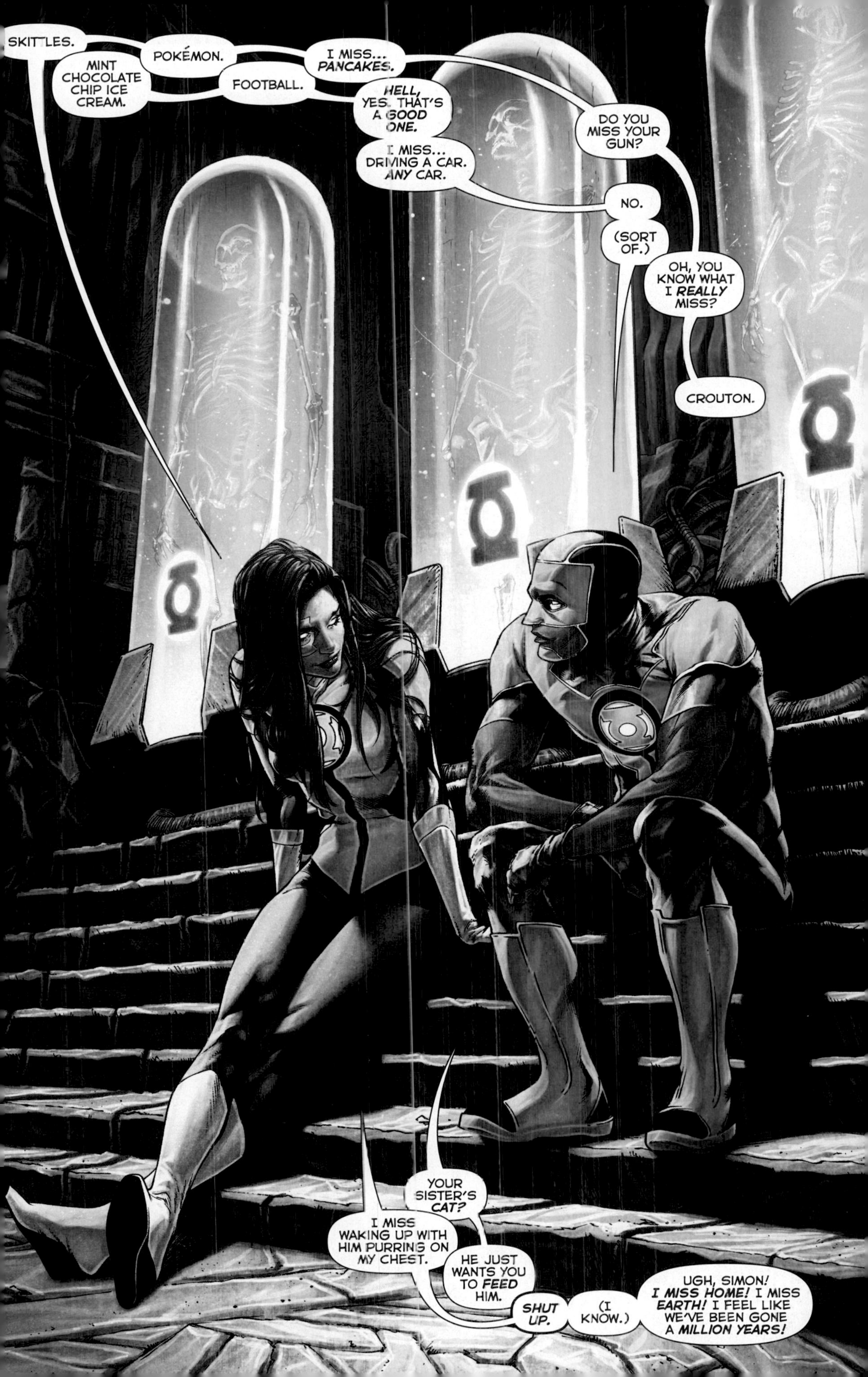
SKITTLES.
MINT CHOCOLATE CHIP ICE CREAM.
POKÉMON.
FOOTBALL.
I MISS... PANCAKES.
HELL, YES. THAT'S A GOOD ONE.
I MISS... DRIVING A CAR. ANY CAR.
DO YOU MISS YOUR GUN?
NO.
(SORT OF.)
OH, YOU KNOW WHAT I REALLY MISS?
CROUTON.
YOUR SISTER'S CAT?
I MISS WAKING UP WITH HIM PURRING ON MY CHEST.
HE JUST WANTS YOU TO FEED HIM.
SHUT UP.
(I KNOW.)
UGH, SIMON! I MISS HOME! I MISS EARTH! I FEEL LIKE WE'VE BEEN GONE A MILLION YEARS!

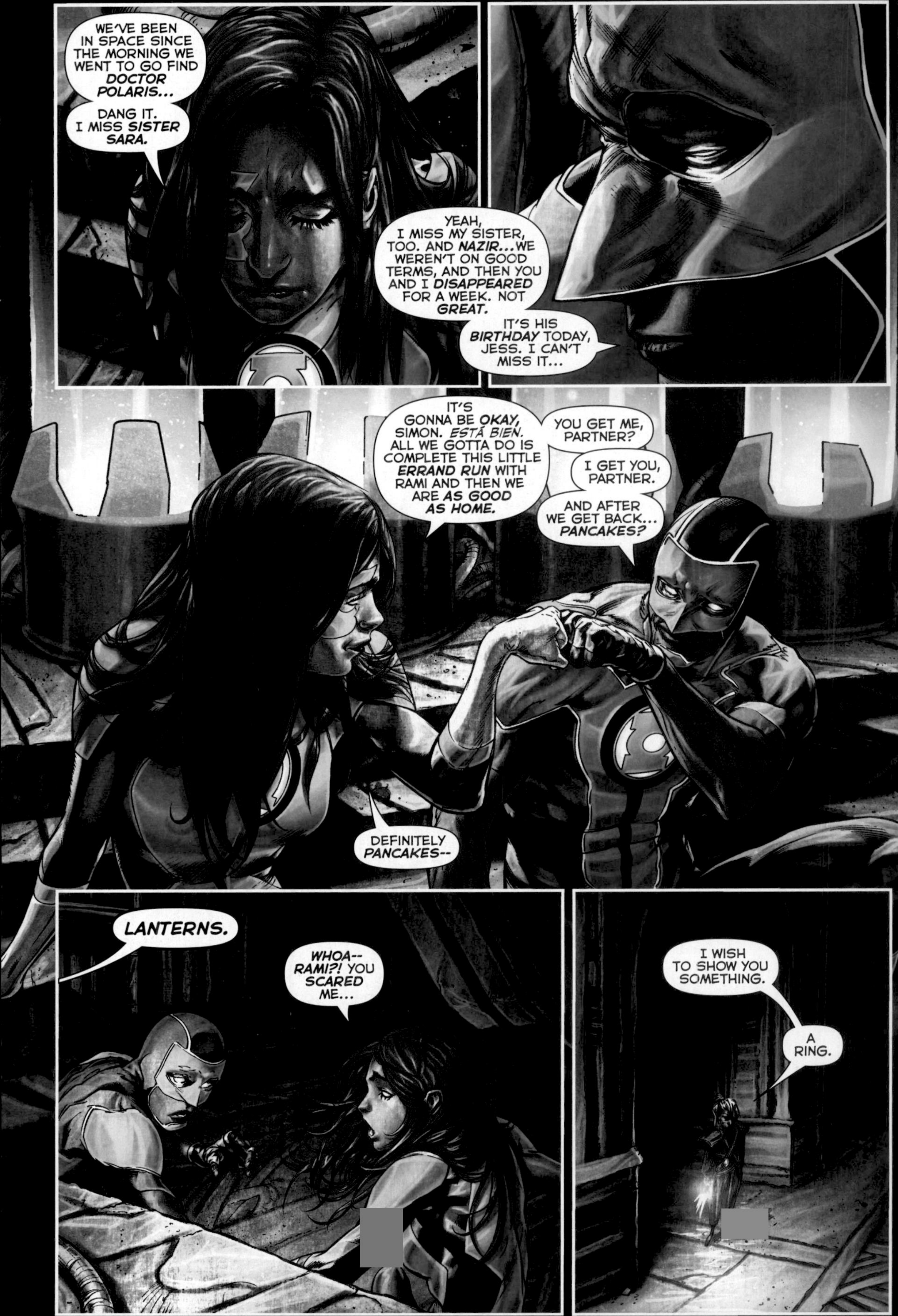
WE'VE BEEN IN SPACE SINCE THE MORNING WE WENT TO GO FIND DOCTOR POLARIS...
DANG IT. I MISS SISTER SARA.
YEAH, I MISS MY SISTER, TOO. AND NAZIR...WE WEREN'T ON GOOD TERMS, AND THEN YOU AND I DISAPPEARED FOR A WEEK. NOT GREAT.
IT'S HIS BIRTHDAY TODAY, JESS. I CAN'T MISS IT...
IT'S GONNA BE OKAY, SIMON. ESTÁ BIEN. ALL WE GOTTA DO IS COMPLETE THIS LITTLE ERRAND RUN WITH RAMI AND THEN WE ARE AS GOOD AS HOME.
YOU GET ME, PARTNER?
I GET YOU, PARTNER.
AND AFTER WE GET BACK... PANCAKES?
DEFINITELY PANCAKES--
LANTERNS.
WHOA-- RAMI?! YOU SCARED ME...
I WISH TO SHOW YOU SOMETHING.
A RING.

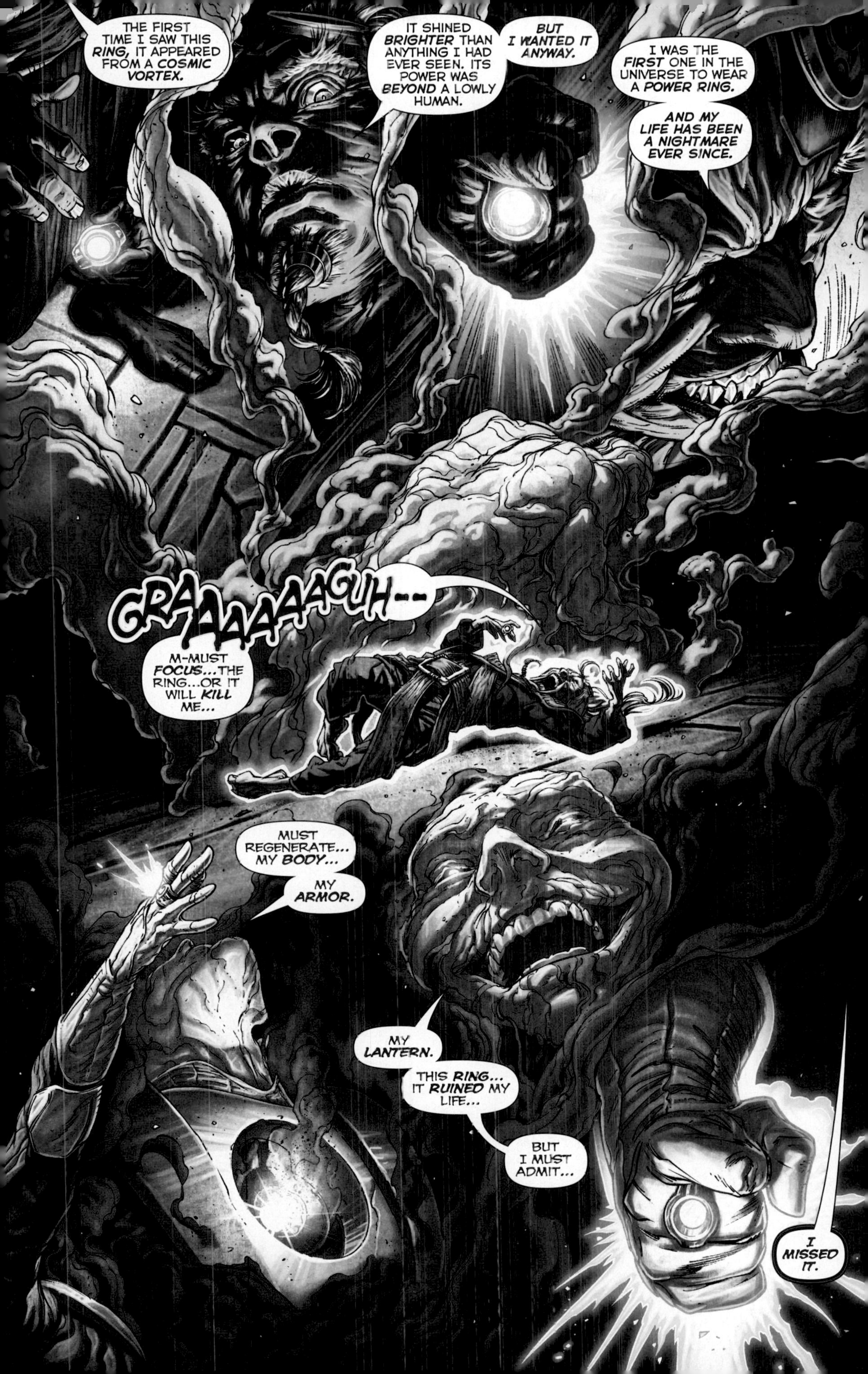
THE FIRST TIME I SAW THIS RING, IT APPEARED FROM A COSMIC VORTEX.
IT SHINED BRIGHTER THAN ANYTHING I HAD EVER SEEN. ITS POWER WAS BEYOND A LOWLY HUMAN.
BUT I WANTED IT ANYWAY.
I WAS THE FIRST ONE IN THE UNIVERSE TO WEAR A POWER RING.
AND MY LIFE HAS BEEN A NIGHTMARE EVER SINCE.
GRAAAAAAAGUH--
M-MUST FOCUS...THE RING...OR IT WILL KILL ME...
MUST REGENERATE... MY BODY...
MY ARMOR.
MY LANTERN.
THIS RING... IT RUINED MY LIFE...
BUT I MUST ADMIT...
I MISSED IT.

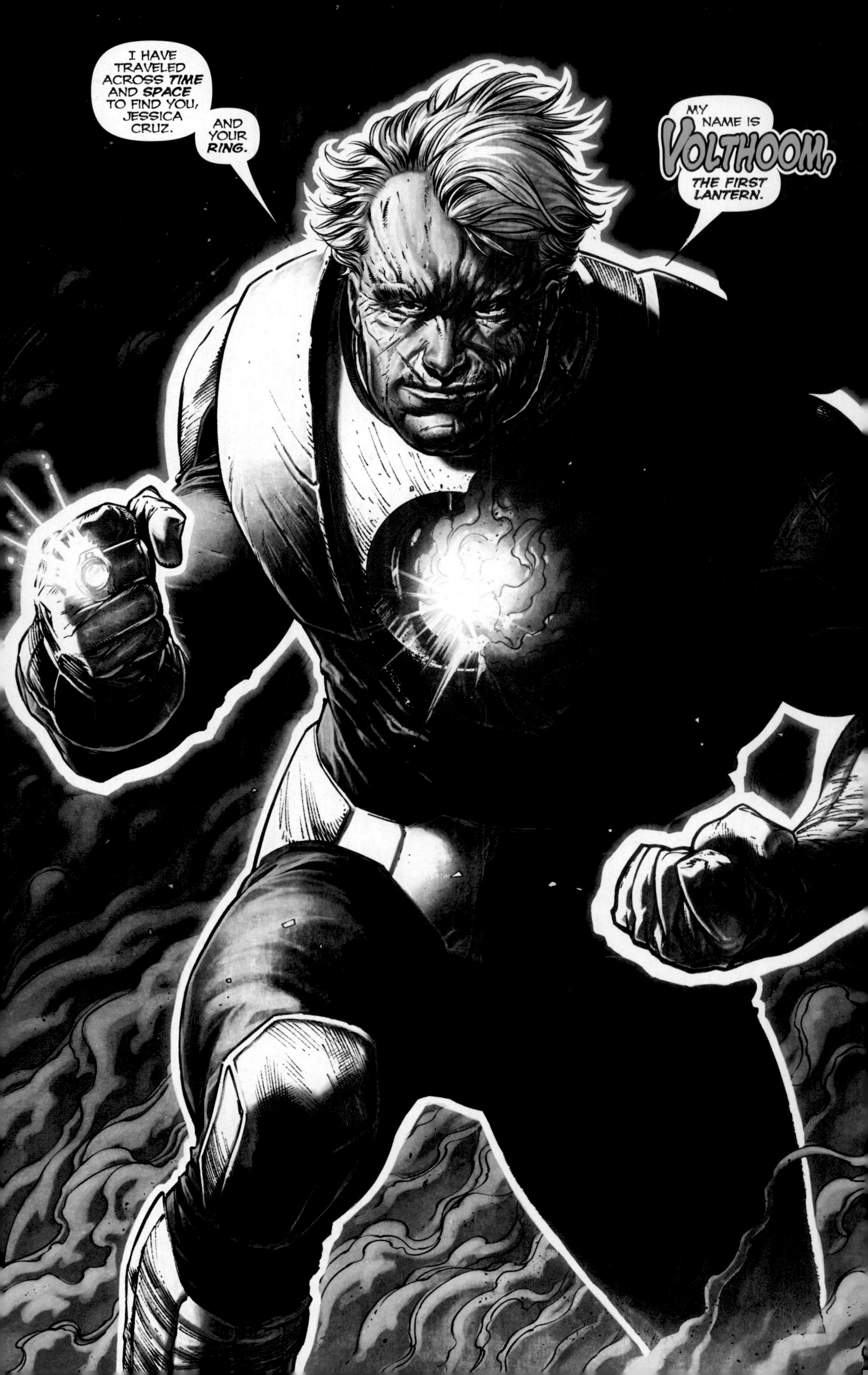
I HAVE TRAVELED ACROSS TIME AND SPACE TO FIND YOU, JESSICA CRUZ.
AND YOUR RING.
MY NAME IS VOLTHOOM, THE FIRST LANTERN.

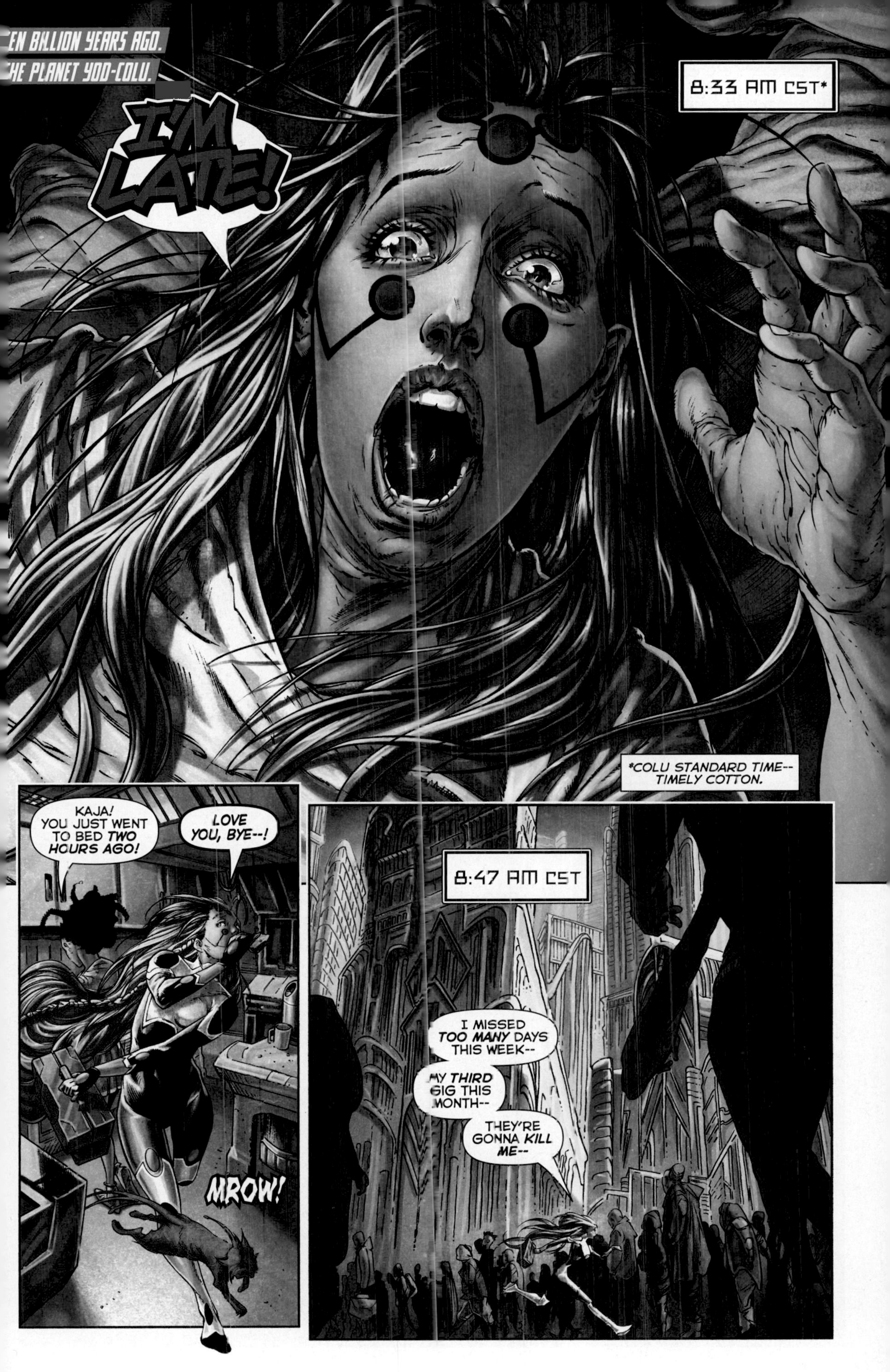
EN BILLION YEARS AGO.
HE PLANET YOD-COLU.
8:33 AM CST*
I'M LATE!
*COLU STANDARD TIME--TIMELY COTTON.
KAJA! YOU JUST WENT TO BED TWO HOURS AGO!
LOVE YOU, BYE--!
MROW!
8:47 AM CST
I MISSED TOO MANY DAYS THIS WEEK--
MY THIRD GIG THIS MONTH--
THEY'RE GONNA KILL ME--

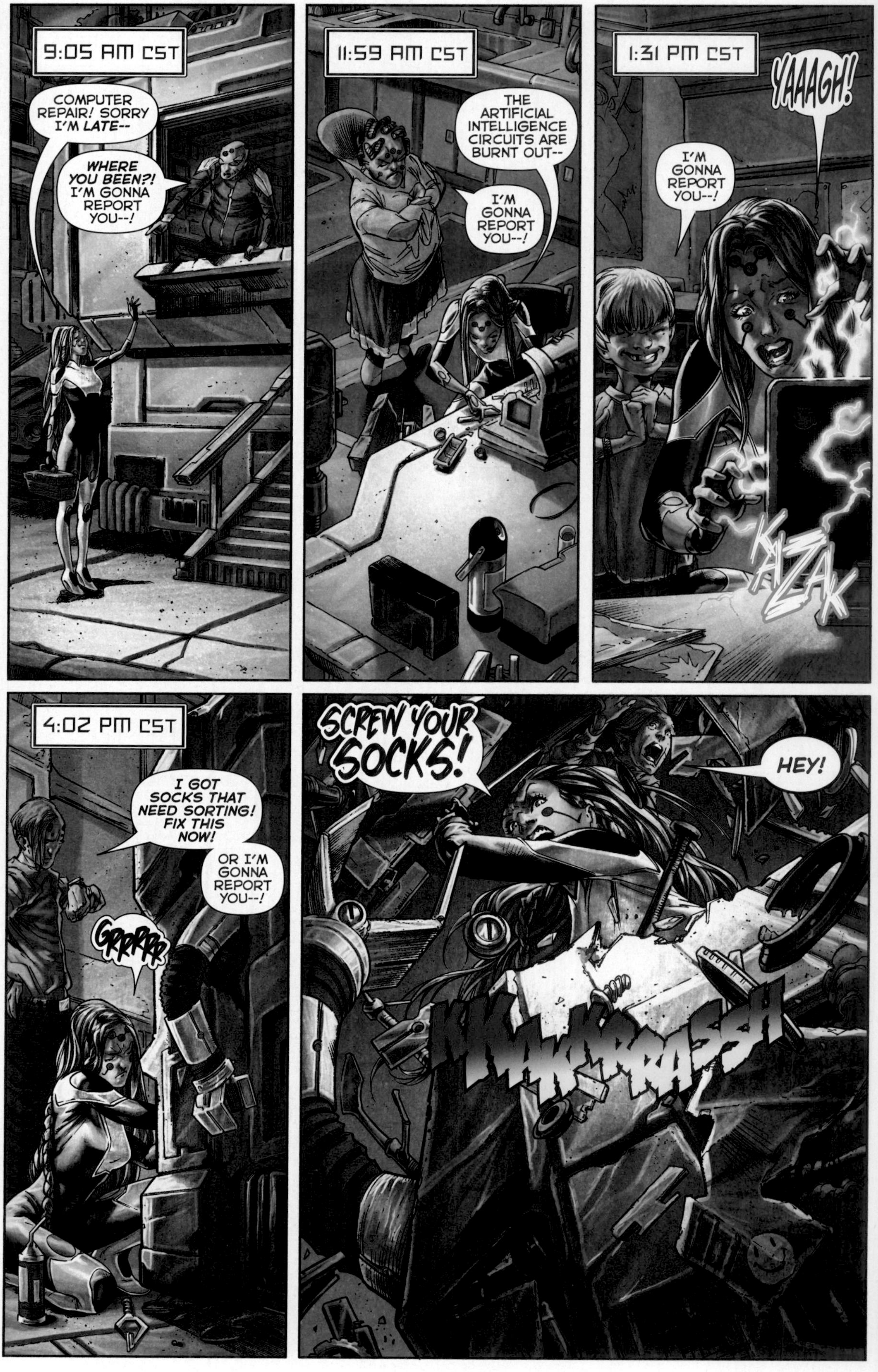
9:05 AM CST
COMPUTER REPAIR! SORRY I'M LATE--
WHERE YOU BEEN?! I'M GONNA REPORT YOU--!
11:59 AM CST
THE ARTIFICIAL INTELLIGENCE CIRCUITS ARE BURNT OUT--
I'M GONNA REPORT YOU--!
1:31 PM CST
YAAAGH!
I'M GONNA REPORT YOU--!
KAZAK
4:02 PM CST
I GOT SOCKS THAT NEED SORTING! FIX THIS NOW!
OR I'M GONNA REPORT YOU--!
GRRRRR
SCREW YOUR SOCKS!
HEY!

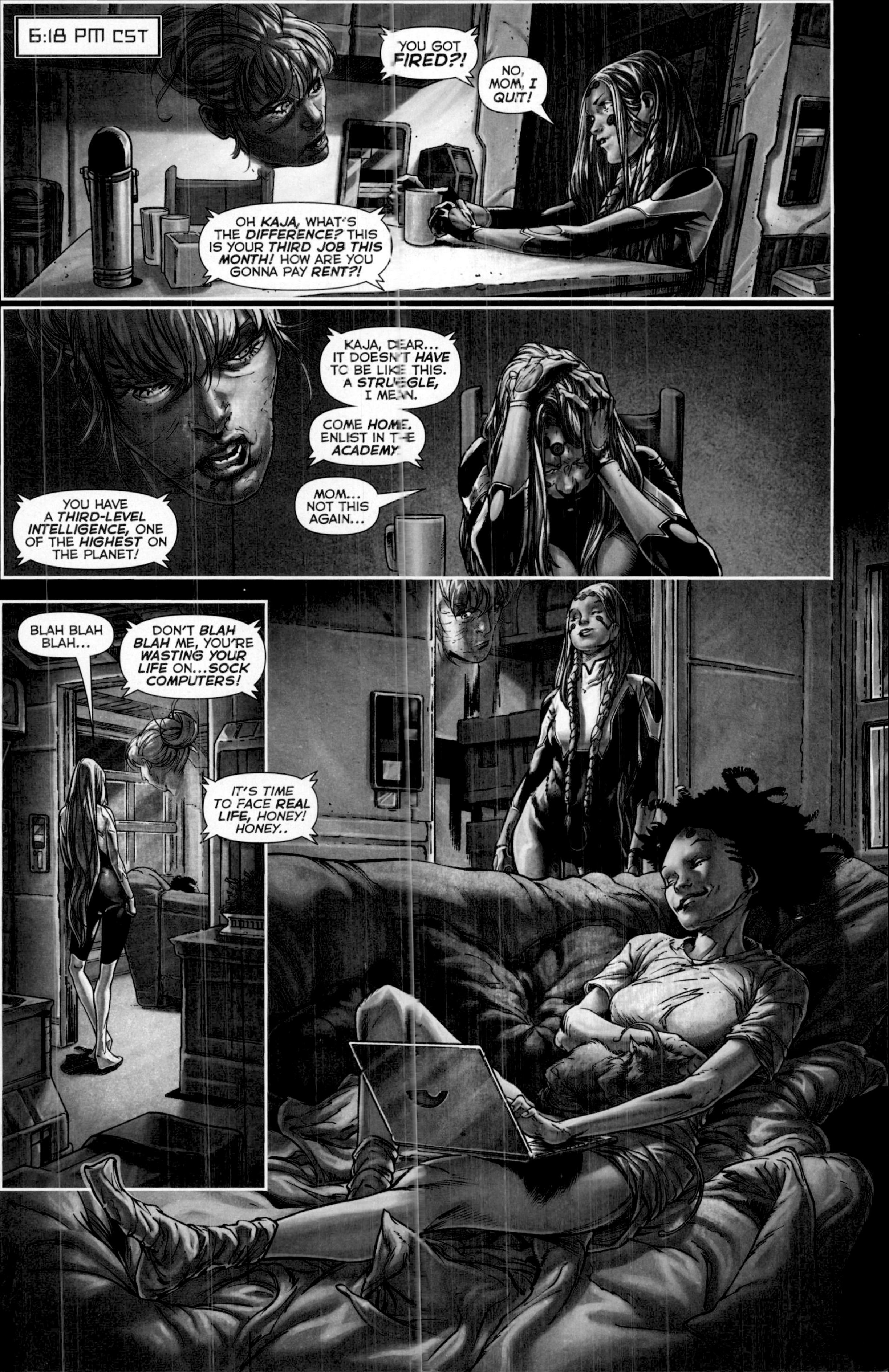
6:18 PM CST
YOU GOT FIRED?!
NO, MOM, I QUIT!
OH KAJA, WHAT'S THE DIFFERENCE? THIS IS YOUR THIRD JOB THIS MONTH! HOW ARE YOU GONNA PAY RENT?!
KAJA, DEAR... IT DOESN'T HAVE TO BE LIKE THIS. A STRUGGLE, I MEAN.
COME HOME. ENLIST IN THE ACADEMY.
YOU HAVE A THIRD-LEVEL INTELLIGENCE, ONE OF THE HIGHEST ON THE PLANET!
MOM... NOT THIS AGAIN...
BLAH BLAH BLAH...
DON'T BLAH BLAH ME, YOU'RE WASTING YOUR LIFE ON...SOCK COMPUTERS!
IT'S TIME TO FACE REAL LIFE, HONEY! HONEY..

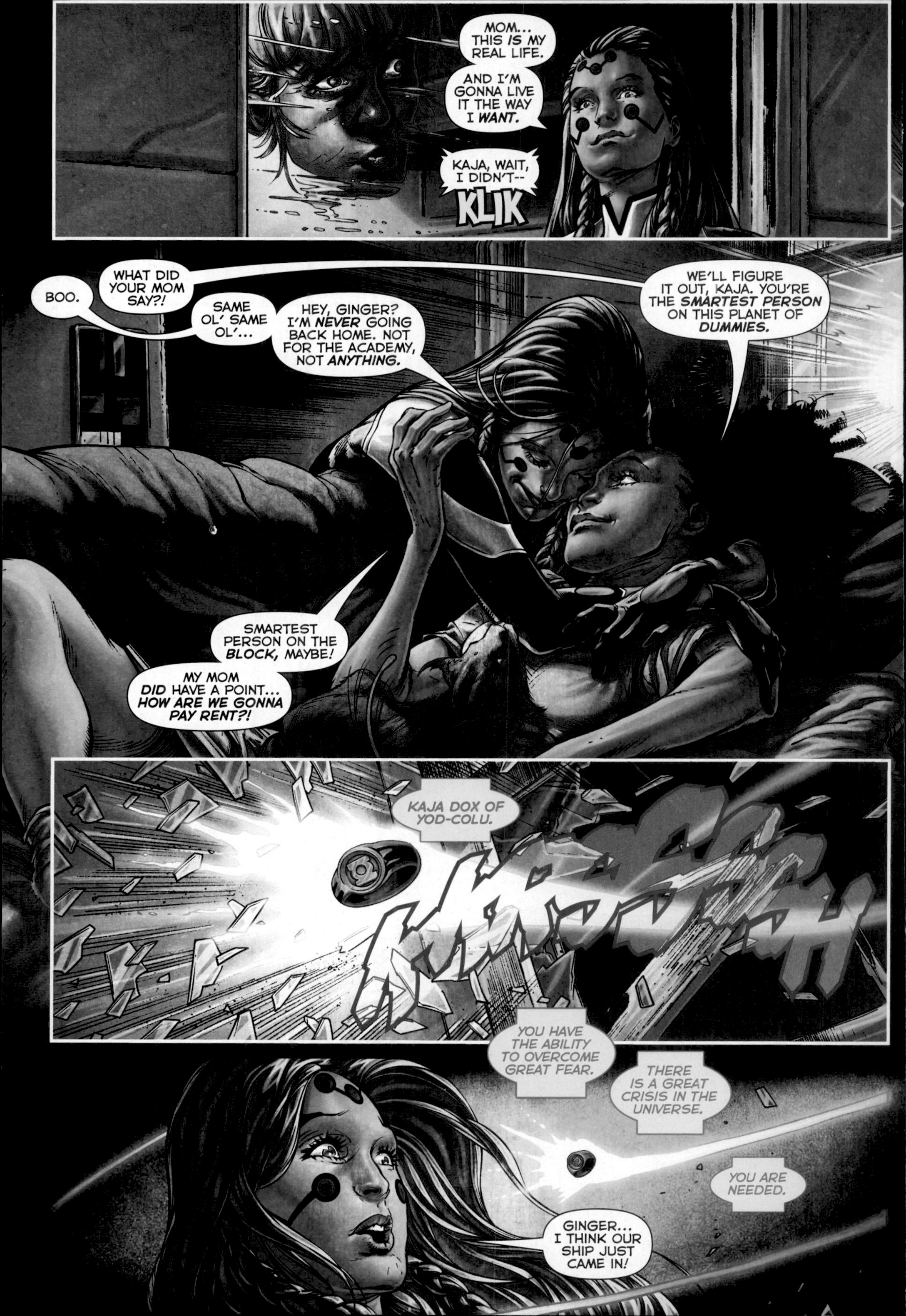
MOM... THIS IS MY REAL LIFE.
AND I'M GONNA LIVE IT THE WAY I WANT.
KAJA, WAIT, I DIDN'T--
KLIK
BOO.
WHAT DID YOUR MOM SAY?!
SAME OL' SAME OL'...
HEY, GINGER? I'M NEVER GOING BACK HOME. NOT FOR THE ACADEMY, NOT ANYTHING.
WE'LL FIGURE IT OUT, KAJA. YOU'RE THE SMARTEST PERSON ON THIS PLANET OF DUMMIES.
SMARTEST PERSON ON THE BLOCK, MAYBE!
MY MOM DID HAVE A POINT... HOW ARE WE GONNA PAY RENT?!
KAJA DOX OF YOD-COLU.
YOU HAVE THE ABILITY TO OVERCOME GREAT FEAR.
THERE IS A GREAT CRISIS IN THE UNIVERSE.
YOU ARE NEEDED.
GINGER... I THINK OUR SHIP JUST CAME IN!

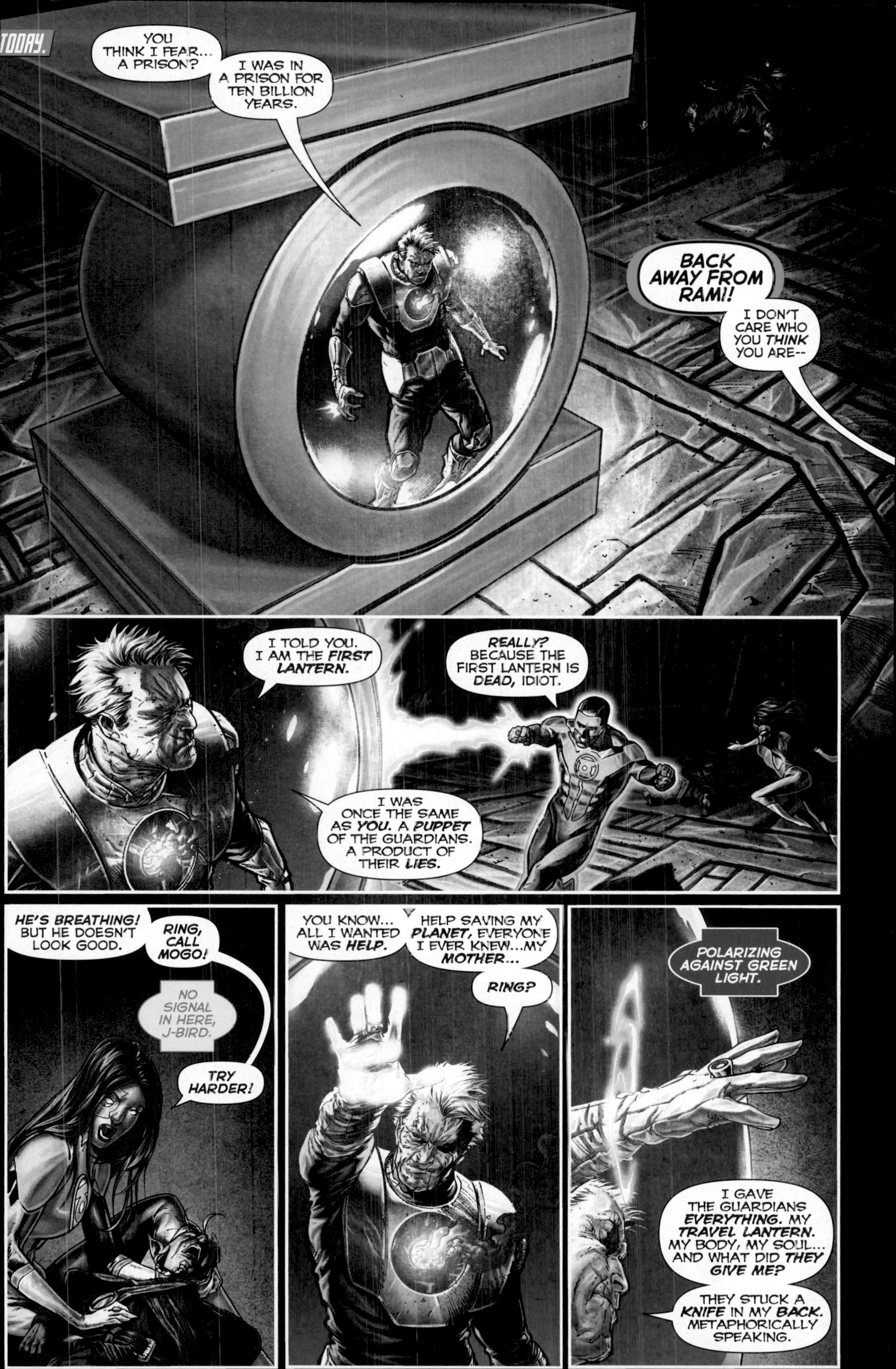
TODAY.
YOU THINK I FEAR... A PRISON?
I WAS IN A PRISON FOR TEN BILLION YEARS.
BACK AWAY FROM RAMI!
I DON'T CARE WHO YOU THINK YOU ARE--
I TOLD YOU. I AM THE FIRST LANTERN.
REALLY? BECAUSE THE FIRST LANTERN IS DEAD, IDIOT.
I WAS ONCE THE SAME AS YOU. A PUPPET OF THE GUARDIANS. A PRODUCT OF THEIR LIES.
HE'S BREATHING! BUT HE DOESN'T LOOK GOOD.
RING, CALL MOGO!
NO SIGNAL IN HERE, J-BIRD.
TRY HARDER!
YOU KNOW... ALL I WANTED WAS HELP.
HELP SAVING MY PLANET, EVERYONE I EVER KNEW...MY MOTHER...
RING?
POLARIZING AGAINST GREEN LIGHT.
I GAVE THE GUARDIANS EVERYTHING. MY TRAVEL LANTERN. MY BODY, MY SOUL... AND WHAT DID THEY GIVE ME?
THEY STUCK A KNIFE IN MY BACK. METAPHORICALLY SPEAKING.

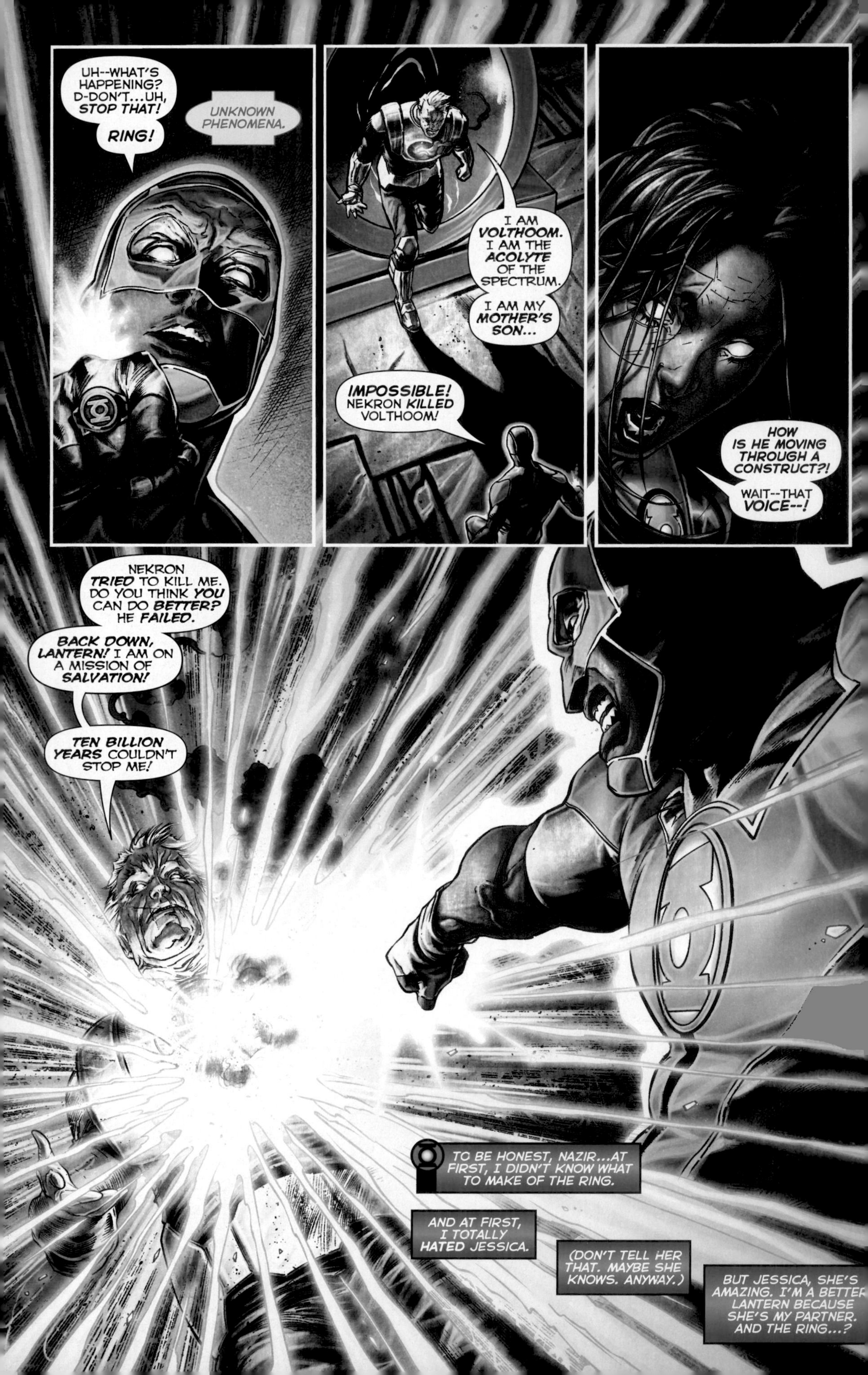
UH--WHAT'S HAPPENING? D-DON'T...UH, STOP THAT!
RING!
UNKNOWN PHENOMENA.
I AM VOLTHOOM. I AM THE ACOLYTE OF THE SPECTRUM.
I AM MY MOTHER'S SON...
IMPOSSIBLE! NEKRON KILLED VOLTHOOM!
HOW IS HE MOVING THROUGH A CONSTRUCT?!
WAIT--THAT VOICE--!
NEKRON TRIED TO KILL ME. DO YOU THINK YOU CAN DO BETTER? HE FAILED.
BACK DOWN, LANTERN! I AM ON A MISSION OF SALVATION!
TEN BILLION YEARS COULDN'T STOP ME!
TO BE HONEST, NAZIR...AT FIRST, I DIDN'T KNOW WHAT TO MAKE OF THE RING.
AND AT FIRST, I TOTALLY HATED JESSICA.
(DON'T TELL HER THAT. MAYBE SHE KNOWS. ANYWAY.)
BUT JESSICA, SHE'S AMAZING. I'M A BETTER LANTERN BECAUSE SHE'S MY PARTNER. AND THE RING...?

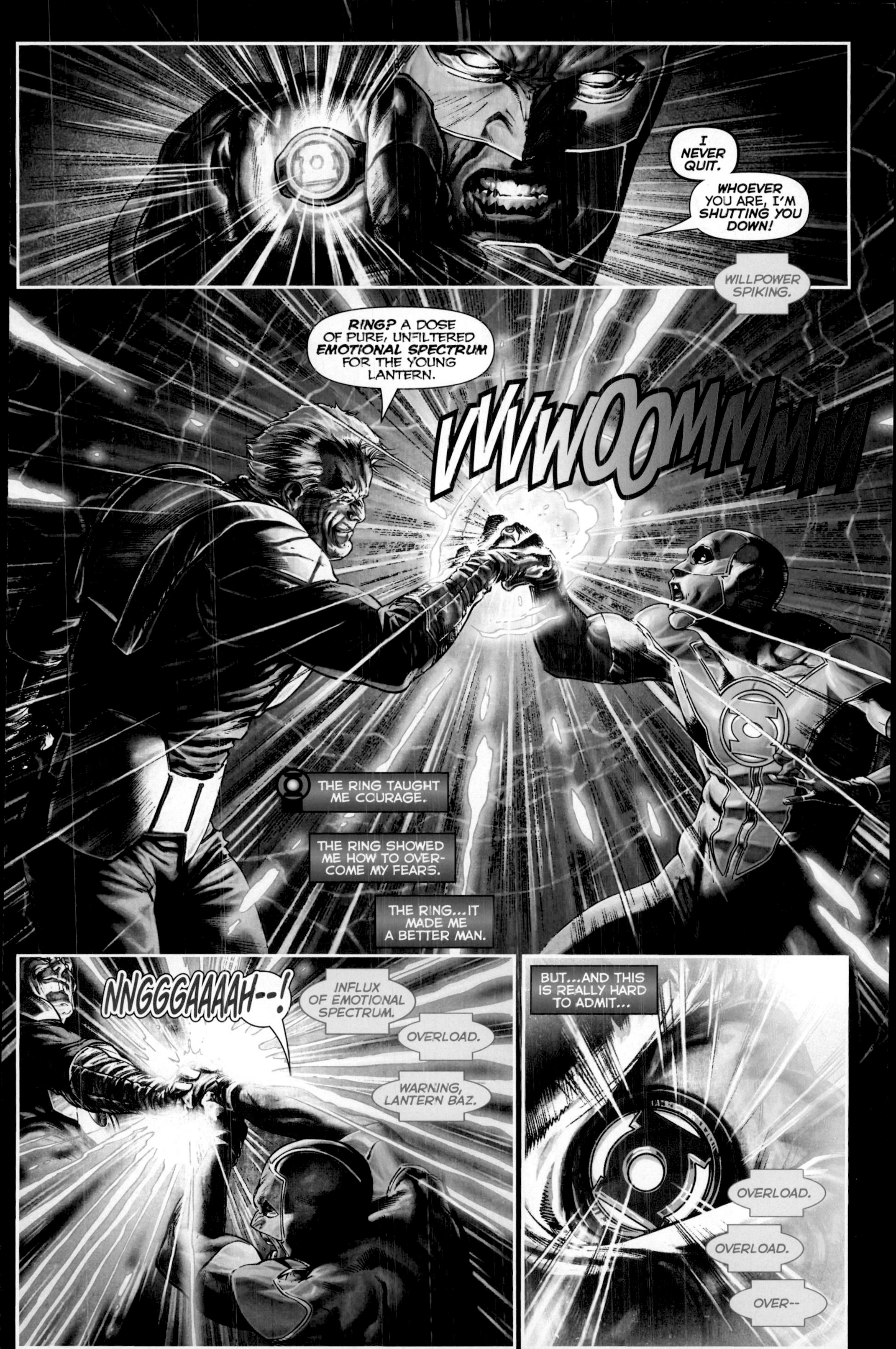
I NEVER QUIT.
WHOEVER YOU ARE, I'M SHUTTING YOU DOWN!
WILLPOWER SPIKING.
RING? A DOSE OF PURE, UNFILTERED EMOTIONAL SPECTRUM FOR THE YOUNG LANTERN.
VVVWOOMMMM
THE RING TAUGHT ME COURAGE.
THE RING SHOWED ME HOW TO OVER-COME MY FEARS.
THE RING...IT MADE ME A BETTER MAN.
NNGGGAAAAH--!
INFLUX OF EMOTIONAL SPECTRUM.
OVERLOAD.
WARNING, LANTERN BAZ.
BUT...AND THIS IS REALLY HARD TO ADMIT...
OVERLOAD.
OVERLOAD.
OVER--

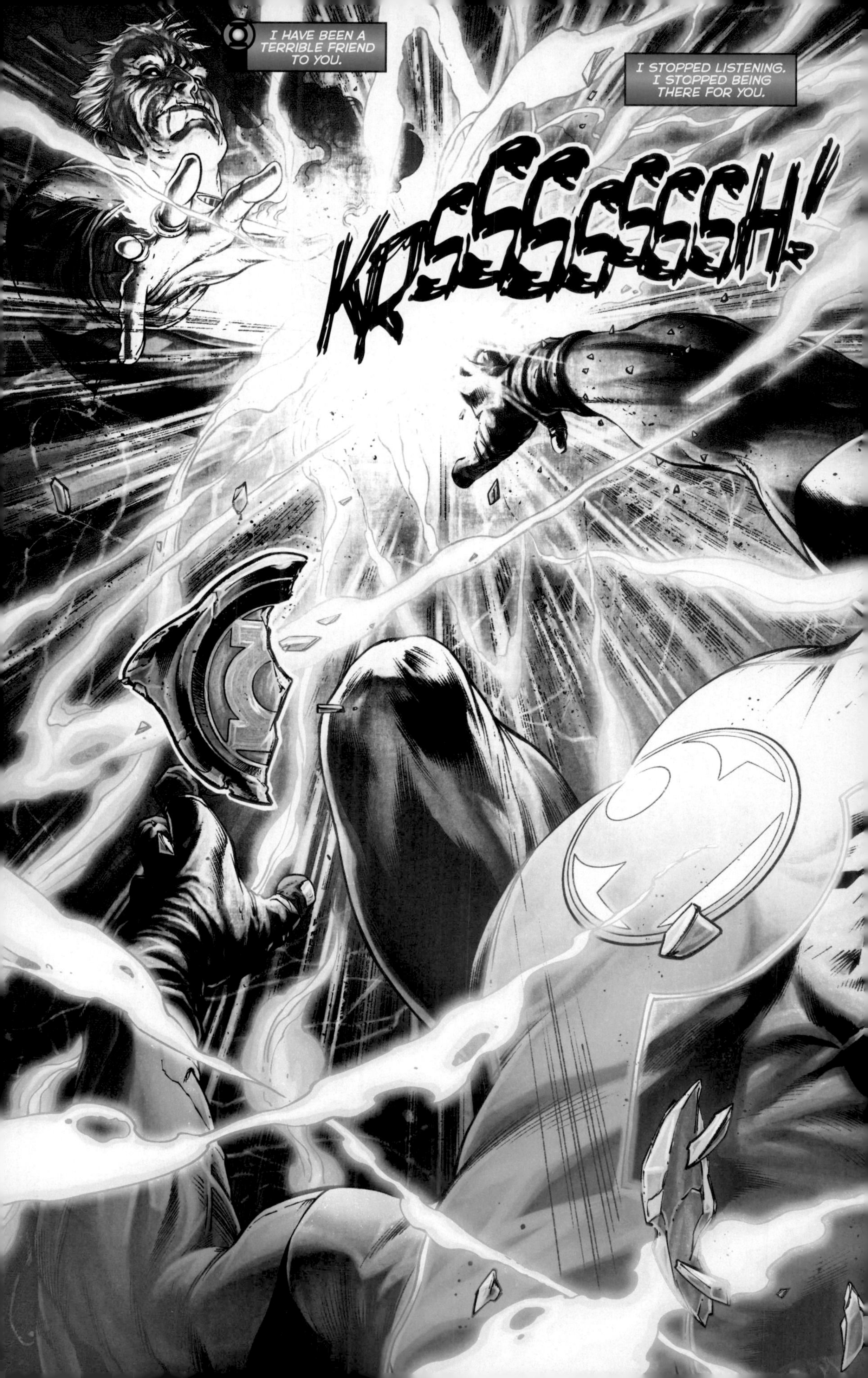
I HAVE BEEN A TERRIBLE FRIEND TO YOU.
I STOPPED LISTENING. I STOPPED BEING THERE FOR YOU.
KOSSSSSSSH!

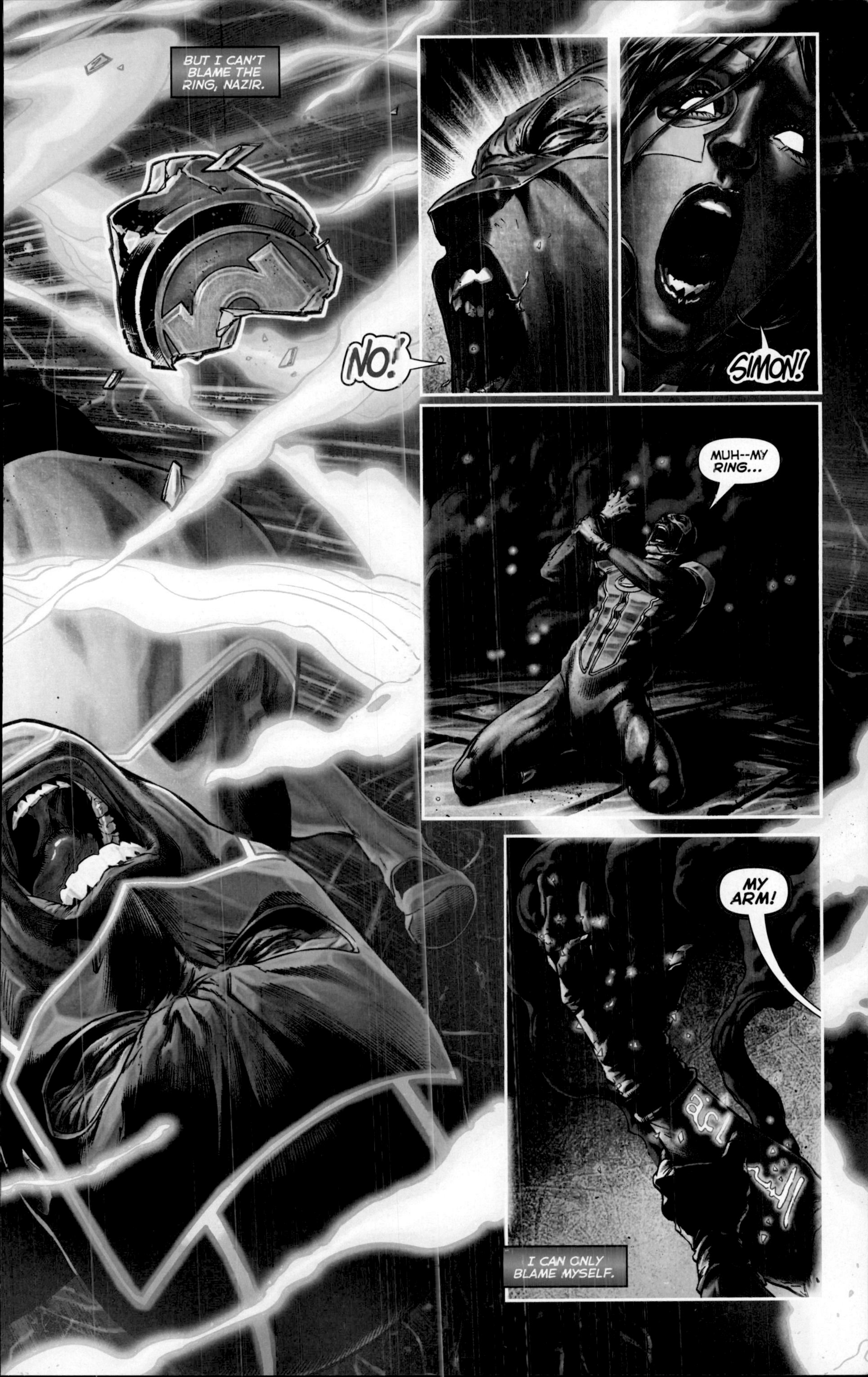
BUT I CAN'T BLAME THE RING, NAZIR.
NO!
SIMON!
MUH--MY RING...
MY ARM!
I CAN ONLY BLAME MYSELF.

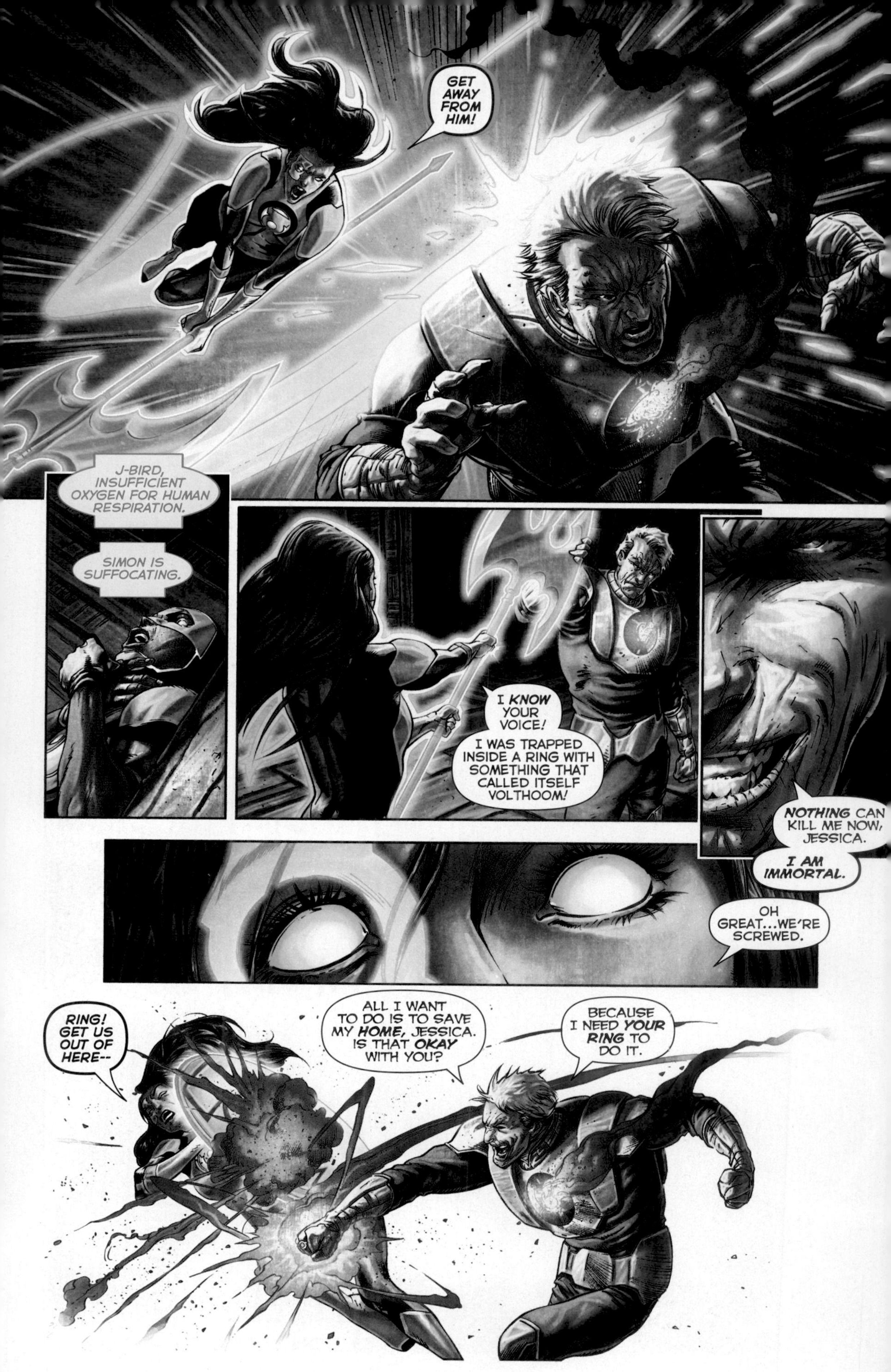
GET AWAY FROM HIM!
J-BIRD, INSUFFICIENT OXYGEN FOR HUMAN RESPIRATION.
SIMON IS SUFFOCATING.
I KNOW YOUR VOICE!
I WAS TRAPPED INSIDE A RING WITH SOMETHING THAT CALLED ITSELF VOLTHOOM!
NOTHING CAN KILL ME NOW, JESSICA.
I AM IMMORTAL.
OH GREAT...WE'RE SCREWED.
RING! GET US OUT OF HERE--
ALL I WANT TO DO IS TO SAVE MY HOME, JESSICA. IS THAT OKAY WITH YOU?
BECAUSE I NEED YOUR RING TO DO IT.

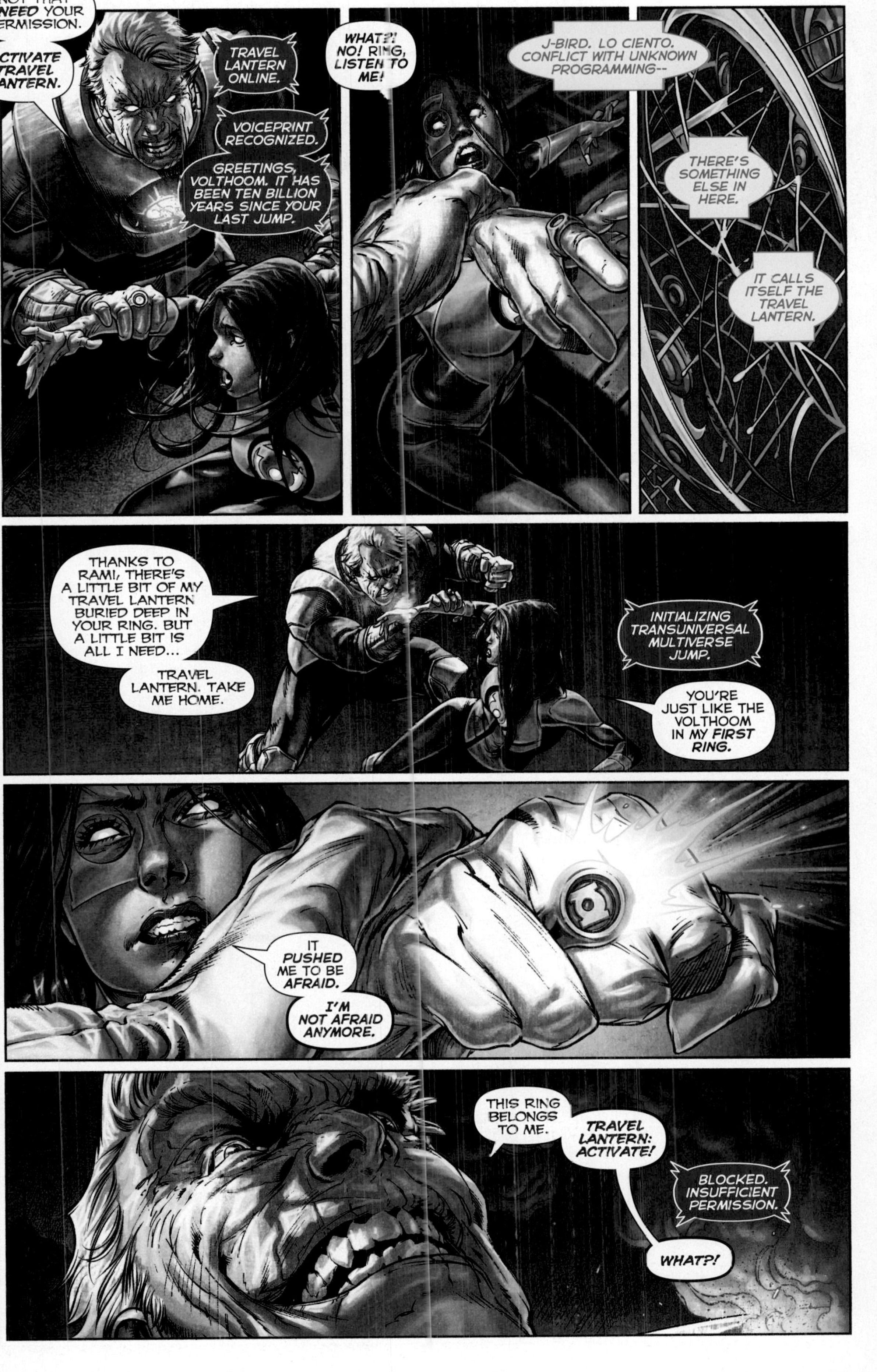
NOT THAT I NEED YOUR PERMISSION.
ACTIVATE TRAVEL LANTERN.
TRAVEL LANTERN ONLINE.
VOICEPRINT RECOGNIZED.
GREETINGS, VOLTHOOM. IT HAS BEEN TEN BILLION YEARS SINCE YOUR LAST JUMP.
WHAT?! NO! RING, LISTEN TO ME!
J-BIRD. LO CIENTO. CONFLICT WITH UNKNOWN PROGRAMMING--
THERE'S SOMETHING ELSE IN HERE.
IT CALLS ITSELF THE TRAVEL LANTERN.
THANKS TO RAMI, THERE'S A LITTLE BIT OF MY TRAVEL LANTERN BURIED DEEP IN YOUR RING. BUT A LITTLE BIT IS ALL I NEED...
TRAVEL LANTERN. TAKE ME HOME.
INITIALIZING TRANSUNIVERSAL MULTIVERSE JUMP.
YOU'RE JUST LIKE THE VOLTHOOM IN MY FIRST RING.
IT PUSHED ME TO BE AFRAID.
I'M NOT AFRAID ANYMORE.
THIS RING BELONGS TO ME.
TRAVEL LANTERN: ACTIVATE!
BLOCKED. INSUFFICIENT PERMISSION.
WHAT?!

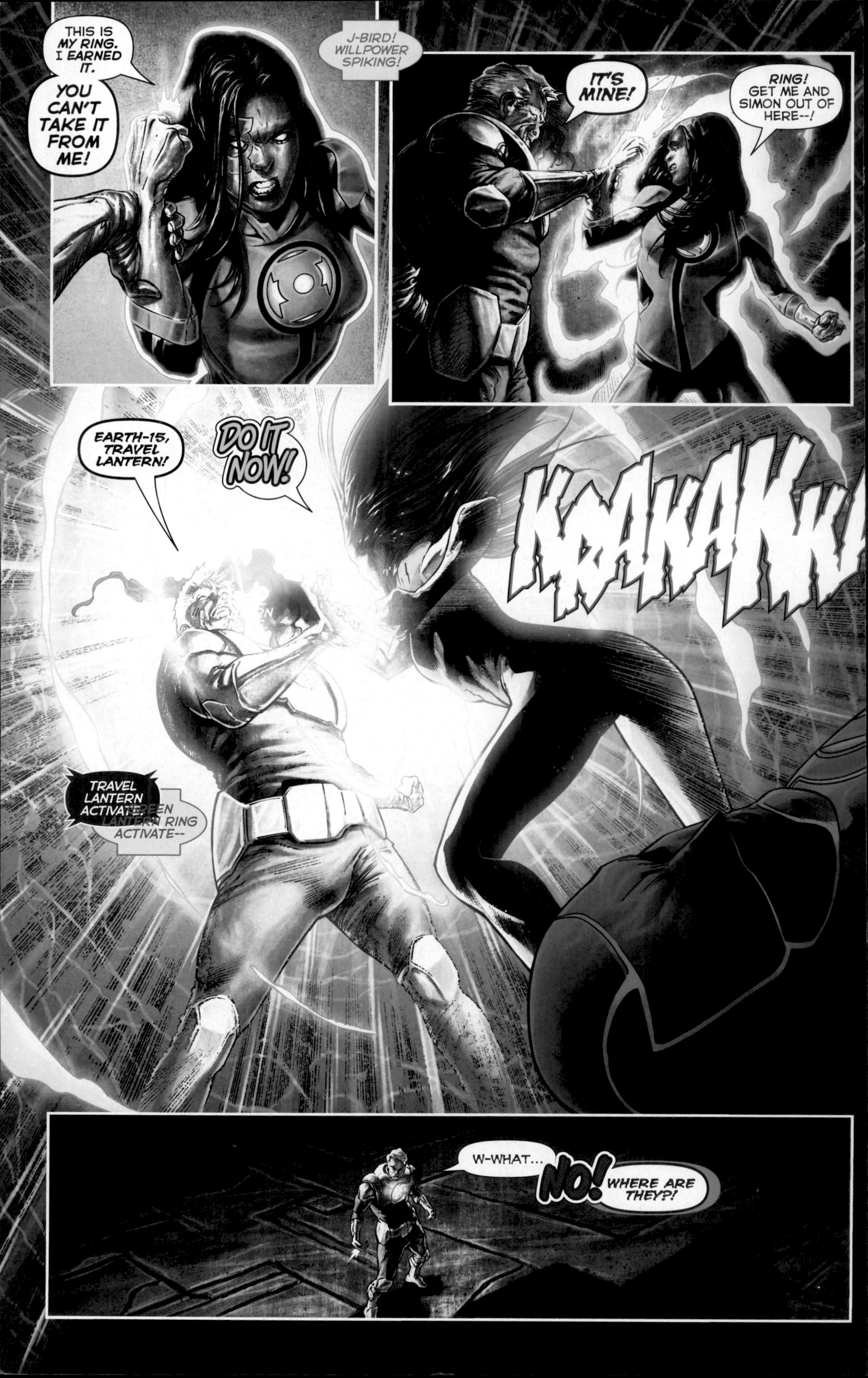
THIS IS MY RING. I EARNED IT.
YOU CAN'T TAKE IT FROM ME!
J-BIRD! WILLPOWER SPIKING!
IT'S MINE!
RING! GET ME AND SIMON OUT OF HERE--!
EARTH-15, TRAVEL LANTERN!
DO IT NOW!
TRAVEL LANTERN ACTIVATE.
LANTERN RING ACTIVATE--
W-WHAT...
NO!
WHERE ARE THEY?!

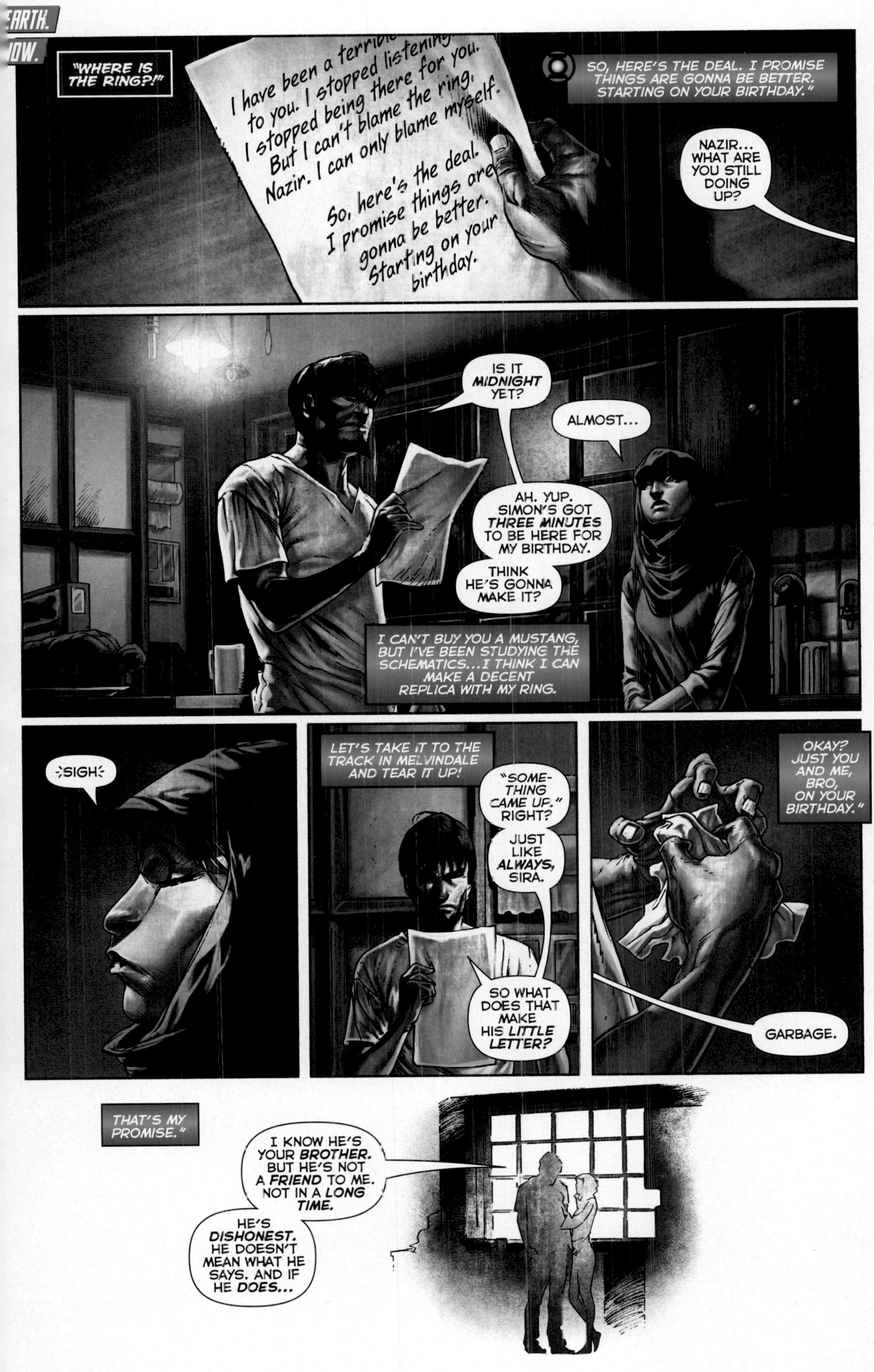
ARTH.
IOW.
"WHERE IS THE RING?!"
I have been a terrib to you. I stopped listening I stopped being there for you. But I can't blame the ring, Nazir. I can only blame myself.
So, here's the deal. I promise things are gonna be better. Starting on your birthday.
SO, HERE'S THE DEAL. I PROMISE THINGS ARE GONNA BE BETTER. STARTING ON YOUR BIRTHDAY."
NAZIR... WHAT ARE YOU STILL DOING UP?
IS IT MIDNIGHT YET?
ALMOST...
AH. YUP. SIMON'S GOT THREE MINUTES TO BE HERE FOR MY BIRTHDAY.
THINK HE'S GONNA MAKE IT?
I CAN'T BUY YOU A MUSTANG, BUT I'VE BEEN STUDYING THE SCHEMATICS...I THINK I CAN MAKE A DECENT REPLICA WITH MY RING.
SIGH
LET'S TAKE IT TO THE TRACK IN MELVINDALE AND TEAR IT UP!
"SOME-THING CAME UP." RIGHT?
JUST LIKE ALWAYS, SIRA.
SO WHAT DOES THAT MAKE HIS LITTLE LETTER?
OKAY? JUST YOU AND ME, BRO, ON YOUR BIRTHDAY."
GARBAGE.
THAT'S MY PROMISE."
I KNOW HE'S YOUR BROTHER. BUT HE'S NOT A FRIEND TO ME. NOT IN A LONG TIME.
HE'S DISHONEST. HE DOESN'T MEAN WHAT HE SAYS. AND IF HE DOES...

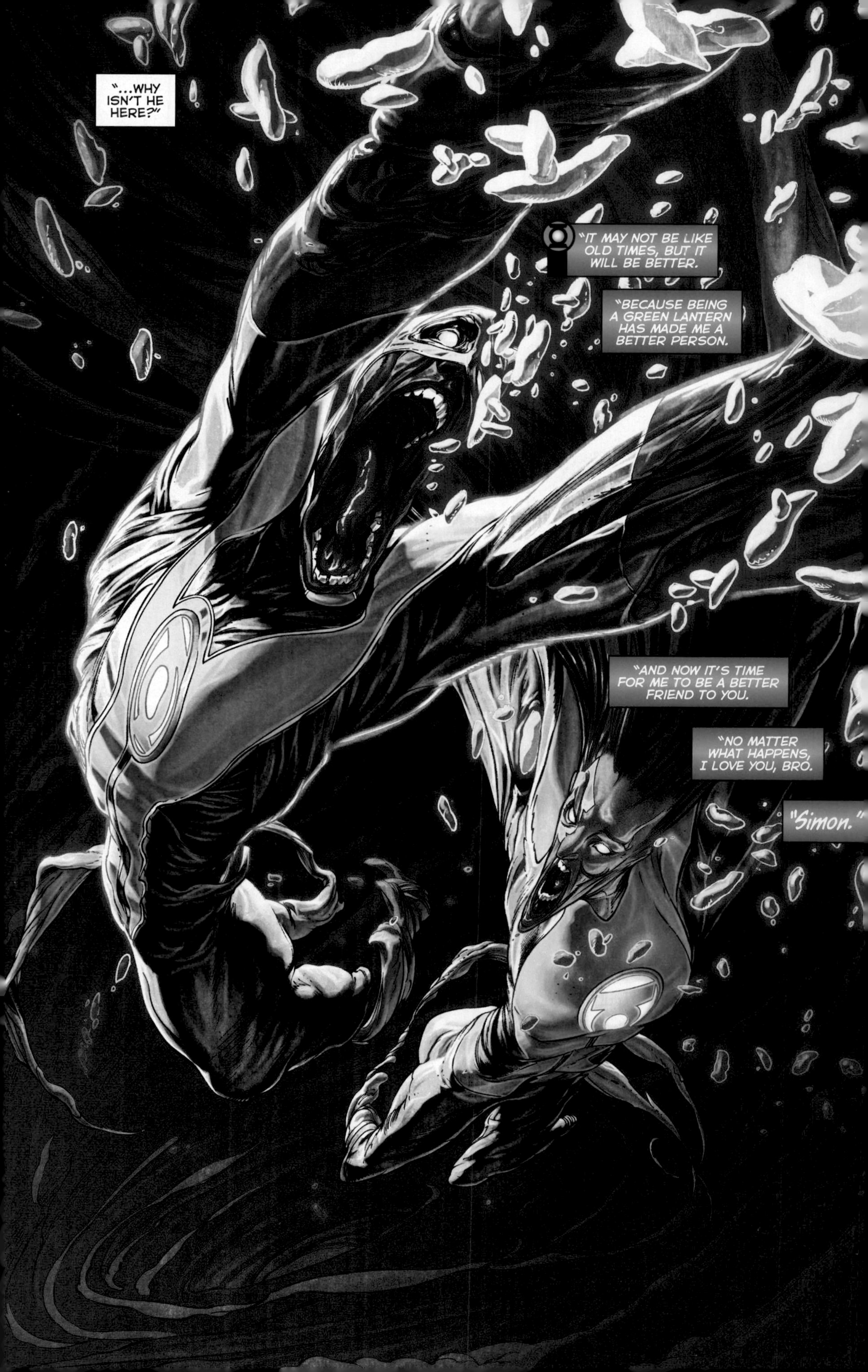
"...WHY ISN'T HE HERE?"
"IT MAY NOT BE LIKE OLD TIMES, BUT IT WILL BE BETTER.
"BECAUSE BEING A GREEN LANTERN HAS MADE ME A BETTER PERSON.
"AND NOW IT'S TIME FOR ME TO BE A BETTER FRIEND TO YOU.
"NO MATTER WHAT HAPPENS, I LOVE YOU, BRO.
"Simon."

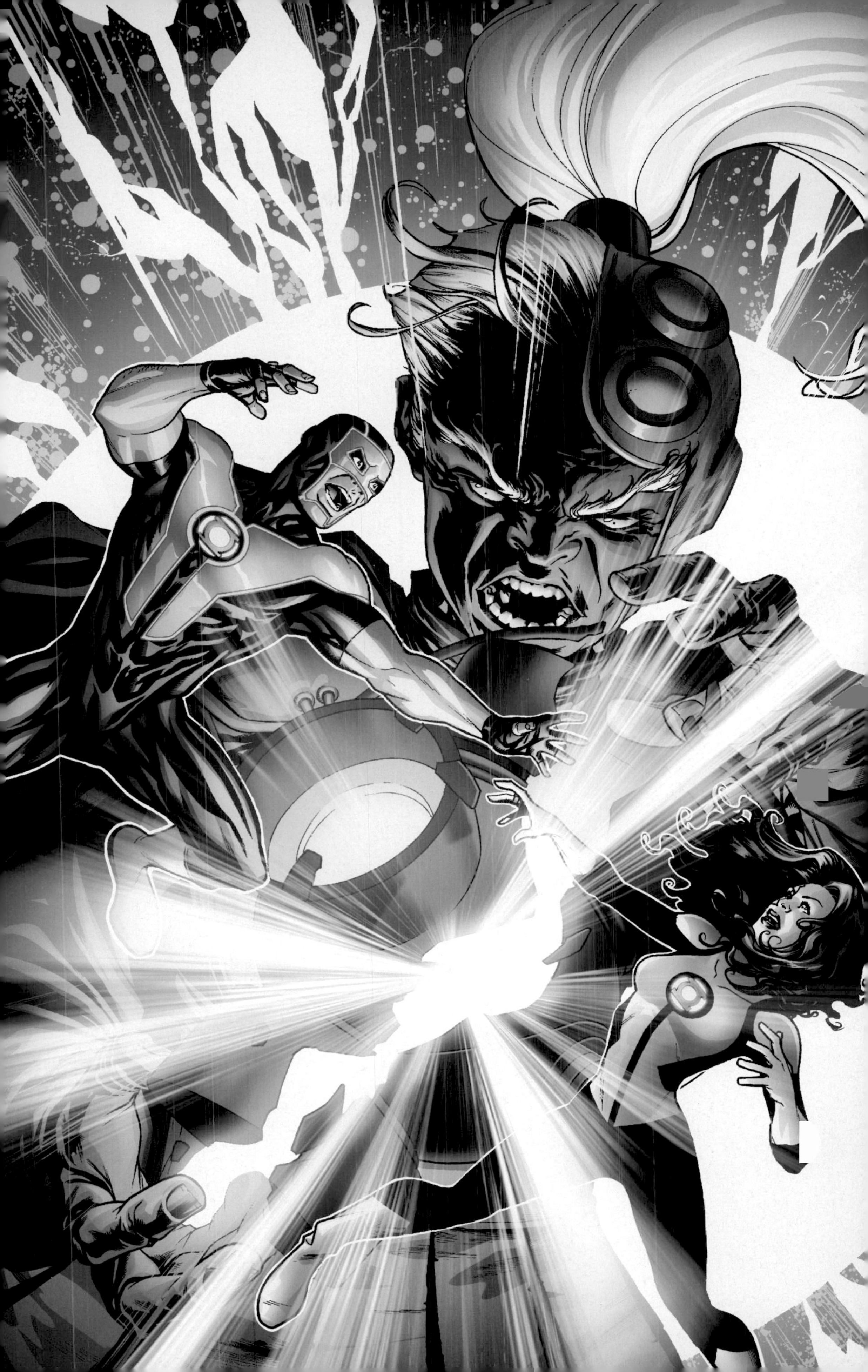

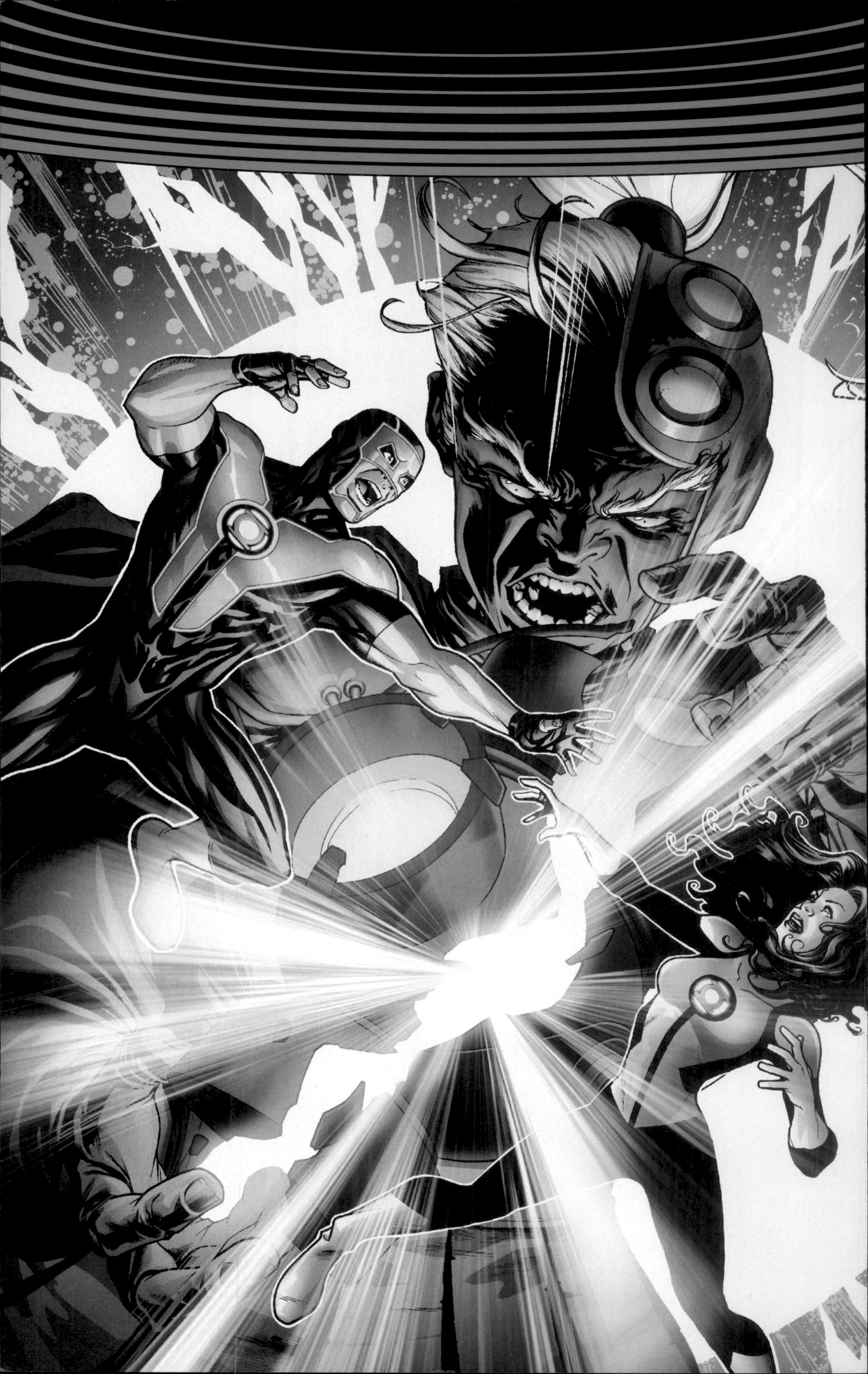

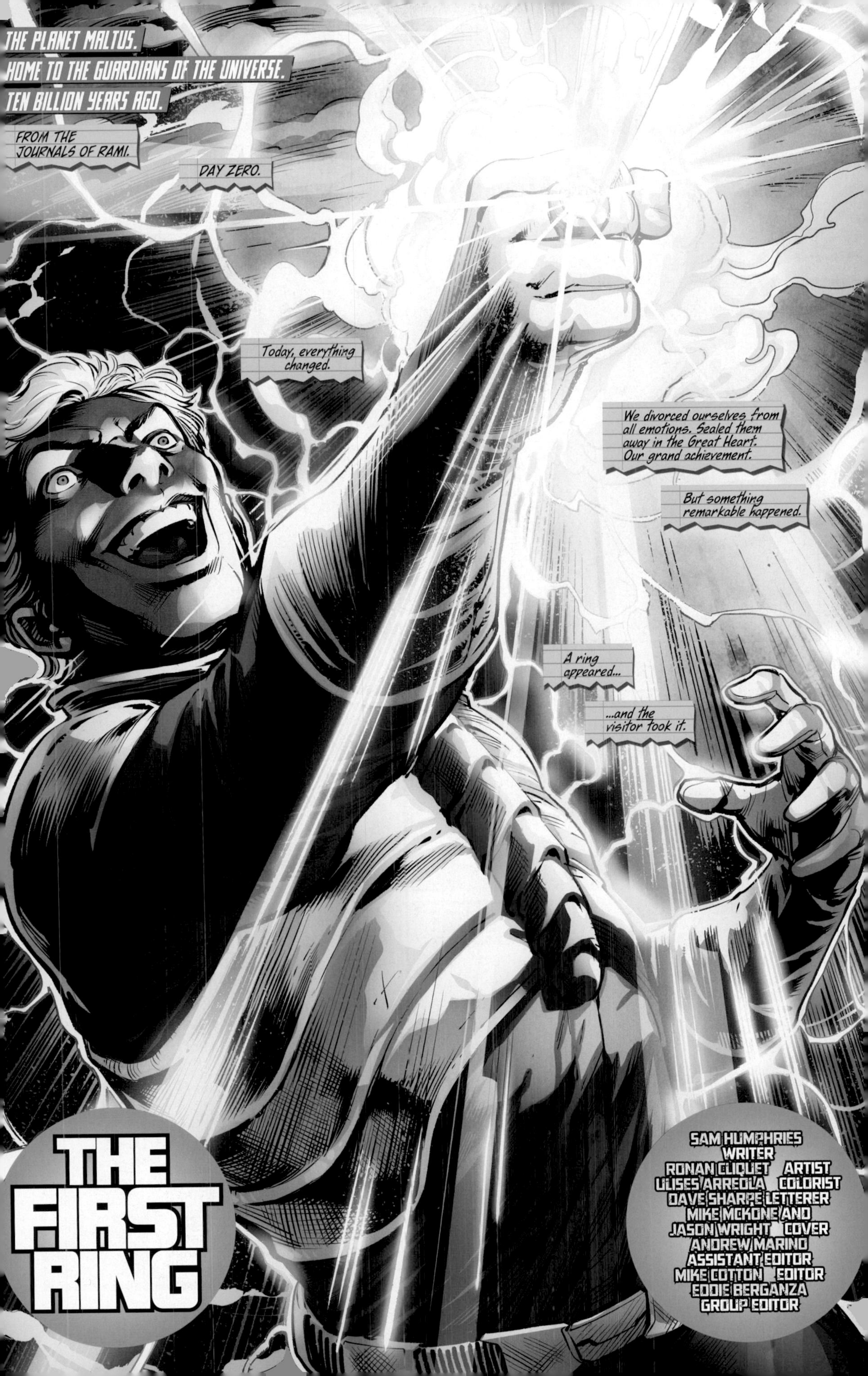
THE PLANET MALTUS.
HOME TO THE GUARDIANS OF THE UNIVERSE.
TEN BILLION YEARS AGO.
FROM THE JOURNALS OF RAMI.
DAY ZERO.
Today, everything changed.
We divorced ourselves from all emotions. Sealed them away in the Great Heart. Our grand achievement.
But something remarkable happened.
A ring appeared...
...and the visitor took it.
THE FIRST RING
SAM HUMPHRIES WRITER
RONAN CLIQUET ARTIST
ULISES ARREOLA COLORIST
DAVE SHARPE LETTERER
MIKE MCKONE AND JASON WRIGHT COVER
ANDREW MARINO ASSISTANT EDITOR
MIKE COTTON EDITOR
EDDIE BERGANZA GROUP EDITOR

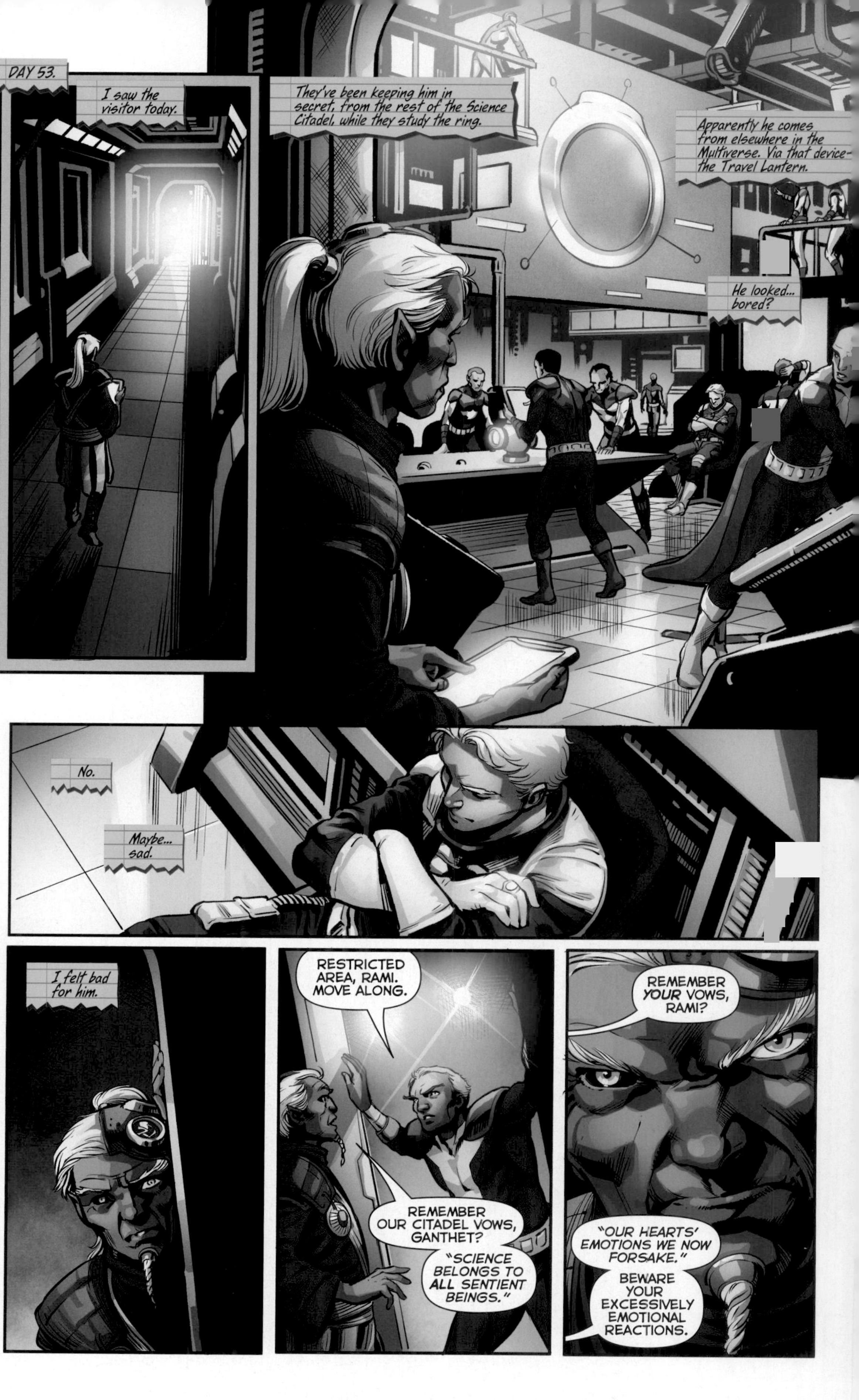
DAY 53.
I saw the visitor today.
They've been keeping him in secret, from the rest of the Science Citadel, while they study the ring.
Apparently he comes from elsewhere in the Multiverse. Via that device– the Travel Lantern.
He looked... bored?
No.
Maybe... sad.
I felt bad for him.
RESTRICTED AREA, RAMI. MOVE ALONG.
REMEMBER OUR CITADEL VOWS, GANTHET?
"SCIENCE BELONGS TO ALL SENTIENT BEINGS."
REMEMBER YOUR VOWS, RAMI?
"OUR HEARTS' EMOTIONS WE NOW FORSAKE."
BEWARE YOUR EXCESSIVELY EMOTIONAL REACTIONS.

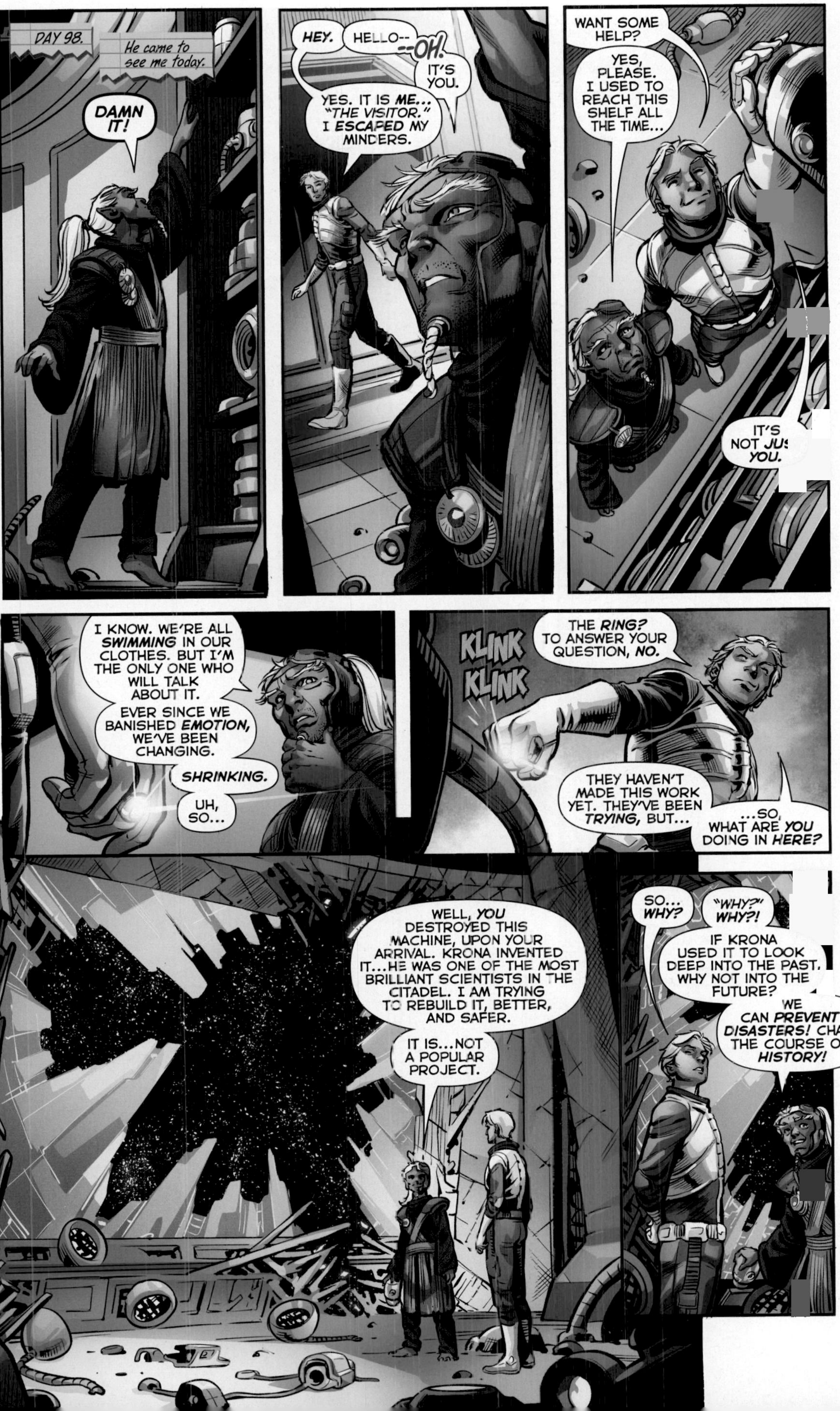
DAY 98.
He came to see me today.
DAMN IT!
HEY.
HELLO--
--OH!
IT'S YOU.
YES. IT IS ME... "THE VISITOR." I ESCAPED MY MINDERS.
WANT SOME HELP?
YES, PLEASE. I USED TO REACH THIS SHELF ALL THE TIME...
IT'S NOT JUS YOU.
I KNOW. WE'RE ALL SWIMMING IN OUR CLOTHES. BUT I'M THE ONLY ONE WHO WILL TALK ABOUT IT.
EVER SINCE WE BANISHED EMOTION, WE'VE BEEN CHANGING.
SHRINKING.
UH, SO...
KLINK KLINK
THE RING? TO ANSWER YOUR QUESTION, NO.
THEY HAVEN'T MADE THIS WORK YET. THEY'VE BEEN TRYING, BUT...
...SO, WHAT ARE YOU DOING IN HERE?
WELL, YOU DESTROYED THIS MACHINE, UPON YOUR ARRIVAL. KRONA INVENTED IT...HE WAS ONE OF THE MOST BRILLIANT SCIENTISTS IN THE CITADEL. I AM TRYING TO REBUILD IT, BETTER, AND SAFER.
IT IS...NOT A POPULAR PROJECT.
SO... WHY?
"WHY?" WHY?!
IF KRONA USED IT TO LOOK DEEP INTO THE PAST, WHY NOT INTO THE FUTURE?
WE CAN PREVENT DISASTERS! CHART THE COURSE OF HISTORY!

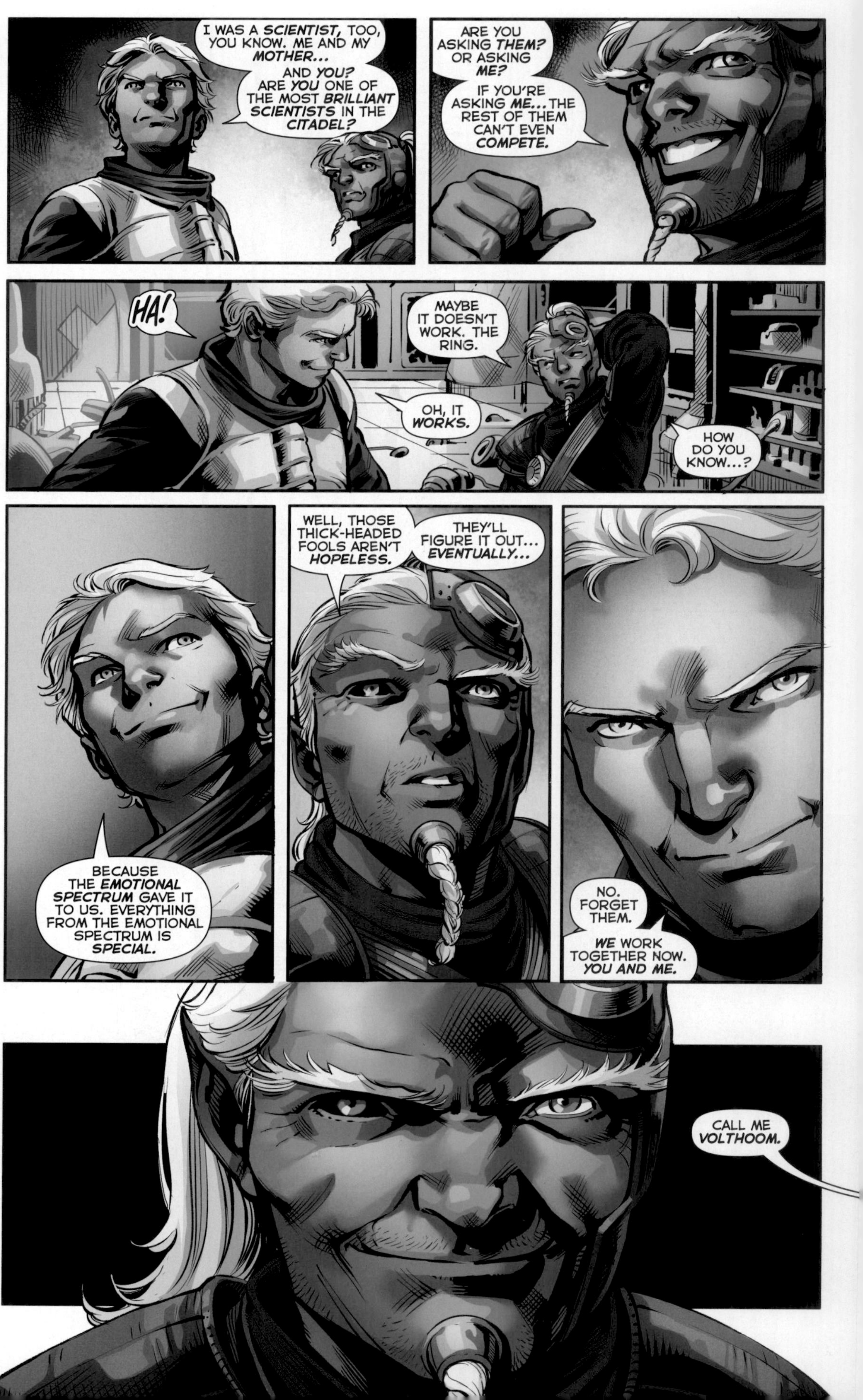
I WAS A SCIENTIST, TOO, YOU KNOW. ME AND MY MOTHER...
AND YOU? ARE YOU ONE OF THE MOST BRILLIANT SCIENTISTS IN THE CITADEL?
ARE YOU ASKING THEM? OR ASKING ME?
IF YOU'RE ASKING ME... THE REST OF THEM CAN'T EVEN COMPETE.
HA!
MAYBE IT DOESN'T WORK. THE RING.
OH, IT WORKS.
HOW DO YOU KNOW...?
BECAUSE THE EMOTIONAL SPECTRUM GAVE IT TO US. EVERYTHING FROM THE EMOTIONAL SPECTRUM IS SPECIAL.
WELL, THOSE THICK-HEADED FOOLS AREN'T HOPELESS.
THEY'LL FIGURE IT OUT... EVENTUALLY...
NO. FORGET THEM.
WE WORK TOGETHER NOW. YOU AND ME.
CALL ME VOLTHOOM.

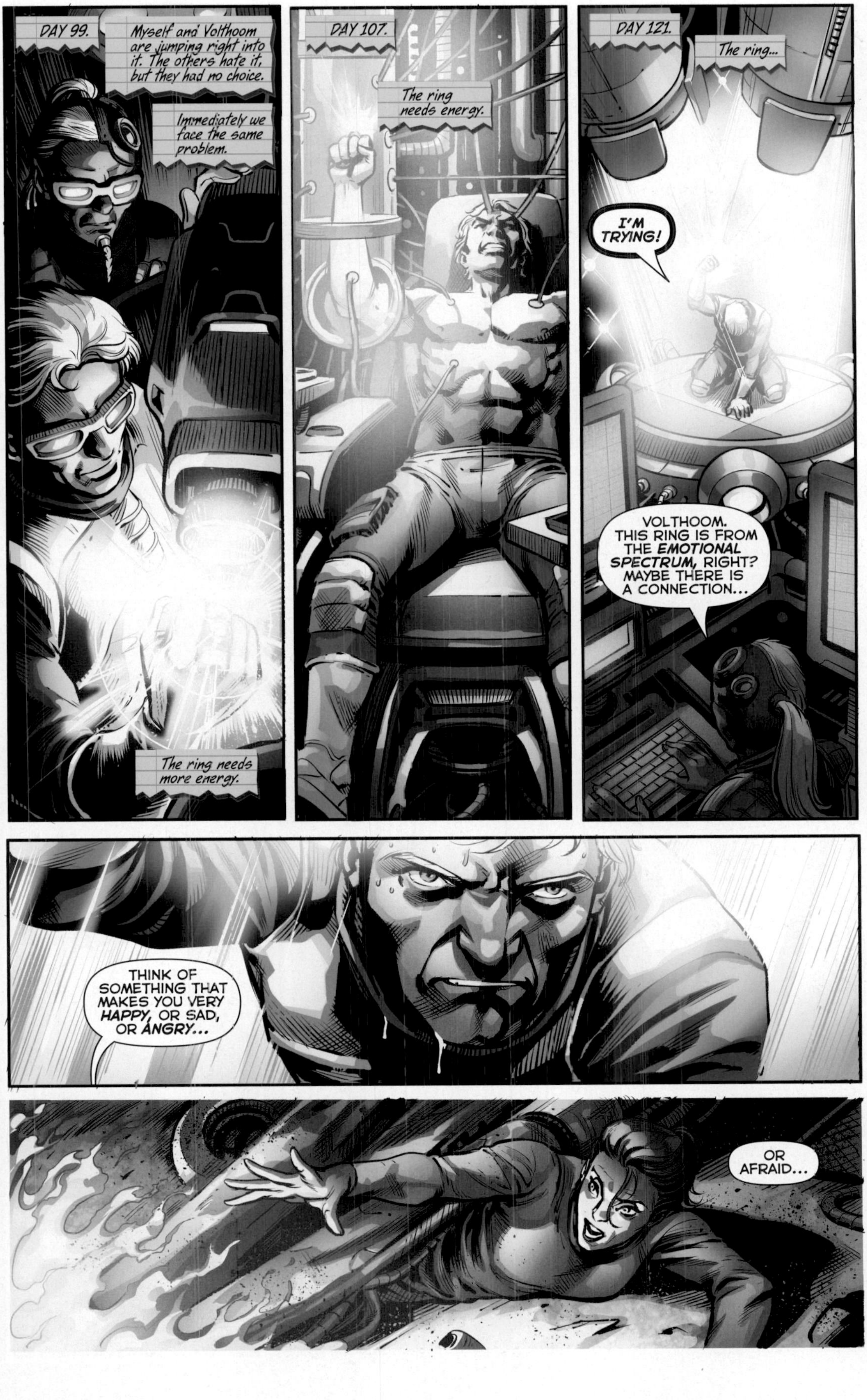
DAY 99.
Myself and Volthoom are jumping right into it. The others hate it, but they had no choice.
Immediately we face the same problem.
The ring needs more energy.
DAY 107.
The ring needs energy.
DAY 121.
The ring...
I'M TRYING!
VOLTHOOM. THIS RING IS FROM THE EMOTIONAL SPECTRUM, RIGHT? MAYBE THERE IS A CONNECTION...
THINK OF SOMETHING THAT MAKES YOU VERY HAPPY, OR SAD, OR ANGRY...
OR AFRAID...

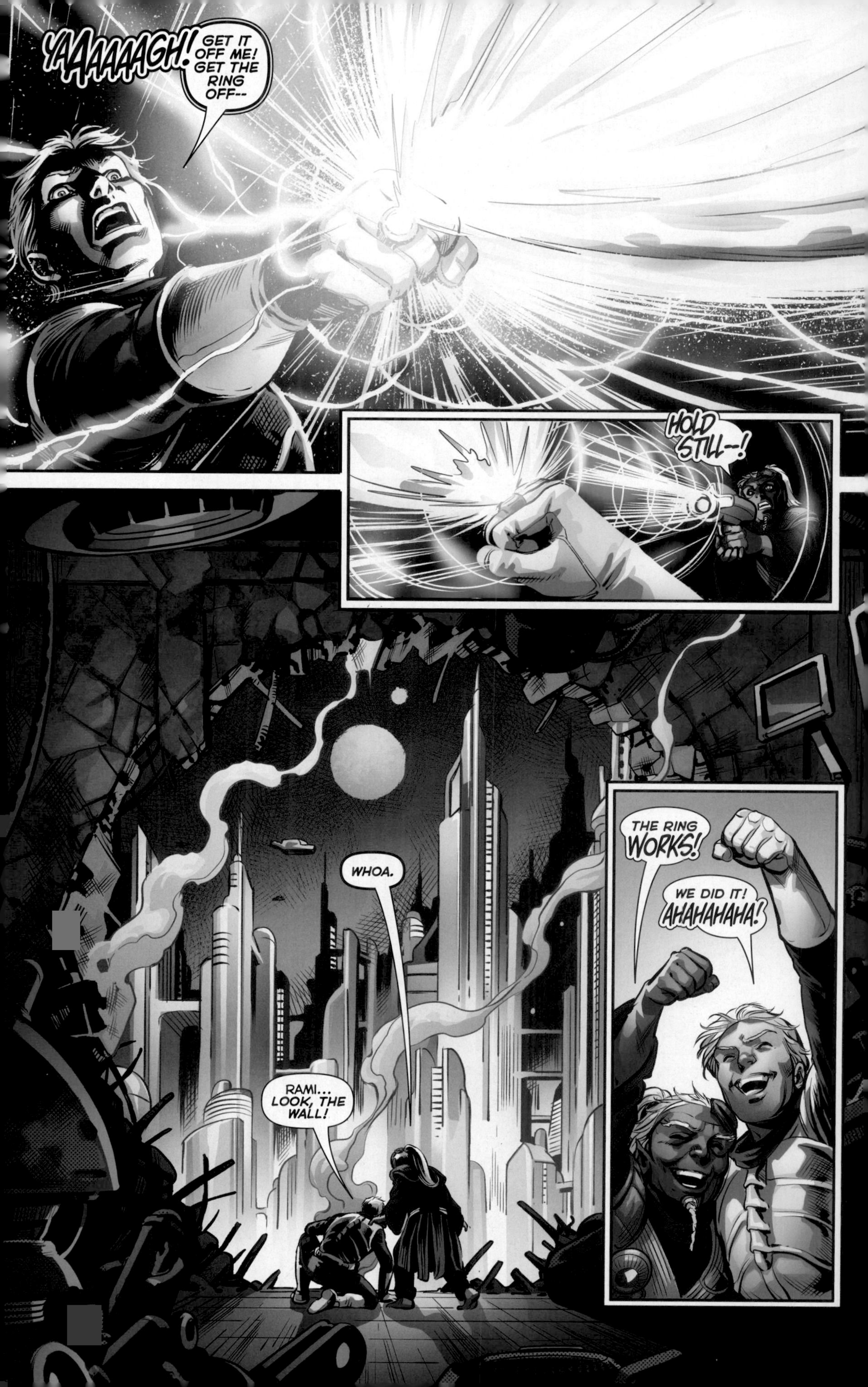
YAAAAAAGH!
GET IT OFF ME! GET THE RING OFF--
HOLD STILL--!
WHOA.
RAMI... LOOK, THE WALL!
THE RING WORKS!
WE DID IT! AHAHAHAHA!

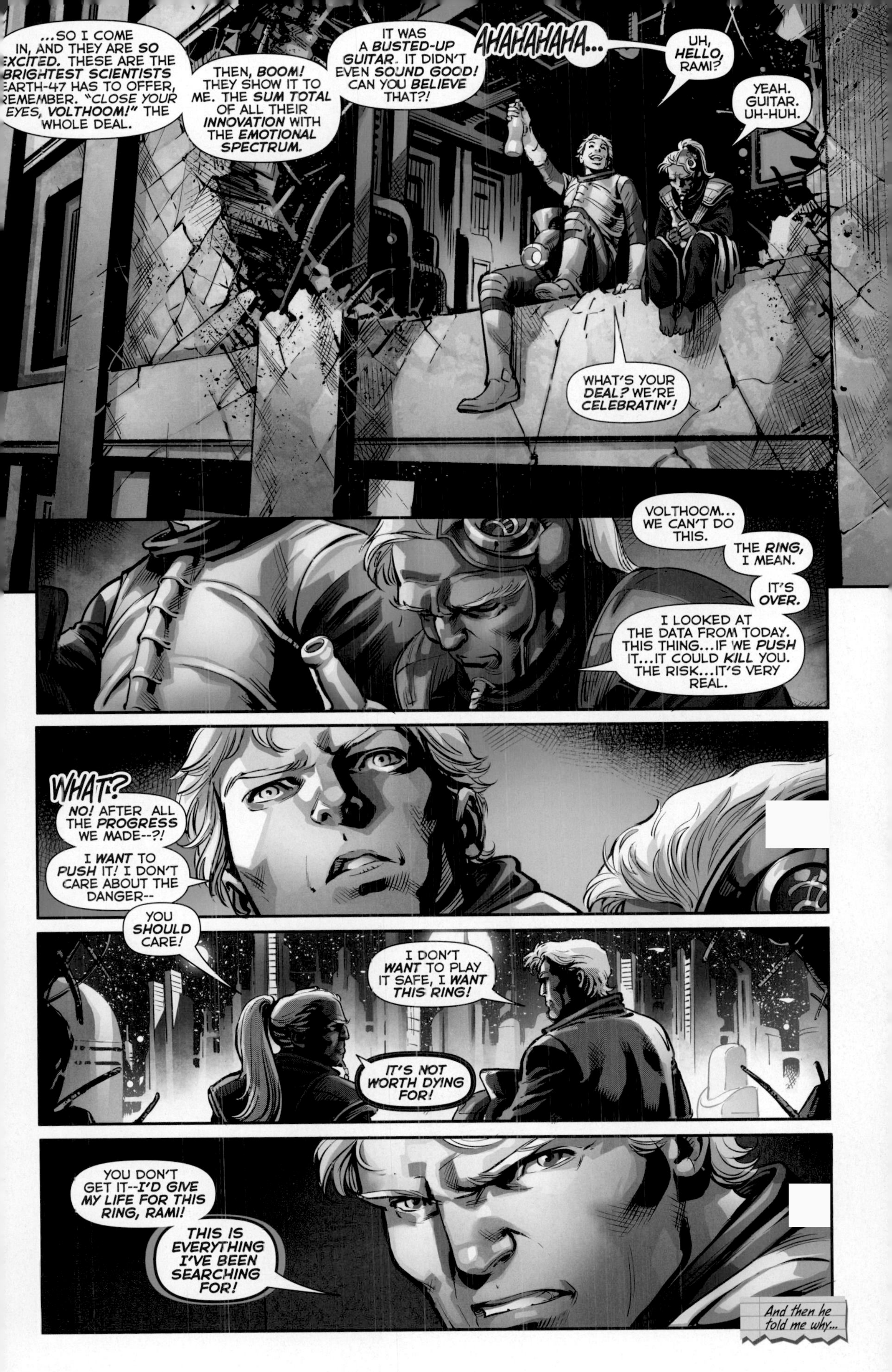
...SO I COME IN, AND THEY ARE SO EXCITED. THESE ARE THE BRIGHTEST SCIENTISTS EARTH-47 HAS TO OFFER, REMEMBER. "CLOSE YOUR EYES, VOLTHOOM!" THE WHOLE DEAL.
THEN, BOOM! THEY SHOW IT TO ME. THE SUM TOTAL OF ALL THEIR INNOVATION WITH THE EMOTIONAL SPECTRUM.
IT WAS A BUSTED-UP GUITAR. IT DIDN'T EVEN SOUND GOOD! CAN YOU BELIEVE THAT?!
AHAHAHAHA...
UH, HELLO, RAMI?
YEAH. GUITAR. UH-HUH.
WHAT'S YOUR DEAL? WE'RE CELEBRATIN'!
VOLTHOOM... WE CAN'T DO THIS.
THE RING, I MEAN.
IT'S OVER.
I LOOKED AT THE DATA FROM TODAY. THIS THING...IF WE PUSH IT...IT COULD KILL YOU. THE RISK...IT'S VERY REAL.
WHAT?
NO! AFTER ALL THE PROGRESS WE MADE--?!
I WANT TO PUSH IT! I DON'T CARE ABOUT THE DANGER--
YOU SHOULD CARE!
I DON'T WANT TO PLAY IT SAFE, I WANT THIS RING!
IT'S NOT WORTH DYING FOR!
YOU DON'T GET IT--I'D GIVE MY LIFE FOR THIS RING, RAMI!
THIS IS EVERYTHING I'VE BEEN SEARCHING FOR!
And then he told me why...

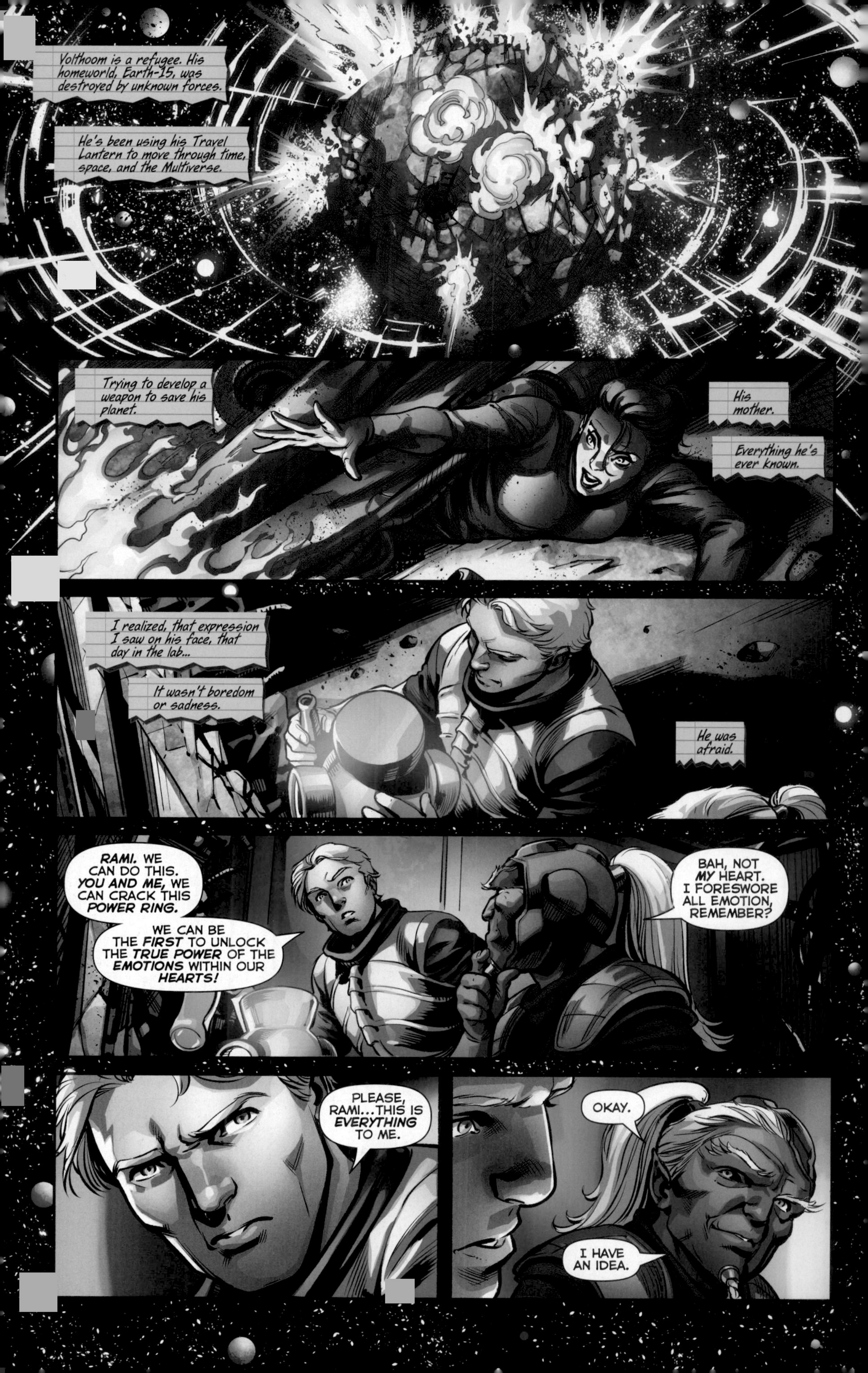
Volthoom is a refugee. His homeworld, Earth-15, was destroyed by unknown forces.
He's been using his Travel Lantern to move through time, space, and the Multiverse.
Trying to develop a weapon to save his planet.
His mother.
Everything he's ever known.
I realized, that expression I saw on his face, that day in the lab...
It wasn't boredom or sadness.
He was afraid.
RAMI. WE CAN DO THIS. YOU AND ME, WE CAN CRACK THIS POWER RING.
WE CAN BE THE FIRST TO UNLOCK THE TRUE POWER OF THE EMOTIONS WITHIN OUR HEARTS!
BAH, NOT MY HEART. I FORESWORE ALL EMOTION, REMEMBER?
PLEASE, RAMI...THIS IS EVERYTHING TO ME.
OKAY.
I HAVE AN IDEA.

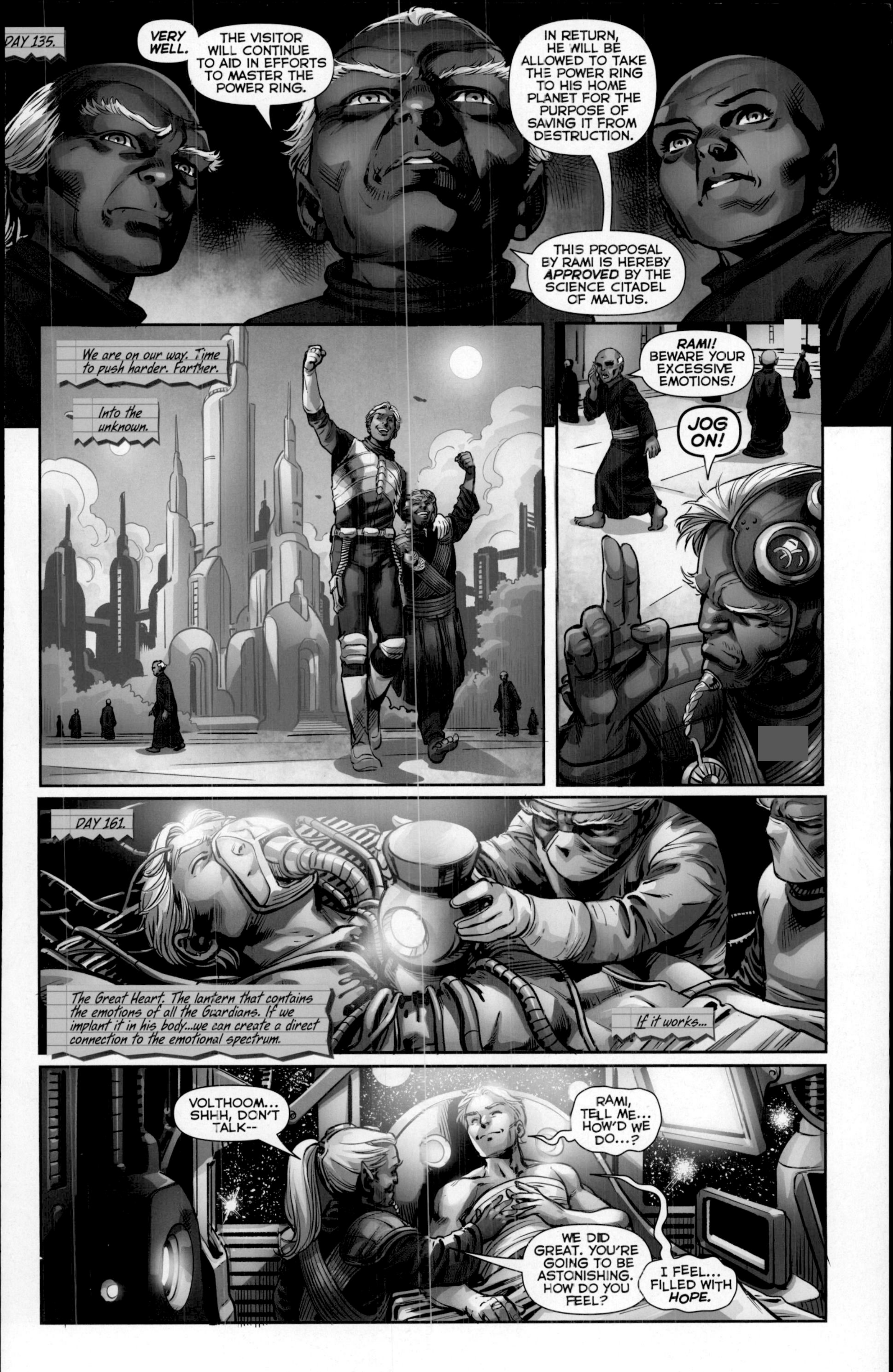
DAY 135.
VERY WELL.
THE VISITOR WILL CONTINUE TO AID IN EFFORTS TO MASTER THE POWER RING.
IN RETURN, HE WILL BE ALLOWED TO TAKE THE POWER RING TO HIS HOME PLANET FOR THE PURPOSE OF SAVING IT FROM DESTRUCTION.
THIS PROPOSAL BY RAMI IS HEREBY APPROVED BY THE SCIENCE CITADEL OF MALTUS.
We are on our way. Time to push harder. Farther.
Into the unknown.
RAMI! BEWARE YOUR EXCESSIVE EMOTIONS!
JOG ON!
DAY 161.
The Great Heart. The lantern that contains the emotions of all the Guardians. If we implant it in his body...we can create a direct connection to the emotional spectrum.
If it works...
VOLTHOOM... SHHH, DON'T TALK--
RAMI, TELL ME... HOW'D WE DO...?
WE DID GREAT. YOU'RE GOING TO BE ASTONISHING. HOW DO YOU FEEL?
I FEEL... FILLED WITH HOPE.

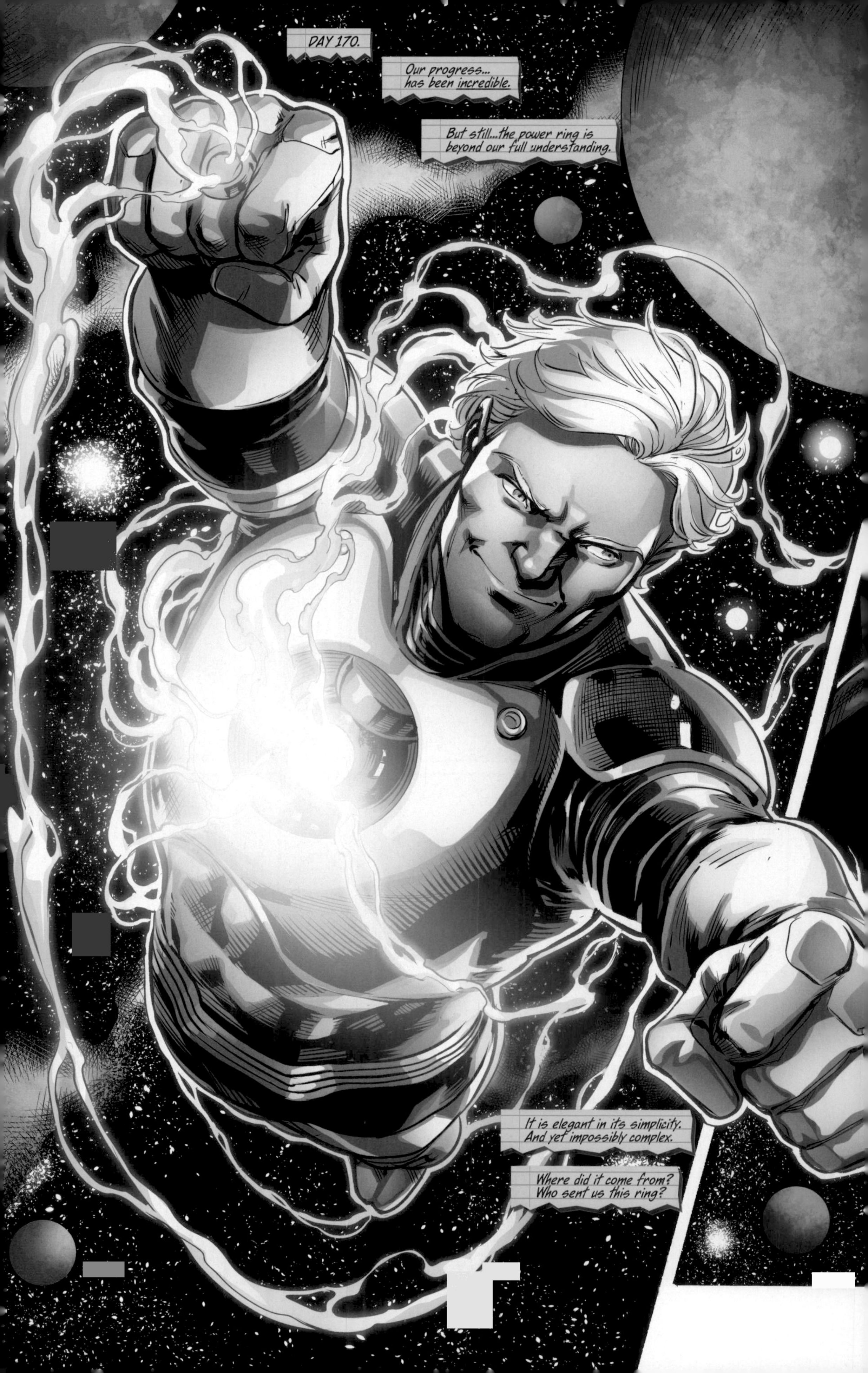
DAY 170.
Our progress... has been incredible.
But still...the power ring is beyond our full understanding.
It is elegant in its simplicity. And yet impossibly complex.
Where did it come from? Who sent us this ring?

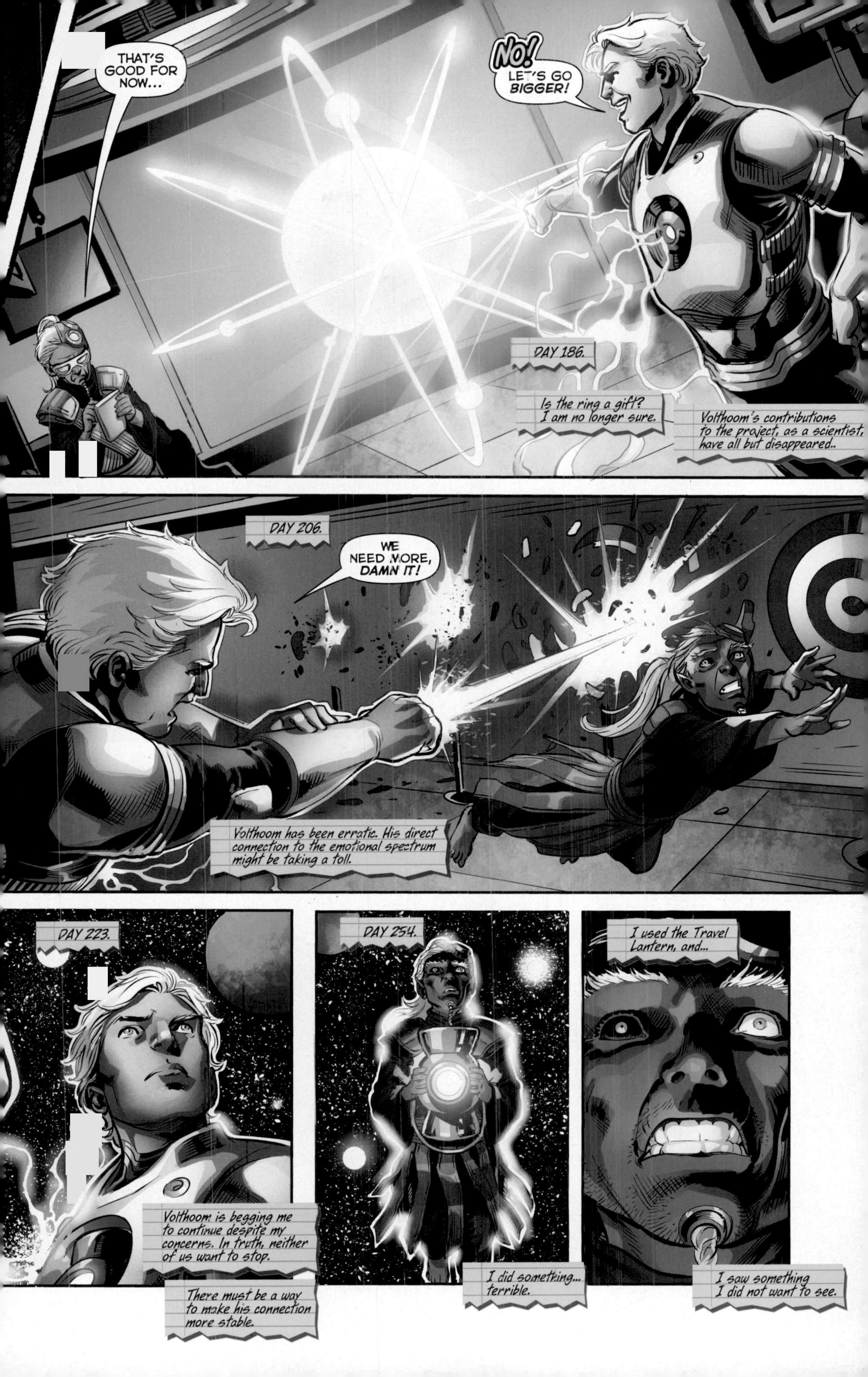
THAT'S GOOD FOR NOW...
NO! LET'S GO BIGGER!
DAY 186.
Is the ring a gift? I am no longer sure.
Volthoom's contributions to the project, as a scientist, have all but disappeared..
DAY 206.
WE NEED MORE, DAMN IT!
Volthoom has been erratic. His direct connection to the emotional spectrum might be taking a toll.
DAY 223.
Volthoom is begging me to continue despite my concerns. In truth, neither of us want to stop.
There must be a way to make his connection more stable.
DAY 254.
I did something... terrible.
I used the Travel Lantern, and...
I saw something I did not want to see.

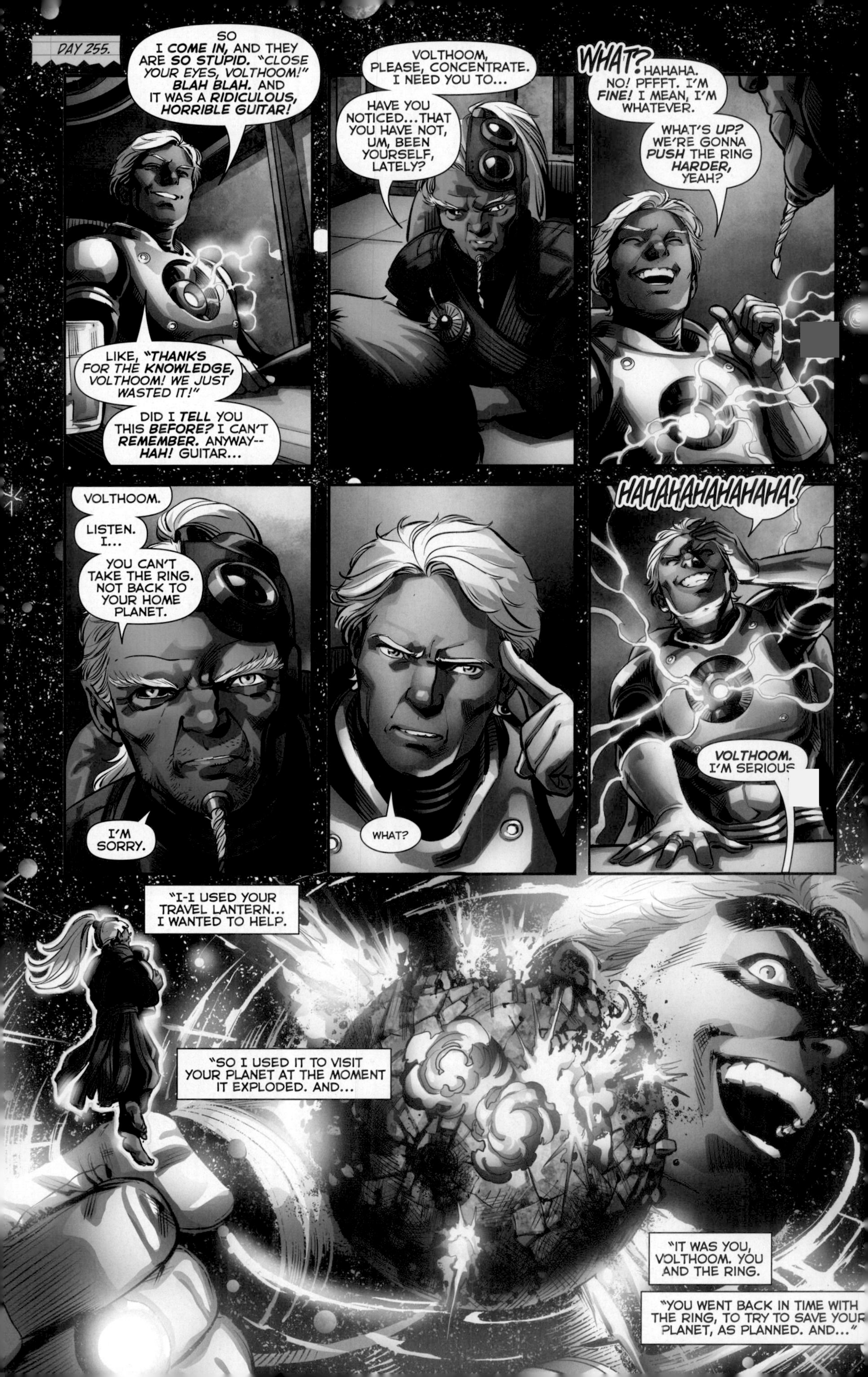
DAY 255.
SO I COME IN, AND THEY ARE SO STUPID. "CLOSE YOUR EYES, VOLTHOOM!" BLAH BLAH. AND IT WAS A RIDICULOUS, HORRIBLE GUITAR!
LIKE, "THANKS FOR THE KNOWLEDGE, VOLTHOOM! WE JUST WASTED IT!"
DID I TELL YOU THIS BEFORE? I CAN'T REMEMBER. ANYWAY-- HAH! GUITAR...
VOLTHOOM, PLEASE, CONCENTRATE. I NEED YOU TO...
HAVE YOU NOTICED...THAT YOU HAVE NOT, UM, BEEN YOURSELF, LATELY?
WHAT?
HAHAHA. NO! PFFFT. I'M FINE! I MEAN, I'M WHATEVER.
WHAT'S UP? WE'RE GONNA PUSH THE RING HARDER, YEAH?
VOLTHOOM.
LISTEN. I...
YOU CAN'T TAKE THE RING. NOT BACK TO YOUR HOME PLANET.
I'M SORRY.
WHAT?
HAHAHAHAHAHAHA!
VOLTHOOM. I'M SERIOUS
"I-I USED YOUR TRAVEL LANTERN... I WANTED TO HELP.
"SO I USED IT TO VISIT YOUR PLANET AT THE MOMENT IT EXPLODED. AND...
"IT WAS YOU, VOLTHOOM. YOU AND THE RING.
"YOU WENT BACK IN TIME WITH THE RING, TO TRY TO SAVE YOUR PLANET, AS PLANNED. AND..."

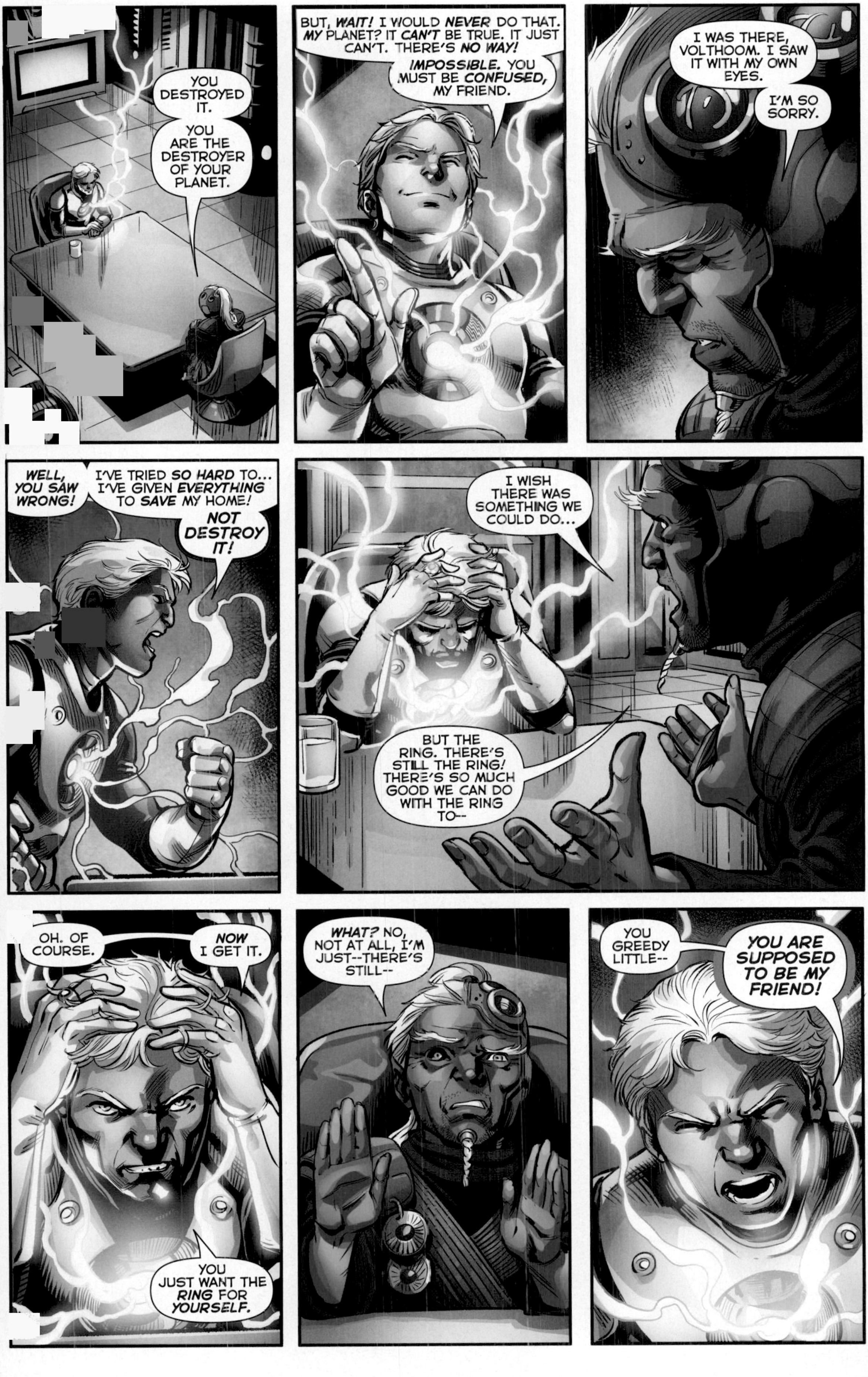
YOU DESTROYED IT.
YOU ARE THE DESTROYER OF YOUR PLANET.
BUT, WAIT! I WOULD NEVER DO THAT. MY PLANET? IT CAN'T BE TRUE. IT JUST CAN'T. THERE'S NO WAY!
IMPOSSIBLE. YOU MUST BE CONFUSED, MY FRIEND.
I WAS THERE, VOLTHOOM. I SAW IT WITH MY OWN EYES.
I'M SO SORRY.
WELL, YOU SAW WRONG!
I'VE TRIED SO HARD TO... I'VE GIVEN EVERYTHING TO SAVE MY HOME!
NOT DESTROY IT!
I WISH THERE WAS SOMETHING WE COULD DO...
BUT THE RING. THERE'S STILL THE RING! THERE'S SO MUCH GOOD WE CAN DO WITH THE RING TO--
OH. OF COURSE.
NOW I GET IT.
YOU JUST WANT THE RING FOR YOURSELF.
WHAT? NO, NOT AT ALL, I'M JUST--THERE'S STILL--
YOU GREEDY LITTLE--
YOU ARE SUPPOSED TO BE MY FRIEND!

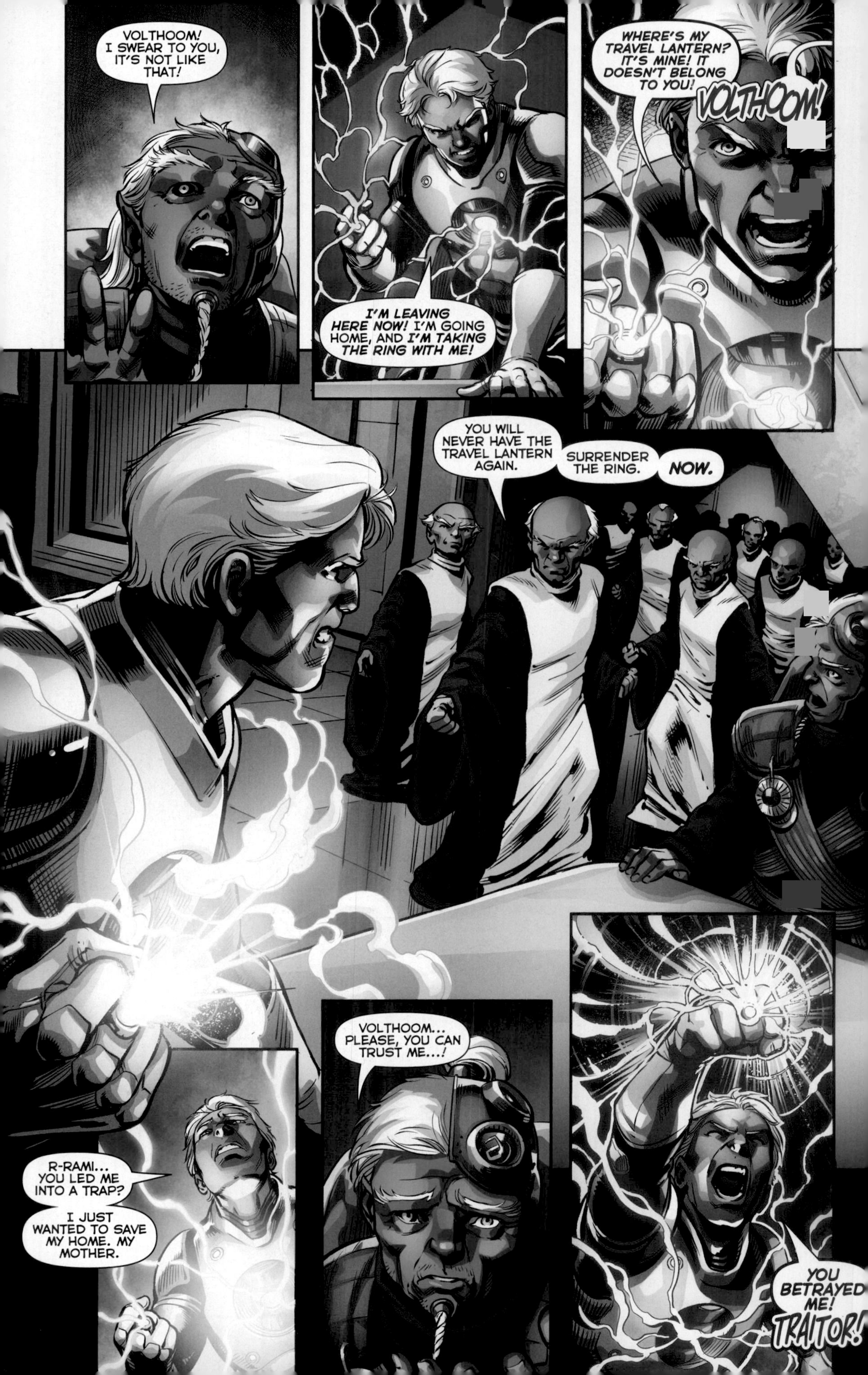
VOLTHOOM! I SWEAR TO YOU, IT'S NOT LIKE THAT!
I'M LEAVING HERE NOW! I'M GOING HOME, AND I'M TAKING THE RING WITH ME!
WHERE'S MY TRAVEL LANTERN? IT'S MINE! IT DOESN'T BELONG TO YOU!
VOLTHOOM!
YOU WILL NEVER HAVE THE TRAVEL LANTERN AGAIN.
SURRENDER THE RING.
NOW.
R-RAMI... YOU LED ME INTO A TRAP?
I JUST WANTED TO SAVE MY HOME. MY MOTHER.
VOLTHOOM... PLEASE, YOU CAN TRUST ME...!
YOU BETRAYED ME!
TRAITOR!

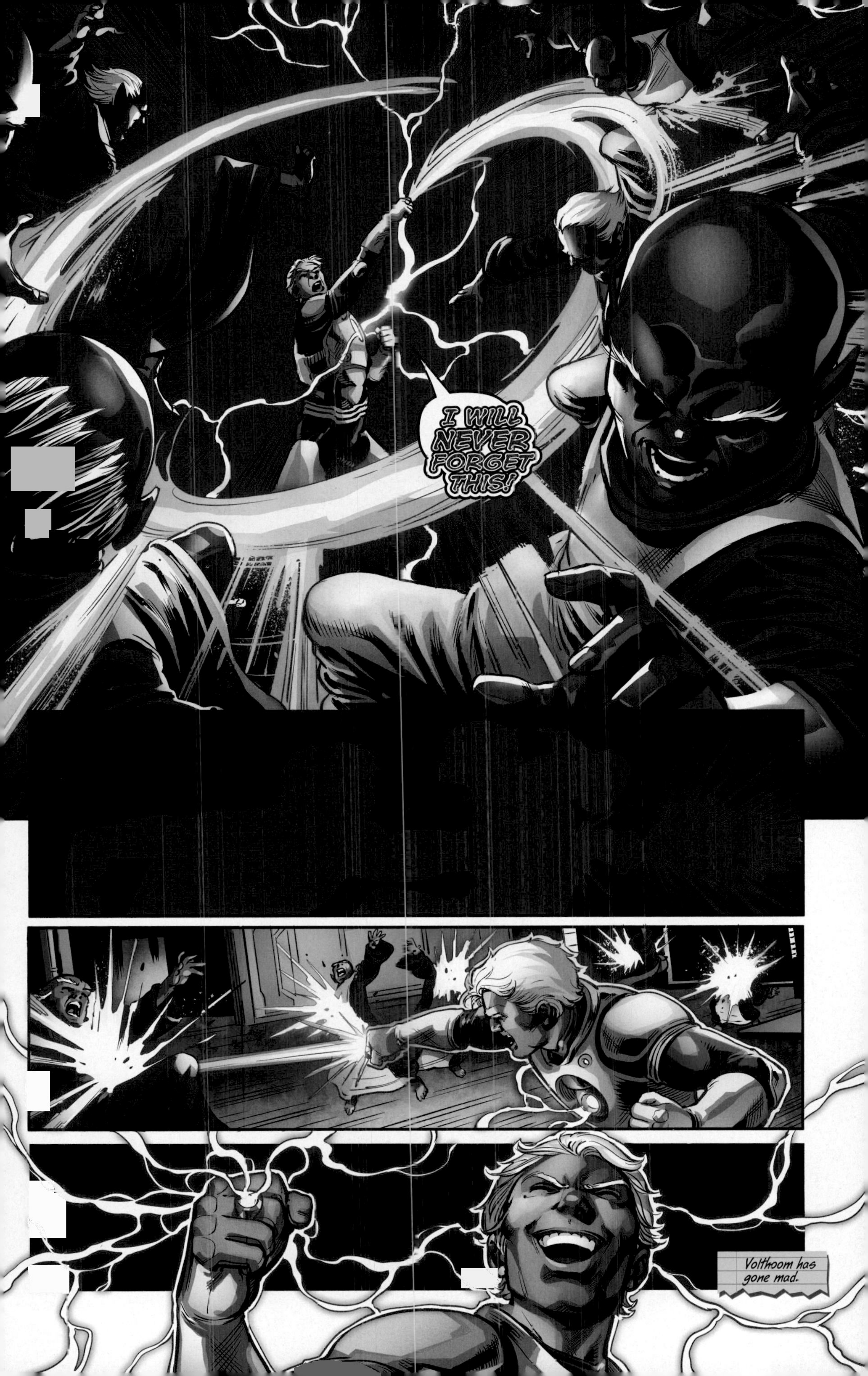
I WILL NEVER FORGET THIS!
Volthoom has gone mad.

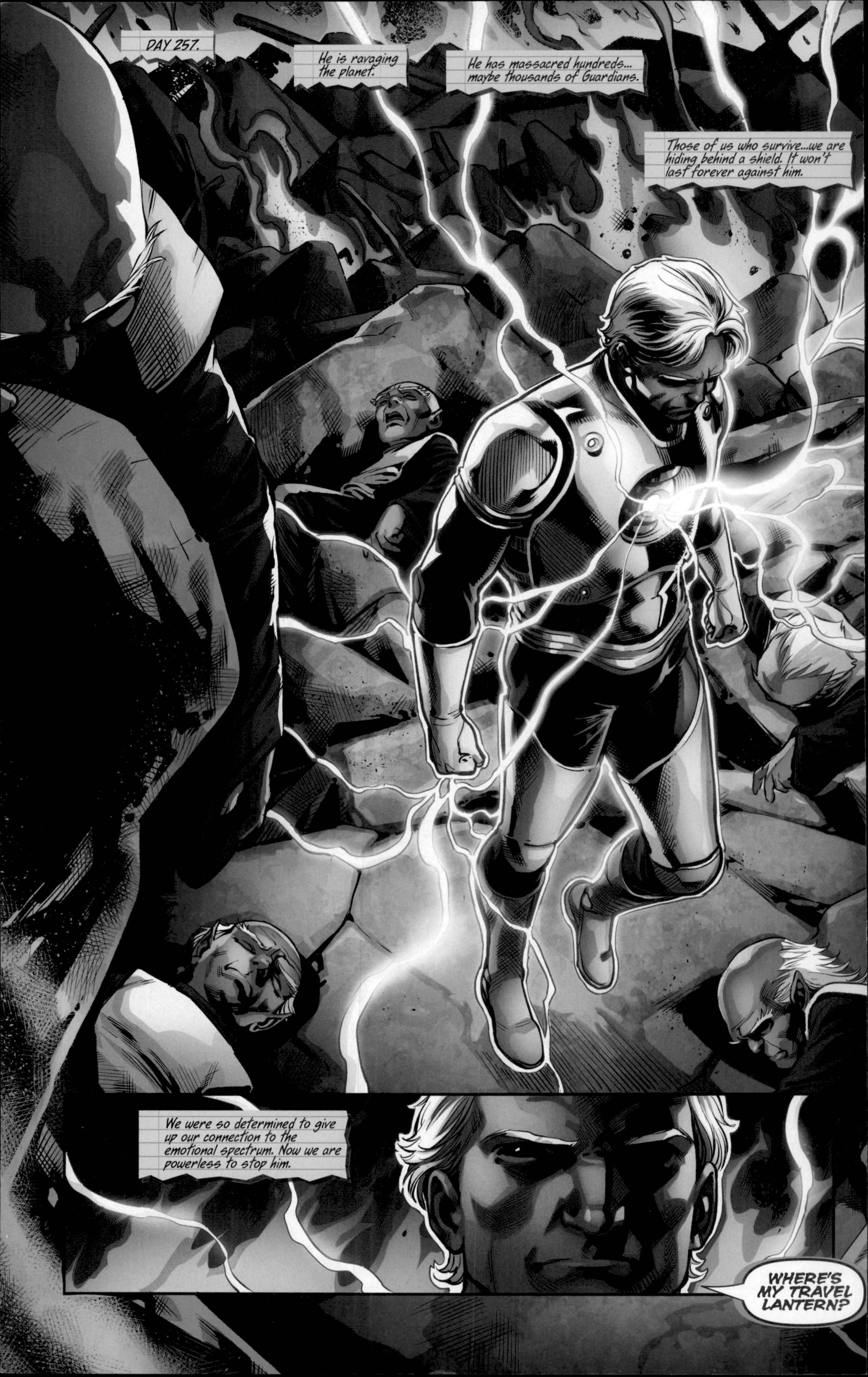
DAY 257.
He is ravaging the planet.
He has massacred hundreds... maybe thousands of Guardians.
Those of us who survive...we are hiding behind a shield. It won't last forever against him.
We were so determined to give up our connection to the emotional spectrum. Now we are powerless to stop him.
WHERE'S MY TRAVEL LANTERN?

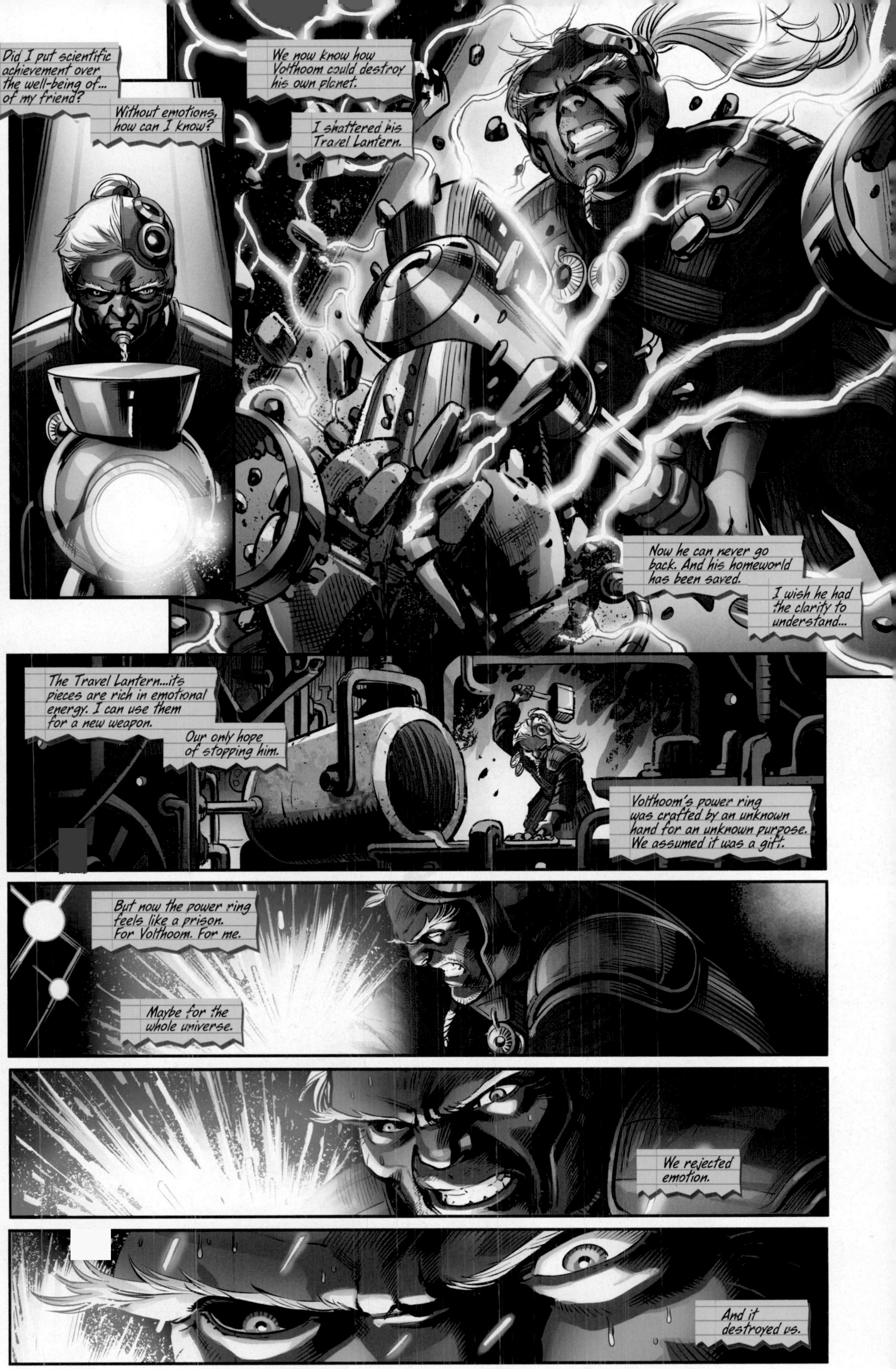
Did I put scientific achievement over the well-being of... of my friend?
Without emotions, how can I know?
We now know how Volthoom could destroy his own planet.
I shattered his Travel Lantern.
Now he can never go back. And his homeworld has been saved.
I wish he had the clarity to understand...
The Travel Lantern...its pieces are rich in emotional energy. I can use them for a new weapon.
Our only hope of stopping him.
Volthoom's power ring was crafted by an unknown hand for an unknown purpose. We assumed it was a gift.
But now the power ring feels like a prison. For Volthoom. For me.
Maybe for the whole universe.
We rejected emotion.
And it destroyed us.

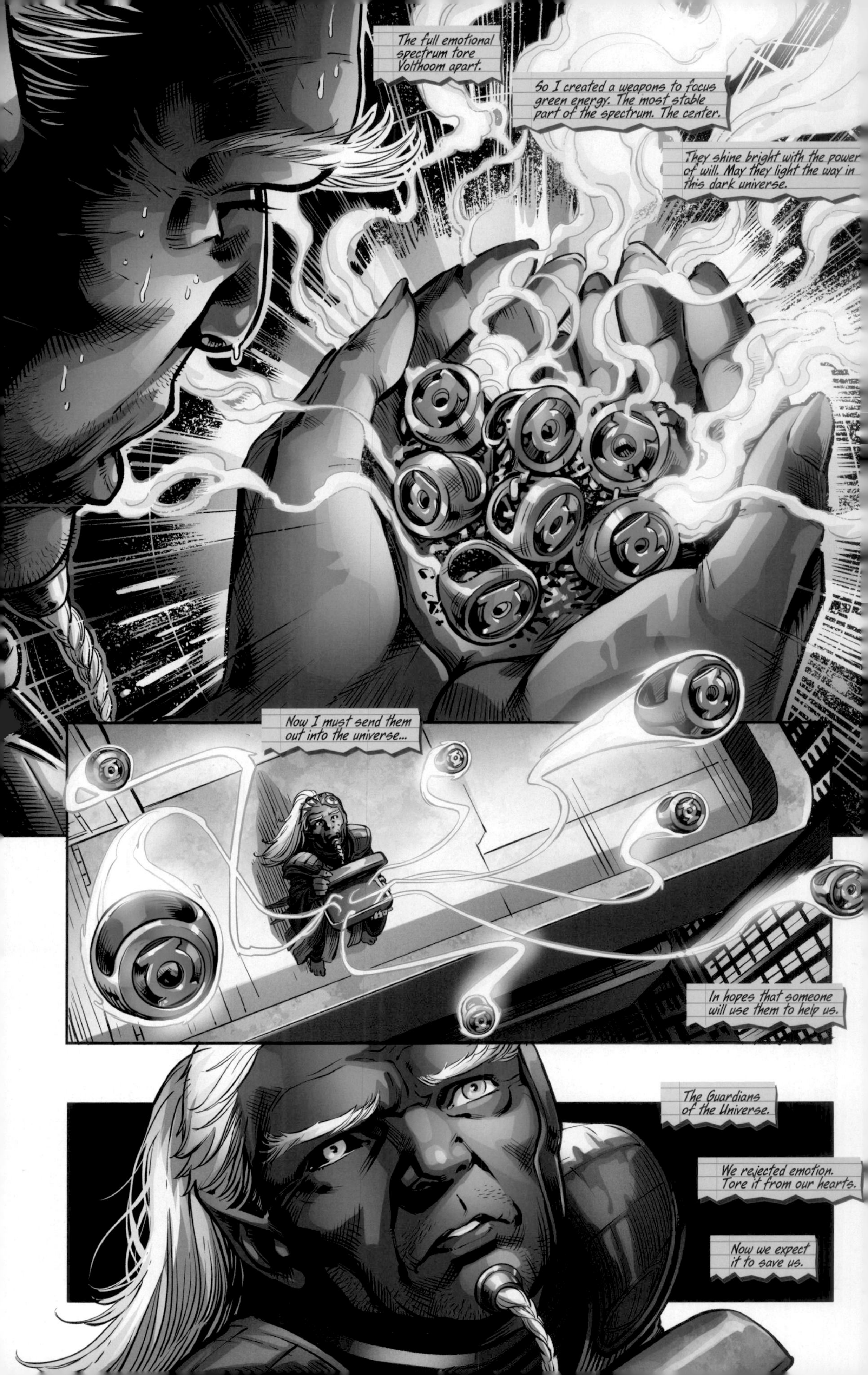
The full emotional spectrum tore Volthoom apart.
So I created a weapons to focus green energy. The most stable part of the spectrum. The center.
They shine bright with the power of will. May they light the way in this dark universe.
Now I must send them out into the universe...
In hopes that someone will use them to help us.
The Guardians of the Universe.
We rejected emotion. Tore it from our hearts.
Now we expect it to save us.

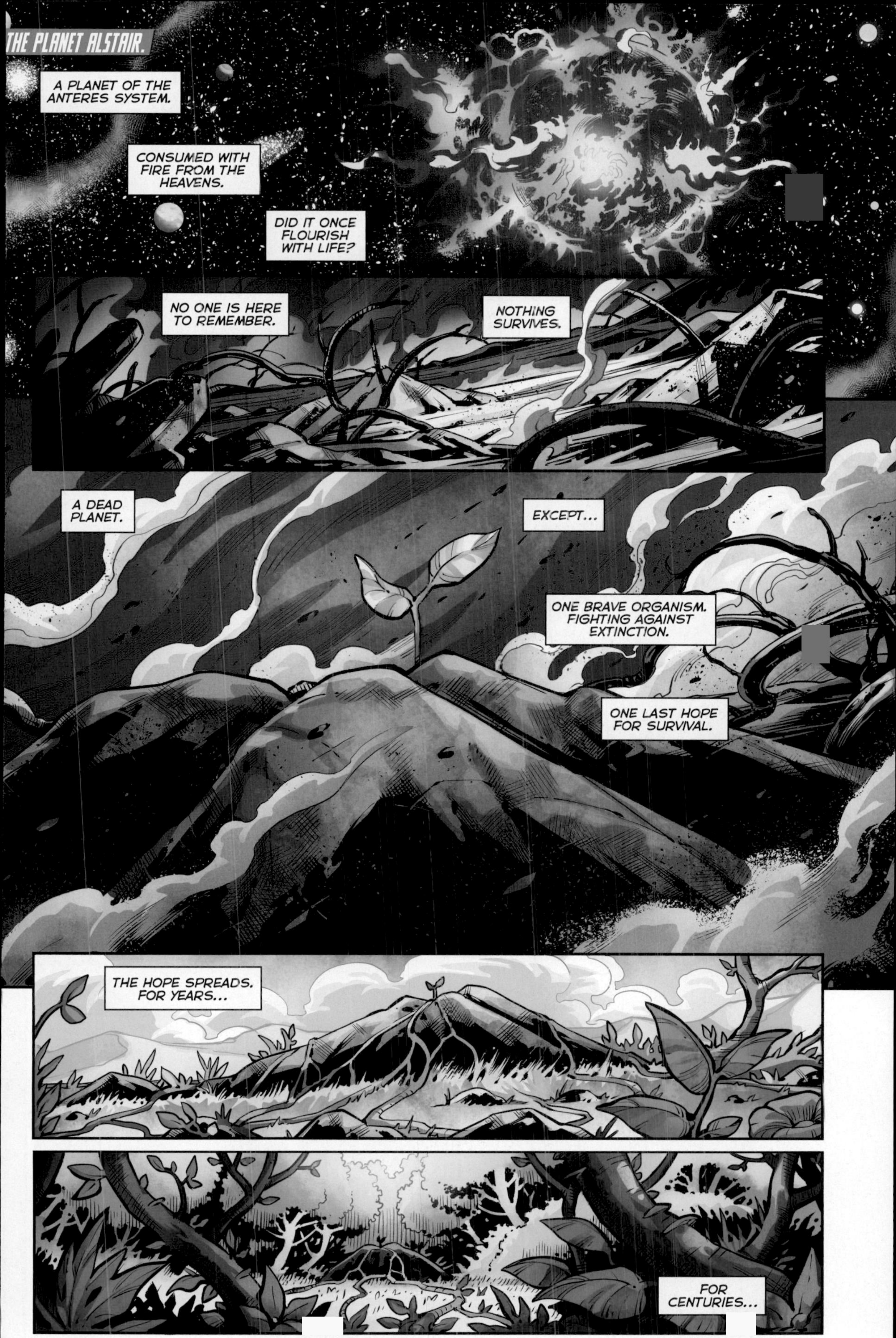
THE PLANET ALSTAIR.
A PLANET OF THE ANTERES SYSTEM.
CONSUMED WITH FIRE FROM THE HEAVENS.
DID IT ONCE FLOURISH WITH LIFE?
NO ONE IS HERE TO REMEMBER.
NOTHING SURVIVES.
A DEAD PLANET.
EXCEPT...
ONE BRAVE ORGANISM. FIGHTING AGAINST EXTINCTION.
ONE LAST HOPE FOR SURVIVAL.
THE HOPE SPREADS. FOR YEARS...
FOR CENTURIES...

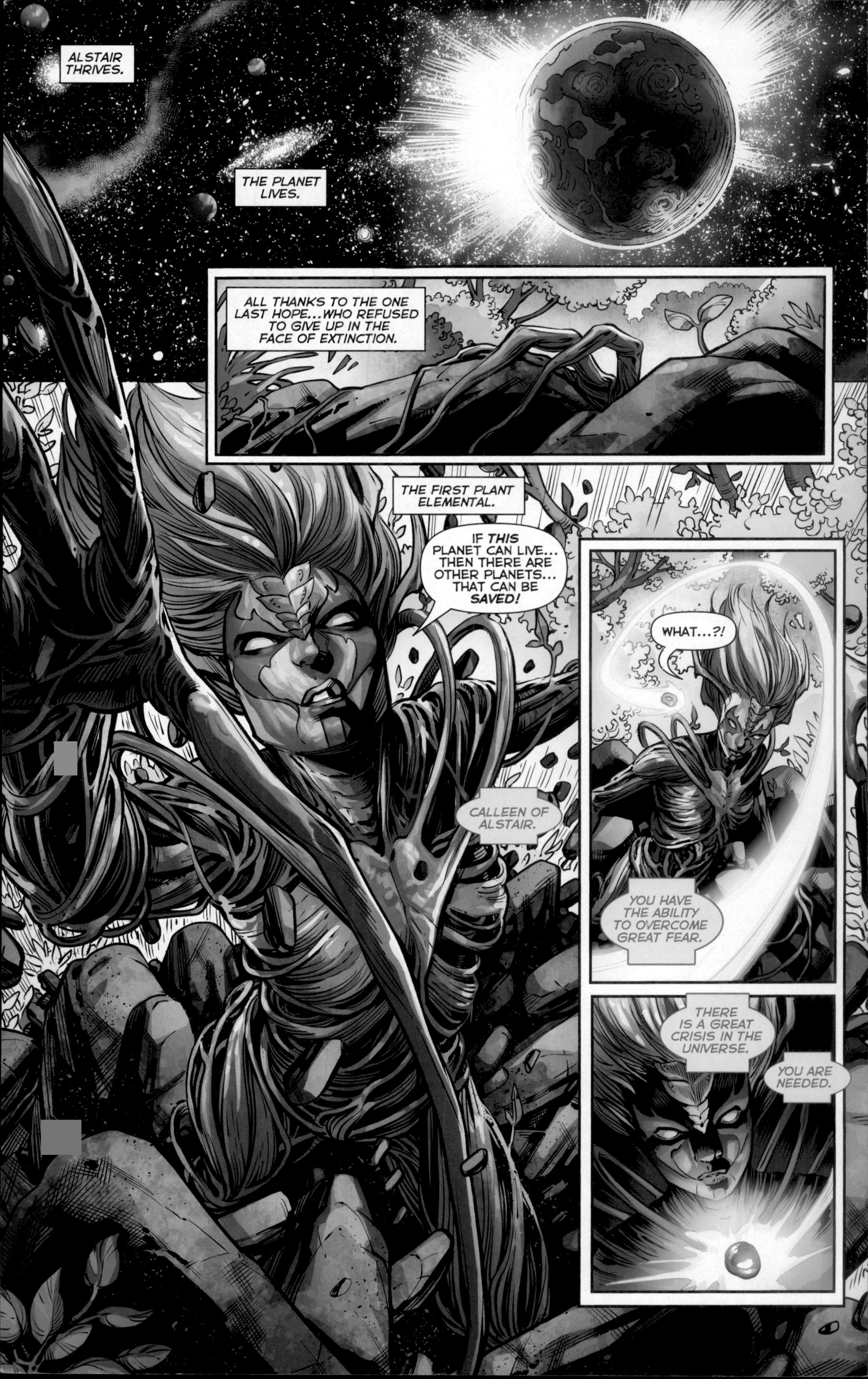
ALSTAIR THRIVES.
THE PLANET LIVES.
ALL THANKS TO THE ONE LAST HOPE...WHO REFUSED TO GIVE UP IN THE FACE OF EXTINCTION.
THE FIRST PLANT ELEMENTAL.
IF THIS PLANET CAN LIVE... THEN THERE ARE OTHER PLANETS... THAT CAN BE SAVED!
CALLEEN OF ALSTAIR.
WHAT...?!
YOU HAVE THE ABILITY TO OVERCOME GREAT FEAR.
THERE IS A GREAT CRISIS IN THE UNIVERSE.
YOU ARE NEEDED.

GREEN LANTERNS

VARIANT COVER GALLERY

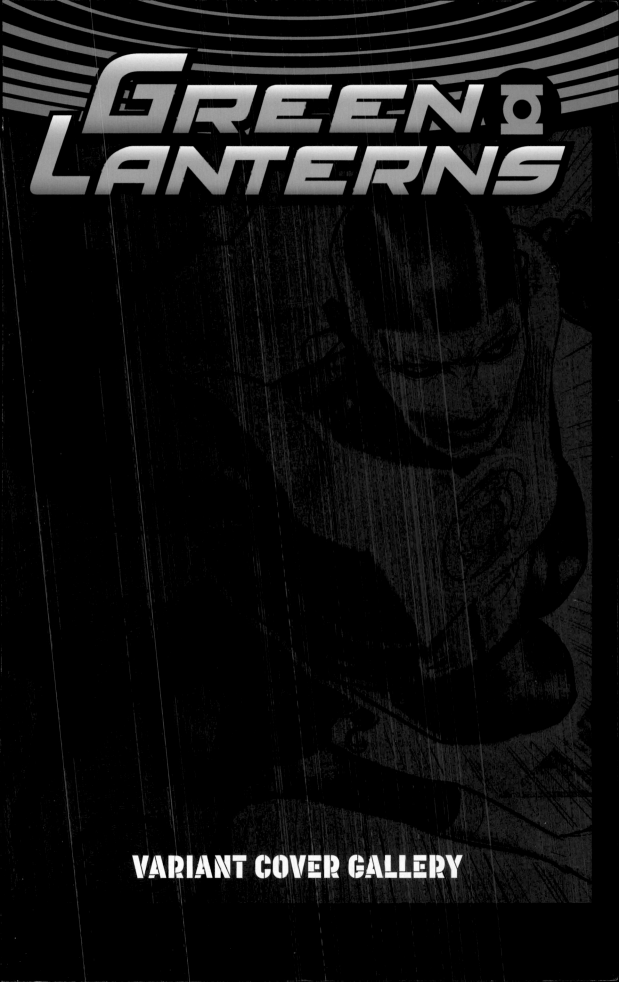

GREEN LANTERNS #[redacted]ant cover art by EMANUELA LUPACCHINO and MICHAEL [redacted]

GREEN LANTERNS #23 variant cover art by EMANUELA LUPACCHINO and MICHAEL ATIYEH

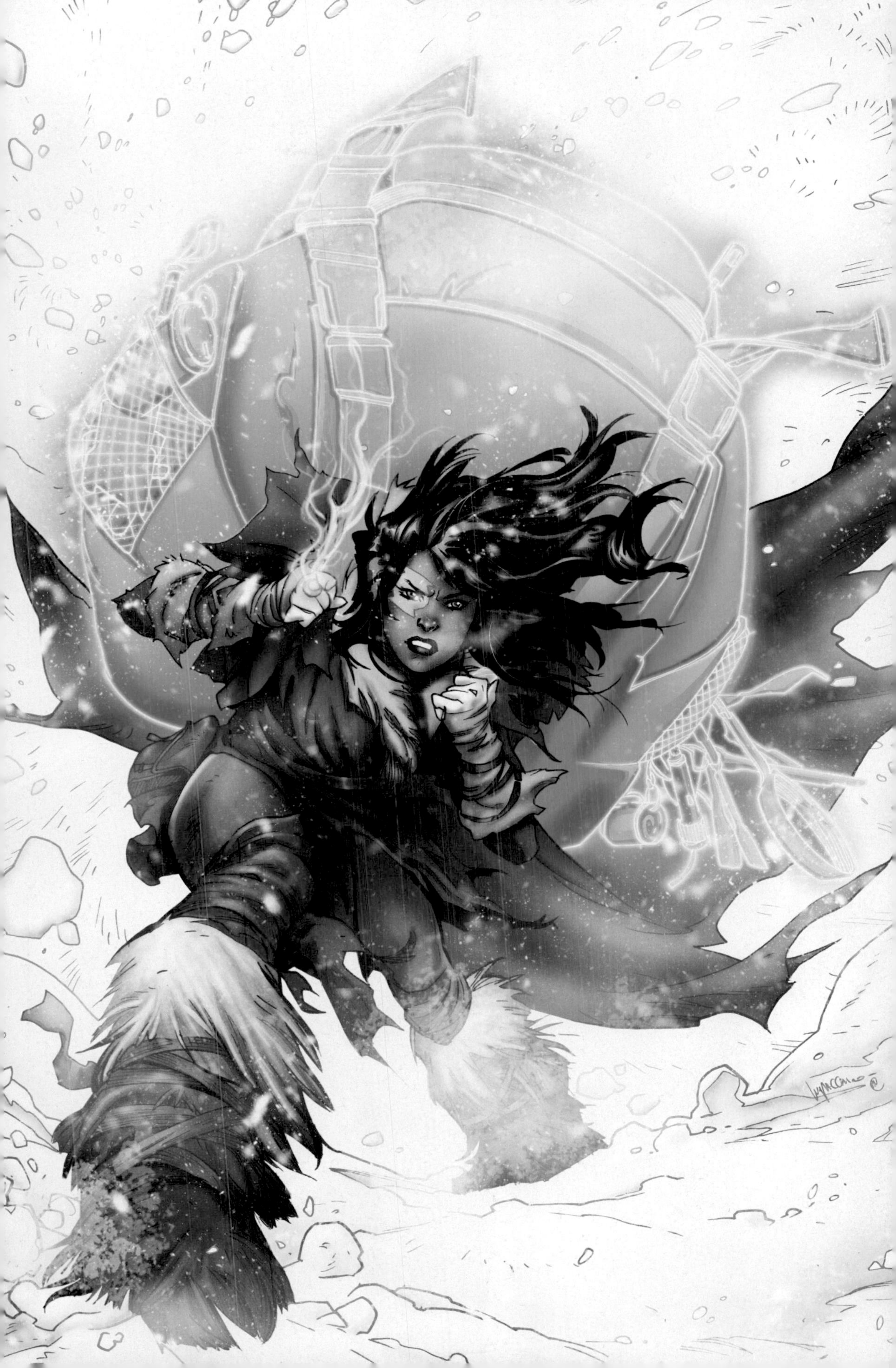

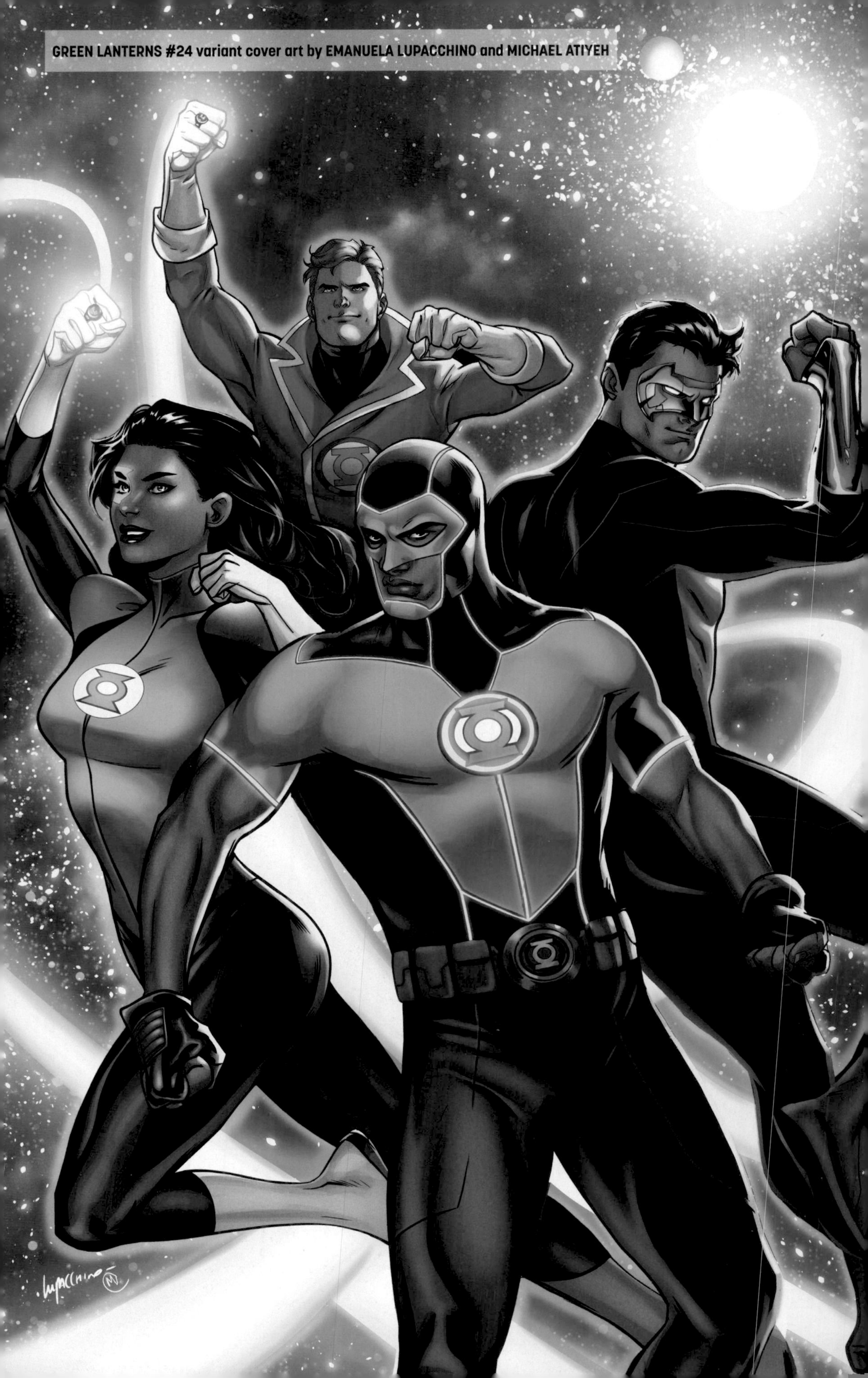

GREEN LANTERNS #24 variant cover art by EMANUELA LUPACCHINO and MICHAEL ATIYEH

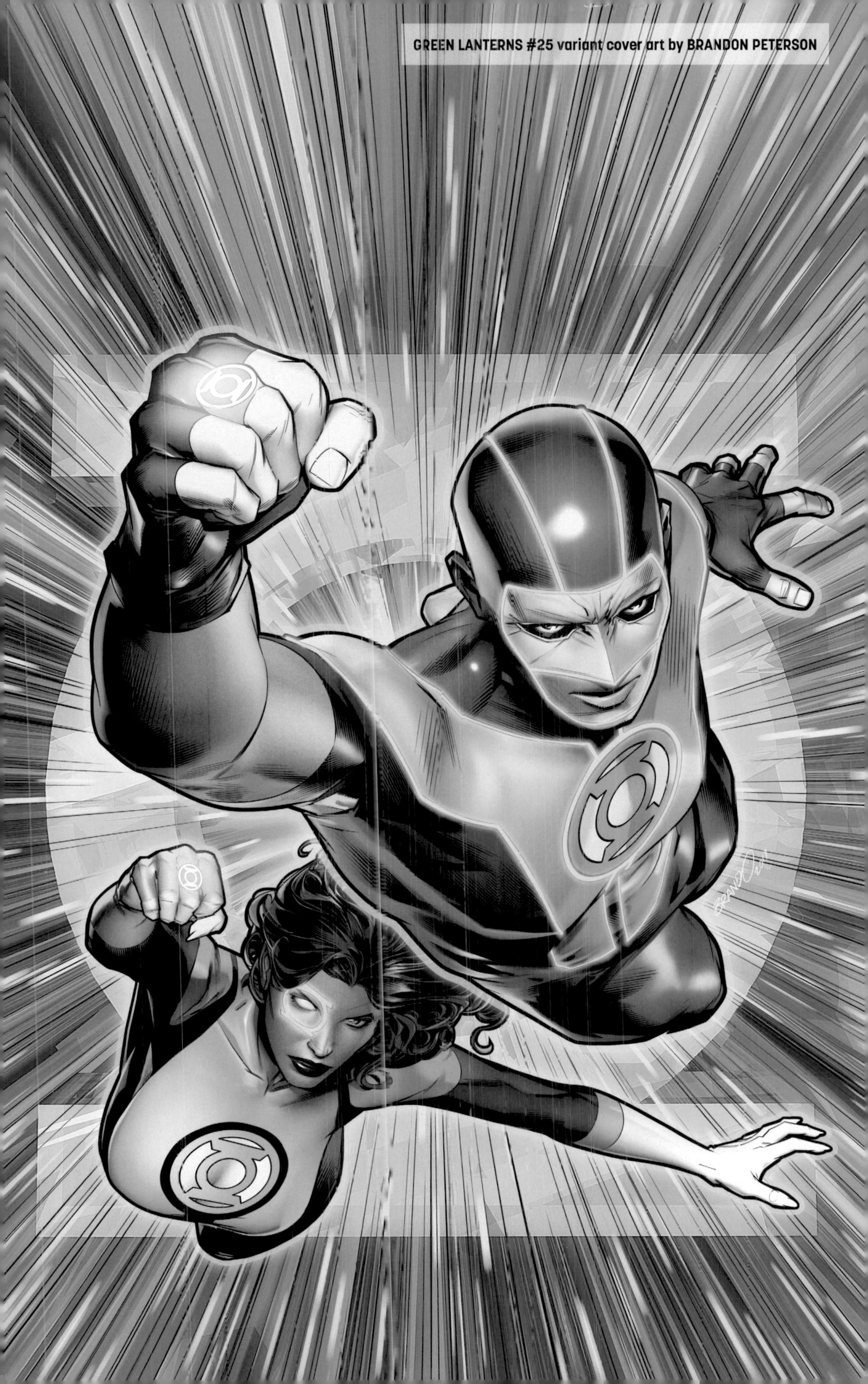

GREEN LANTERNS #25 variant cover art by BRANDON PETERSON

GREEN LANTERNS #26 variant cover art by BRANDON PETERSON

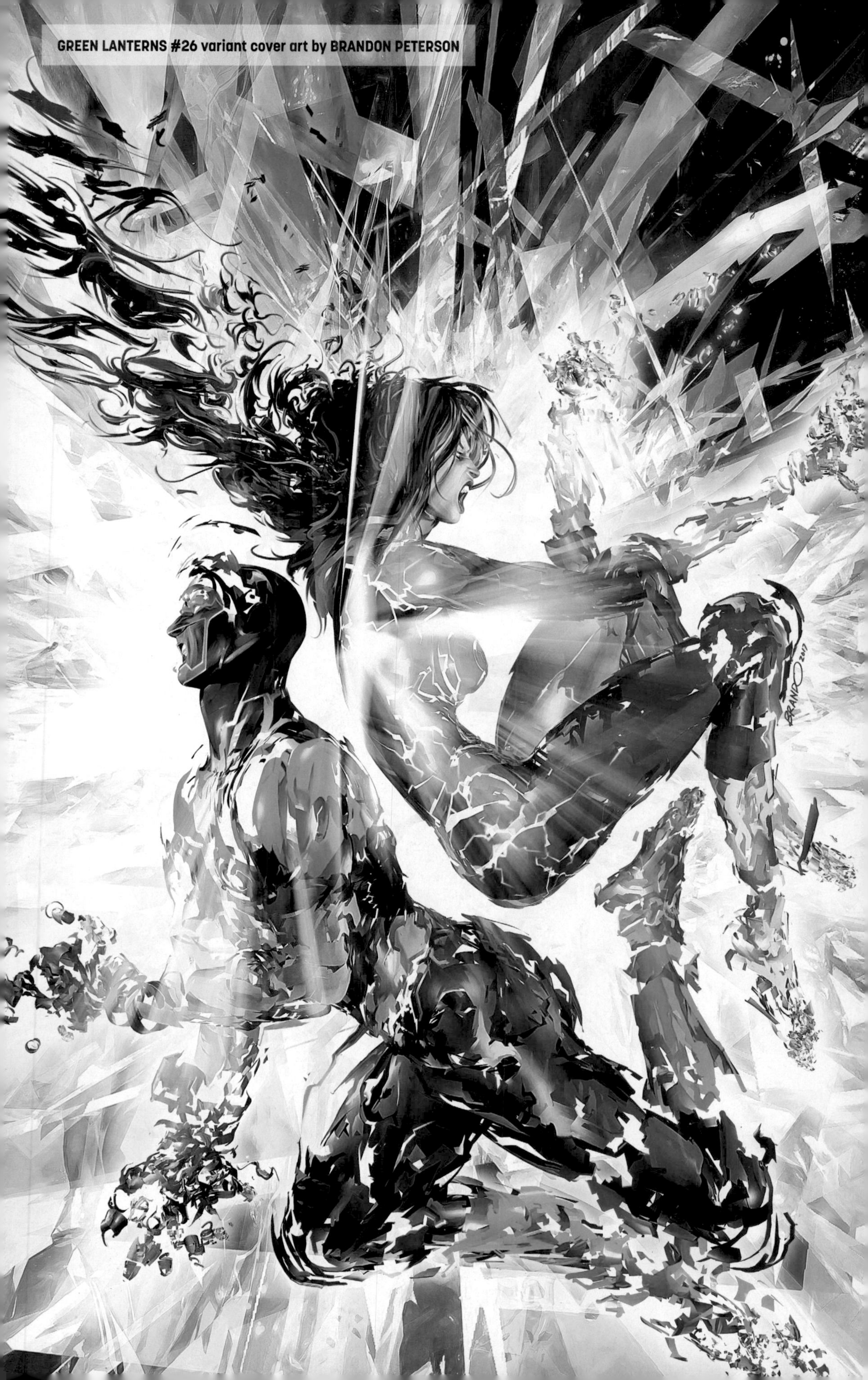